INVASION
1982

The Falkland Islanders' Story

Graham Bound

Foreword by Frederick Forsyth

Pen & Sword
MILITARY

First published in Great Britain in 2002 as
Falkland Islanders at War by LEO COOPER

Reprinted in 2007 and again in this format in 2016 by
PEN & SWORD MILITARY
An imprint of
Pen & Sword Books Ltd
47 Church Street, Barnsley
South Yorkshire
S70 2AS

ISBN 978 1 47385 343 0

Typeset in 10.5/12.5pt Plantin by
Phoenix Typesetting, Auldgirth, Dumfriesshire

Printed and bound in England
By CPI Group (UK) Ltd, Croydon, CR0 4YY

Pen & Sword Books Ltd incorporates the Imprints of Pen & Sword Aviation,
Pen & Sword Family History, Pen & Sword Maritime, Pen & Sword Military,
Pen & Sword Discovery, Pen & Sword Politics, Pen & Sword Atlas,
Pen & Sword Archaeology, Wharncliffe Local History, Leo Cooper,
Wharncliffe True Crime, Wharncliffe Transport, Pen & Sword Select,
Pen & Sword Military Classics, The Praetorian Press, Claymore Press,
Remember When, Seaforth Publishing and Frontline Publishing

For a complete list of Pen & Sword titles please contact
PEN & SWORD BOOKS LIMITED
47 Church Street, Barnsley, South Yorkshire, S70 2AS, England
E-mail: enquiries@pen-and-sword.co.uk
Website: www.pen-and-sword.co.uk

Dedicated with love to Nadia
who supports me in every possible way.

Contents

Acknowledgements

Many people gave their time to talk to me about their memories of the 1982 war. Most of them are Falkland Islanders (this is, after all, their story), but I was also helped by Argentine and British veterans.

I have quoted directly from many of these interviews, in some cases extensively. Other people have not been quoted directly, but their memories and opinions gave me important background information.

To all of the people listed below, my thanks.

In the Falklands:

Lorraine McGill; Brian Hewitt; June McMullen; Bob Smith; Bill and Barbara Curtis; Anna King; Tracy Porter; Frances Biggs; Bill Luxton; Anton Livermore; Mario Zuvic; Brook Hardcastle; John Leonard; Christopher Harris; Michael McKay; Pappy Minto; David and Pat Gray; Pat Whitney; Don Bonner; Eileen Vidal; Eric Goss; Robin Pitaluga; Robert Wilkinson; Finlay Ferguson; Fraser Wallace; Ted Carey; Fred Ford; Gerald Cheek; Bob Stewart; Grizelda Cockwell; Gus Reid; Sam and Carol Miller; Jan Cheek; Les and Jill Harris; Terry and Joan Spruce; Jock and June McPhee; John Fowler; Charles Coutts (Jnr); Bill Morrison; Len McGill; Charlie and Maude McKenzie; Brian Summers; Marvin Clark; Christine Peck; Mike Butcher; Neil and Glenda Watson; Nobby Clark; David and Carol Eynon; Denzel Clausen; Derek Rozee; Phillip Middleton; Phillip Miller; Raymond Evans; Fred Clarke; Ron Buckett; Ron Dixon; Rodney Lee; Dennis and Sharon Middleton; Sharon Halford; Tim and Sally Blake; Stuart Wallace; Susan Binnie; Taff Davies; Terry Peck; Roy Buckett; Tim Miller; Tony and Ailsa Heathman; Norma Edwards; Trevor Browning; Trudy McPhee; Charles Dixon; Velma Malcolm; Bob and Janet McLeod; Willy Bowles; John and Mandy McLeod; Neil Hewitt;

Vernon and Gail Steen; Tony Pole-Evans; Mike Summers; Clara and Bill McKay.

In Europe:

Mike Norman; Bob North; Roger Patton; Dick and Connie Baker; John Pettinger; Pat Butler; Reg Silvie; Gareth Noott; Rachel Aspogard; Sir Rex Hunt; Kevin Browning; Nidge Buckett; Geordie Gill.

In Argentina:

Carlos Bloomer Reeve; Barry Melbourne Hussey; Manuel Dorrego; Mario Benjamin Menendez.

In Australia:

Alison and Mike Bleaney.

Several people lent me photographs, documents and recordings. They are: Phil Middleton, Mike Butcher, Peter King, Terry and Joan Spruce, Ron Buckett, Bob McLeod, Vernon Steen, Eric Goss, Carlos Bloomer Reeve and Juan Manuel Ipina. Thanks to them.

Finally, a number of people made my work much easier with their help and kindness. In Stanley, my mother, Joan, looked after me (it was good to be home); Cynthia O'Shea helped me greatly with transcriptions, and Rosemary King was at the end of the line ready to help in important ways. Trudy McPhee and Trudy Butcher were also very helpful.

In England Jill Campion helped in many ways, not least by taking a flattering photo of me for the biographical notes that appear on the cover. John Ezard of the Guardian gave me valuable advice, and Dave Barlow drew maps that I believe make life much easier for the reader.

In Buenos Aires, Juan Manuel Ipina put me up and helped in many other ways (if you are typical of a new generation of Argentines, Juan, then there is indeed hope). Bernardo and Susana Mayer also reminded me that politics are one thing, but family friendships persevere.

I'm grateful to my employers and colleagues at Focus, the Ministry of Defence's newspaper, who held the fort while I took a lengthy period off to pursue this project.

The staff at Pen and Sword were always a pleasure to deal with, and Tom Hartman, my editor, delivered his criticism and advice in a remarkably painless way.

And, of course, my friends in Britain tolerated me for the best part of a year when my mind was in another place and another time.

My thanks to everyone.

Additional acknowledgements for the 2007 edition

I was only too aware that mistakes found their way into the original edition of this book, and I asked readers in the Falklands to help me correct them. A number of kind people did so. I appreciated that. Unfortunately I cannot promise that no errors remain.

I was aware of several gaps in the narratives. In particular I was missing comment about the months leading up to the invasion and the invasion itself from the vantage point of the Governor, Sir Rex Hunt. I sent him a list of questions, which he answered in considerable detail. His comments can now be read in the early chapters. Nidge Buckett, Gail and Vernon Steen, Tony Pole Evans, Geordie Gill and Kevin Browning also helped me to add substance to some chapters. Their names have been added to the list of interviewees.

For this edition I have drawn from accounts by a few other authors – mostly acknowledged in the text. Particularly helpful books (and therefore recommended) were: *My Falkland Days*, by Sir Rex Hunt (Politico's); *Razor's Edge, the Unofficial History of the Falklands War*, by Hugh Bicheno (Weidenfeld and Nicolson); *At Her Majesty's Secret Service*, by Nigel West (Greenhill), *The Official History of the Falklands Campaign*, by Sir Lawrence Freedman (Routledge) and *Argentine Forces in the Falklands*, by Nick van der Bijl (Osprey).

For the postscript to chapter 12, I drew heavily from reports published on-line by the excellent Uruguayan press agency Mercopress. To be found at www.mercopress.com, this service is recommended to anyone wishing to be informed about current affairs in Argentina and the Falklands.

My sincere thanks to everyone mentioned.

Foreword

by Frederick Forsyth

As the twenty-fifth anniversary of the Argentine invasion of the Falkland Islands comes upon us, it is only natural that thoughts will stray back that quarter century to contemplate once again and maybe reassess those events.

Masses of material has already been written, but most of it concerned the British Expeditionary Force, the fighting units involved, the details of the reconquest and the final triumph of liberation.

Too little perhaps has dwelt upon the Islanders themselves, so the reissue of this book is apposite.

Those seeking to understand why the invasion was so offensive and required such a huge and hazardous response from Britain would be quite wrong to think the British have any animus towards the Argentine people as a whole. Far from it; relations between our two peoples are traditionally warm and friendly.

But in the Seventies Argentina fell prey to a succession of brutal military dictatorships in which the names of Generals Viola, Videla and Galtieri are rightly wreathed in disgust. By 1982 there were 25,000 so-called 'disappeared ones' inside Argentina. Unionists, students, academics, journalists and foreign visitors, who had fallen foul of a neo-Nazi regime, had been snatched from the streets, imprisoned, tortured and murdered.

This was the regime that, in the spring of 1982, was finally at bay before domestic Argentine opinion and desperately sought to divert the public mood in a different direction. And this was the brutal tyranny that sought to impose itself on the few hundred peaceable farmers and traders of the Falklands. And that was why the thraldom of Galtieri and people like him could simply not be tolerated over British citizens.

Reading the text, one is struck by the hitherto overlooked story of a small island people never trained for war, resistance or espionage, rising to levels of quiet heroism neither they nor anyone else could have expected of them. That is why it is such a good story, and a perfect complement to what the British soldiers, sailors and airmen accomplished in a hundred days.

INVASION
1982

Chapter One

The 150-Year Echo

At five minutes past six on the morning of 2 April 1982 several loud explosions ripped through the Royal Marines barracks at the west end of Stanley Harbour.

It was a calm pre-dawn morning and the noise of the grenades and rockets launched by the Argentine special forces as they attacked Moody Brook rolled across the still harbour, echoing off the ridge on the north shore, disturbing logger ducks and kelp geese along the beach, and rattling windows in the cottages of Stanley.

At the headquarters of the Falkland Islands Defence Force (FIDF), a rambling weatherboard and corrugated iron building in the centre of Stanley, Major Phil Summers, Assistant Government Chief Secretary by day and commander of the forty-strong civilian militia on weekends, heard the explosions.

The senior officer had been at the HQ since about 7.30 the night before, having dutifully turned out in response to the news that an Argentine invasion was imminent. After a short briefing by Governor Rex Hunt, Phil Summers and his officers had allocated key positions for the men to guard and issued weapons and ammunition.

Major Summers could have been a figure from Dad's Army – there were shades of Captain Mainwaring. Indeed the Defence Force was affectionately known as that. Rotund and not cutting a fine figure in uniform, he was more at home in his daytime environment, the Government Secretariat. But, like the other ill-prepared men who turned out that night, he was no coward and he accepted without question that he was to do his duty.

As the explosions faded, the CO found a dignity that sometimes eluded him and strode out of the drill hall onto John Street. In a steady and firm voice, calculated to instil a little more confidence in the un-fortunates who defended the road with ancient Lee Enfield bolt-action rifles, he said, "Right lads, it's started."

1

In his voice was resignation, and perhaps even a hint of relief. Like other Falkland Islanders, he had been waiting years for 'it'; the final day of reckoning in the long-simmering dispute with Argentina. They had never discussed invasion; it was a taboo word. Like cancer, there was not a lot that could be done to avoid it and not much point in talking about it. If 'it' happened, it had to be faced bravely.

The sounds of aggression had, in a sense, echoed not just across Stanley's still harbour, but across the decades.

Argentines insist that 2 April was simply the latest act in a drama that had begun 149 years earlier in 1833. Then, they allege, British forces sacked the settlement at Puerto Soledad which the infant country had inherited from the Spanish, and deported the colonists.

That the British had never abandoned their earlier claim to the Islands, and the Argentine inheritance of all Spanish claims in the area is at the very least of debatable legality, matters not at all. The loss of the Malvinas was a slap in the face of the nation, never to be forgotten.

But the Malvinas only emerged as an Argentine *cause célèbre* in 1946, soon after the charismatic *caudillo* Juan Domingo Peron had placed the sky-blue sash of the presidency across his chest. Searching for an issue which would unite all Argentines, he set his diplomats to work rejuvenating the Malvinas dispute.

From then on Argentina harried the British Government. In 1964 they succeeded in placing the issue on the agenda of the United Nations. Britain protested, but the following year the UN General Assembly formally urged the two countries to discuss their dispute.

In the Falklands, where the main concerns of life had nothing to do with such arcane history, the Argentine claim was ignored. There was a vague awareness that the neighbours were best avoided, but who needed them anyway? Trading links were happily and firmly established with Montevideo in Uruguay.

Monthly steamers travelled the 1,000 miles to and from Montevideo, carrying exported wool, sick Islanders for treatment at the British Hospital, children for education at the British School, and holidaying colonial administrators who caught the Royal Mail ships on from the River Plate to Southampton.

In 1966 things changed. A bizarre event brought the dispute and the threat home. On 26 September, a clear early spring day, the rumble of multiple aero-engines disturbed the peace of tiny sheep farming settlements on the west of the Islands. Reports of the strange sound reached Stanley shortly before a large four-engined Douglas DC4 aircraft, bearing the colours of Aerolineas Argentinas, appeared over the town.

It circled, losing height and apparently searching for an airport. People poured onto the streets for a better view.

The airliner, by far the largest aircraft ever seen over the Falklands, was carrying about forty passengers, fresh produce and crates of newly hatched chicks. It had taken off several hours earlier from the northern Patagonian town of Bahia Blanca for a flight to Rio Gallegos in the far south. Soon after take-off a number of the passengers emerged from their seats, reached into their hand luggage and produced guns.

The hijackers, including a vivacious young blonde woman (Islanders were later shocked by the rumour that a generous stock of condoms had been found along with the ammunition in her bag), were the extreme right-wing Condor Group. They ordered the captain to change course for the Malvinas, where they intended to reclaim the Islands for the motherland.

The crew must have had concerns, but the Argentine guerrillas appeared blissfully unaware that Stanley had no airport. In those days the only aircraft to operate within the Falklands were the De Havilland Beaver floatplanes of the Government Air Service, a bush-style operation that linked the farm settlements and tiny island communities.

But the DC4 needed to put down somewhere and Islanders felt a mixture of alarm and relief when it began to descend in the direction of the racecourse. Landing such a large aircraft on a soft stretch of grass with fences and grandstands on each side was desperately dangerous – better, though, than running out of fuel in mid-air. Showing remarkable skill, the pilots touched down lightly and managed to reduce the DC4's speed before the undercarriage began ploughing into the soft turf. Eventually it came to a jarring stop, still upright but with its wheels well and truly stuck. Remarkably, there were no injuries.

Falkland Islanders have rarely been criticised for their lack of hospitality and on this day they excelled. Clearly the passengers and crew were in trouble and many locals leapt into their Land Rovers and sped to the racecourse, intent on doing whatever they could to help. To their horror, guerrillas waving guns met them. Many well-intending locals, including Police Officer Terry Peck (who would later make his name in the 1982 war) were herded aboard the aircraft to join the innocent passengers and crew as hostages. Outside the plane, the Argentines raised an Argentine flag and began distributing leaflets stating their purpose.

It was a dangerous situation with elements of farce. The Governor and his second in command, the Colonial Secretary – both London appointees – were in Britain, and the senior civil servants were two

3

local men, Financial Secretary Les Gleadell and Assistant Colonial Secretary HL 'Nap' Bound. This was one of the first cases of terrorists hijacking an airliner; it may have been the first. Whether it was or not, the crime had not yet taken on the sinister significance that is attached to it today, and the two men struggled to find a phrase to describe the incident. Eventually they cabled the Foreign Office in London to say that there had been a case of 'air piracy'. In a reply that was strangely similar to the unhelpful advice given to Governor Rex Hunt on the eve of the 1982 invasion, the two senior locals were told to manage as best they could.

Stanley's meagre military force was mobilised to support the handful of unarmed policemen. It was a moment of glory for the Defence Force. Only six Royal Marines were then based in Stanley, training the local men and advising the Governor on issues of security and defence. They suggested the Defence Force stake out the DC4, denying the 'pirates' water, warmth and sleep.

This may have been the only terrorist incident that ended thanks to Jimmy Shand, Russ Conway and the Beatles. The Force set up loud-speakers around the plane and a DJ maintained a constant flow of furious Scottish jigs and rinky-tink piano tunes. This was a low trick and the Argentines could not hold out for long.

Hostage Terry Peck waited until his captors' attention was diverted and secreted himself beneath the ample robes of the local Anglican priest, who had gained access to the aircraft and was attempting to negotiate. The policeman was a small, wiry young man, but the priest was still left looking little short of pregnant. Moving in awkward unison the two crossed the FIDF lines successfully.

As light faded, the temperature dropped, the plane's toilets backed up, water became short and the DJ introduced his *pièce de résistance* – his collection of Beatles' singles. The next morning the guerillas asked the priest to convey their surrender to the authorities.

In the same self-serving and appeasing fashion that characterised policy in the months before the 1982 invasion, London decided that Argentina was not to be provoked with a stiff response. There would be no local trial and the hijackers were held in an annexe to the Catholic church rather than in prison. A few days later an Argentine steamer, the *Bahia Buen Suceso*, dropped anchor in Port William, Stanley's outer harbour, and embarked the hijackers.

Back home, the Condor group were heroes and the authorities charged them only with relatively minor offences. Some of the group received suspended sentences and even the vivacious blonde deputy leader was free within a few years.

The Islanders had handled the first Argentine assault on the Islands well and with very little help from London. Indeed, in the aftermath of the incident, they had been let down by the British Government.

It had been no invasion, but the incident had brought the Argentine threat into the open. Soon afterwards, the town's fire alarms were altered to give an optional wavering tone, which would be the invasion alarm. Large timber obstructions were placed on the racecourse to stop any future landing.

Slowly but inexorably the threat increased, not only from the near neighbour, but – in a political sense – from London as well. Later in 1966 it became clear that British diplomats were manoeuvring to solve the problem of a colony which was of no further use to Britain. If necessary, they would do this by conceding to Argentine demands.

There was the small matter of the Islanders to consider, but handling them should not be beyond the wit of Whitehall. 2,000 sheep farmers would be encouraged to be reasonable and accept that reliance on Britain 8,000 miles away no longer made sense. A warmer relationship with Argentina, on the other hand, really was rather a good idea.

In 1968 Foreign Secretary Michael Stewart shocked Parliament and the Islanders by admitting that he had initiated talks about sovereignty during a visit to Buenos Aires the previous year. He said Britain was confident about the justice of its claim, but so was Argentina, and both sides had to address this if there was to be any dialogue at all.

It was the beginning of a Machiavellian diplomatic process, continued dogmatically by whatever government was in power until the outbreak of war in 1982.

Missions to the Falklands by junior foreign office ministers became relatively routine. They would arrive with, at best, a message of watery support and appeals for realism, at worst with details of a new and unsavoury political reality or proposal. It was easy for the ministers and their men to convey their messages without the inconvenience of debate or criticism, because local government was dominated by the Governor and other officials nominated by London. Executive Council meetings, upon which few democratically elected members sat, were conducted in secret. Independent news media did not exist. The local radio station was owned and controlled by the government, and (in the early days, at least) the only newspaper was the *Monthly Review*, a duplicated paper of dry record that occasionally carried government statements without comment, and was otherwise notable for its "hatched, matched and despatched" column.

But ministers and officials underestimated the Islanders. Knowing that they could not successfully fight the Foreign Office alone, a group of leading Islanders mobilised influential friends in Britain, including back-bench Members of Parliament, into a remarkably effective pressure and lobby group.

The Argentines hated the Emergency Committee, as it was known, sneering that it was actually the instrument of the Falkland Islands Company who simply want to continue plundering the Islands' economy. But the committee became a permanent thorn in the side of the Foreign Office. It countered every official move with public reminders that the Islanders were loyal subjects of the Queen who had settled in a none-too comfortable colony when the crown valued its empire, and who did their bit in support of the mother country during two world wars. Their 'wishes', not just their 'interests,' had to be respected.

Assessments of the military threat at that time are not known, but in 1968 London beefed up the Royal Marines detachment, calling it Naval Party 8901 and basing it in the long abandoned and virtually derelict wireless transmitting station at Moody Brook. It is slightly puzzling that London bothered to increase the garrison at all, but it is possible that a force of less than platoon size would find it difficult to sustain itself economically and with any degree of independence. In any case, as a signal to the Argentines, the lightly armed force of about thirty men did not seem to be saying much. It was easy to assume that because Britain had committed such a meagre force it cared little about the Islands.

London still hoped that the Islanders would come to depend on their big neighbour. In 1971, following more secret talks, the pressure was ratcheted up. Falkland Islanders were told that their subsidised shipping link with Uruguay could not continue. They were presented with a new arrangement, one that pushed them firmly into bed with Buenos Aires. No one in the Islands liked it, but there was no choice.

The Communications Agreement was dressed up as a joint commitment to support the Islands. The Argentines would build a temporary airstrip so that its state airline, Lineas Aereas del Estado (LADE), could operate a weekly service to and from the mainland. For its part, Britain would build a permanent airport, and (to counter the argument that too much reliance was being placed on Argentina) also provide a passenger-cargo ship operating to South America. It was implied that the new ship would be capable of trading with Uruguay if the Argentines ever abused their monopoly over air services.

This fooled no one. The small print was alarming: to travel through Argentina locals would need a *'tarjeta provisorio,'* a provisional card, bearing their personal details and the Argentine coat of arms. Issued in Buenos Aires, the much-hated 'white card,' as locals knew it, was a *de facto* Argentine passport. The Argentines would also set up an office in Stanley to run LADE and even mail would be routed through Argentina, where it would be rubber-stamped twice with lavish English and Spanish cachets. The agreement allowed the Argentines to continue viewing Islanders as Argentine citizens, but with patronising generosity Buenos Aires said it would not insist that Falklands men endure military service. This only suggested that they were really a special kind of Argentine citizen.

With the new dawn in relations came agreements that medical treatment unavailable in Stanley would be provided in Argentina and scholarships would be available for local children to study in Buenos Aires, Cordoba and other Argentine cities.

A little later YPF, the Argentine state oil company, was given a monopoly to provide petrol and diesel in the Islands, while Gas del Estado, another state company, began an attempt to wean Islanders off their free supply of peat.

Some observers have characterised the British policy towards the Falklands before 1982 as one of 'benign neglect'. This is too generous. By the early 1970s British policy was thoroughly malignant. Chief Secretary at the time was Tom Laing. His brief was to do all he could to foster relations between the Islands and the Argentines. "Do what you can to get people together," his Whitehall bosses told him.

The master plan was not subtle. Given a decade or two, Falklanders would accept the Argentines; indeed those who had been educated there would virtually *be* Argentines. Problem solved.

Not surprisingly, deep political anger was directed at the British Government – particularly the deceitful Foreign Office, which had conceived and carried out the strategy. Local rage increased when the Foreign Office reneged on its side of the Communciations Agreement. Although Britain did eventually fund the building of a small permanent airstrip at Stanley (notably too small to allow flights from Britain), the shipping link, which would have weakened the Argentine grip, never materialised. This was, quite simply, a broken promise.

Periodically over the next decade, Islanders requested – indeed almost demanded – the extension of territorial waters beyond the negligible few miles. This would have enabled Stanley to issue licences to the fishing fleets that were scooping up hugely valuable catches within sight of the Islands. The resulting revenue would almost certainly reverse the declining economy, and the move was within London's power, as was shown in the aftermath of the 1982 war, when a zone covering thousands of square miles of valuable ocean was declared posthaste. But, of course, no one in Whitehall wanted the Islanders to prosper.

Notwithstanding the skulduggery and the anger, the decade

between 1971 and 1981 was not entirely unhappy in Stanley. Emigration to better lives in Britain and New Zealand continued, but (on a human level at least) many of those who stayed got along reasonably well with the Argentines who were posted to Stanley to maintain the air and fuel services. Politics was politely avoided and the 'I-word,' the threat made real by the DC4 incident, was put to the back of most people's minds.

It was during this period that an Argentine Air Force officer who would go on to become an unlikely local hero during the 1982 war made his first appearance in Stanley. Vice Comodoro Carlos Bloomer Reeve was an Argentine of Scottish and French descent who spoke fluent English and was something of an anglophile. Bloomer Reeve was an inspired choice to head the Argentine airline LADE in Stanley and be the senior representative of Buenos Aires during 1974 and 1975. Amiable, always smiling and not politically driven, he and his family settled easily in Stanley. They enjoyed the distinctly old-fashioned and charming community. Here the pace of life was slower and it was possible to enjoy the simpler things in life.

In Stanley Bloomer Reeve and his wife Mora fitted into the expatriate British social scene. They were regulars at Government House cocktail parties. In socially stratified Stanley, ordinary Islanders might have held this against him, but his children attended the local school and Bloomer Reeve visited the shops, and easily made friends at all levels.

Running a weekly air service was not exactly hard work. As a pilot Bloomer Reeve had been used to tough operational tours in the Antarctic and, during the Congo crisis in the early 1960s, he had flown transport planes for the United Nations.

One of the two Argentine teachers working in the local school (Argentine Spanish teachers were another result of the Communications Agreement) remembers the friendly atmosphere that prevailed. The young teacher, who is now a diplomat, also enjoyed the way of life. She happily remembered the novelty of conducting classes with farm ('camp' in the local vernacular) children by radio. There was also the chance to learn from local women how to make bread and spin wool. She remembers locals politely avoiding discussion of the dispute: "You could tell there was apprehension, but on a one-to-one basis there was not really any hostility. After a few months you could see the divide. But we could work with it."

Bloomer Reeve and the handful of Argentines who lived and worked in Stanley simply did their jobs. Lives were saved by LADE evacuating patients to Argentine hospitals; children gained at least a smattering of a second language and some even spent a few years attending private schools in Argentina. There were a few marriages between local girls and the YPF and Gas del Estado staff. As a bonus, the Stanley team regularly thrashed the Argentine residents at football.

But if anyone mistook this peaceful coexistence for proof that the sly British and Argentine policy was working, they were dangerously mistaken.

In spite of the Argentine military coup of 1976, which led to the 'dirty war', the notorious campaign of abduction, murder, torture and total suppression of human rights, London continued to talk to Buenos Aires. The talks often involved Islander councillors (such had been the success of the Falkland Islands Committee pressure group that Islanders 'wishes' were now important and they could not be left out of talks). There was no obvious raising of the military threat from Buenos Aires, but the hard-line regime, which obviously had little time for niceties, insisted that substantial progress must be made. There was, however, no breakthrough. Enter stage right in 1980 a Thatcherite junior Foreign Office minister, who will be forever associated with the Falklands. Nicholas Ridley arrived in the Foreign Office to find a fat file marked 'Falklands' requiring his attention. To his mind the issue had meandered along for too long and he intended to solve it.

The politician, one of Margaret Thatcher's favourite lieutenants, set off for Stanley via Buenos Aires in November of that year and was met there by impatient and irritated Argentines. They had not been told in advance of his visit and wasted no time in telling him that he could go to Stanley on the Argentine airline if he wished, but he must come to the next round of talks with some positive proposals to solve the dispute.

Even if Ridley had not received this quasi-ultimatum, a shrewd look at the Argentine press might have caused a few alarm bells to ring. A curiously mixed message had emerged from the Institute for the Malvinas Islands and Southern Argentine Territories in June 1980, and was reported by the English-language *Buenos Aires Herald*:

> An armed invasion of the Malvinas Islands would not be too much of a problem, according to retired admiral Jorge Fraga, President of the Institute. But that would not be the right way to recover them.

It seemed that some people, at least, were giving thought to the pros and cons of military action.

When Ridley arrived in Stanley, the local paper *Penguin News* reported that "the burning question is, what is he here for?". Rex Hunt

9

received him graciously, but undoubtedly aware that Islanders were every bit as suspicious as the *Penguin News* editor. Their impression was that Ridley and Rex were spending long hours in discussion, but Rex later told the author in 2006 that this was not so. "He spent most of his time between 22 and 29 November 1980 fishing and sketching," said Rex. "I took every opportunity to tell him that Falkland Islanders would not accept his 'leaseback' proposal." This was a legal and diplomatic device whereby titular sovereignty would be ceded to Buenos Aires only to be immediately leased back for a very long period of time, satisfying Argentine pride but allowing life in the Islands to continue unchanged.

"But," continued Rex, "he seemed to believe that he could persuade them by himself. His message to the Islanders was simple: 'The dead hand of the sovereignty dispute was stagnating the Islands' economy.' I replied that it was the dead hand of the Foreign Office, who were reluctant to declare a fishing zone."

Nevertheless, Ridley seemed sanguine and confident – disastrously so, as became clear when he eventually addressed the Islanders in public. A meeting was convened in the Town Hall and the turnout was large. Ridley stood on the stage looking confident. Rex Hunt stood alongside him, looking uncomfortable. Islanders were told that the dispute had rumbled on for far too long and now some accommodation *had* to be reached. Ridley repeated his 'dead hand of the sovereignty dispute' argument. There were, he said, three strategies that he might be able to sell to the Argentines, but some stood less chance of being accepted than others. In fact, two were red herrings, patently hopeless concepts that served only to show how sensible was the leaseback proposal.

There was the 'freeze' idea, whereby both sides would agree to disagree and take no action to further their claims for a specified time. But the minister pointed out that at the end of the moratorium period the old problem would return with a vengeance.

Then there was the possibility of 'condominium,' joint government. The Argentine flag would need to fly alongside the Union Flag. There would also need to be two police forces, two governors, and two official languages. Even Ridley believed this was a non-starter.

Finally he explained his preferred idea: 'leaseback'. This, he suggested, was a workable solution. Britain would formally cede sovereignty to Buenos Aires, and before the ink had dried on that document would sign another, leasing the Islands back for an agreed period, say 99 years. The Falklands' way of life would be maintained and everyone would be happy.

Across Ridley's face spread a cadaverous grimace, which was as near as he could get to a smile.

Until this climactic point the hundreds of Islanders in the hall had been relatively quiet. But now men and women fought to be heard.

None of the proposals was acceptable to Islanders – and certainly not leaseback. Islanders were stunned by what they heard. "Doesn't the Minister know that the Argentine government is a bunch of murdering thugs? Are they going to honour an agreement?" shouted one man.

"Are we going to leave a political time bomb as an inheritance for our grandchildren? No fear!"

Ridley was visibly shaken. Rex Hunt had been right and Islanders were not as supine and malleable as he had thought. He tried to answer the questions, but was shouted down. Eventually he lost his temper. If Islanders did not accept a solution, preferably leaseback, then they would be to blame for the consequences. "They [the Argentines] cannot be strung along for much longer," he shouted. Some who were there believed he alluded to the possibility of an invasion.

The next day, the minister, accompanied by the Governor, embarked on a tour of the camp settlements. But he was met everywhere with the same hostility. The people of Green Patch, for example, issued a statement saying they would have nothing to do with any of his three proposals.

Meanwhile, the now late and legendary local musician Des Peck had dedicated his latest 'composition' to the hapless Minister, and sung it with gusto in Stanley pubs. To the tune of Tom Dooley, it went: "Hang down your head Nicholas Ridley, hang down your head in shame . . ." Despite the congested syllables, the song hit the spot.

Ridley was not going to stay a day longer than necessary, but shortly before leaving he told *Penguin News* of his assessment of the situation. He studiously avoided the 'I-word', but in doing so could not find another to adequately describe the threat. "It's a mood of impatience," he said of the climate in Argentina. "No, not of impatience; it's a mood of . . . sooner or later, sometime, one way or another, we have to get further on. We have to make more progress. That's their mood, not my mood."

Asked whether the deadlock might lead the Argentines to tighten the screw on the Falklands by removing the air, fuel and medical services, Nicholas Ridley thought carefully before answering with words that, even then, seemed ominous.

I am a man of peace. I would feel I had failed if that happened. I can't foresee what Argentina would do. Your guess is as good as mine, because you live near them and know them perhaps better even than I do. I merely say that in the long term one has to come to terms with one's neighbours and one has to live in peace with them. What one cannot do is live in a perpetual state of siege and antagonism, suspicion and bellicosity.

As the envoy arrived at the new Stanley Airport to board the Argentine LADE Fokker, an angry crowd of people jeered him. They honked Land Rover horns and waved Union Flags and defiant placards. Recently resigned Police Chief Terry Peck had attached a loudspeaker to his Land Rover and belted out his coordination of the protest.

Before boarding the LADE plane Ridley bravely addressed the crowd, saying that he had not discussed the three possible solutions with the Argentines and that he had no intention of raising them while transiting Buenos Aires on his way home. Nevertheless, the BBC World Service's man in Argentina, Harold Briley, reported that the Minister did meet with the Argentines.

Whether the Islanders liked it or not, the ball had for the first time been placed in their court. Councillors were required to consult their people in a more considered way and respond formally to London. The most senior councillor, Adrian Monk, went on local radio and told Islanders he would not agree with any of the Ridley proposals. He summed up the ideas succinctly: "They stink!" He roundly condemned the British government and said that his condemnation extended to the Foreign Office agents in the Falklands: the Governor and his administrators. Other Islanders, he suggested, should also have the courage to say this.

By too close an association with Nicholas Ridley, even Governor Rex Hunt was losing his authority. He too went on local radio with a carefully constructed speech:

> Let me assure you that if I am ever instructed by Her Majesty's Government to pursue policies which are against the best interests of the Falkland Islanders, and I cannot persuade them to change these policies, I shall have no hesitation in tendering my resignation. So please do not suspect the Minister's motive or my own.

This certainly helped Rex Hunt's image locally, but his use of the subjective 'interests' in place of 'wishes' raised more than a few eyebrows.

Rex told the author much later that he had been forced to tread extremely carefully and was actually fully supportive of Adrian Monk. But he knew that anything he said publicly would get back to the Foreign Office in London. He recalled:

> I had already heard that rumour had spread in Whitehall that I had 'gone native'. The last thing I wanted was to be replaced by a new governor who might well have been more interested in his career than the Falkland Islanders.

At their next meeting in January 1981, a little over a year before the invasion, councillors agreed a motion stating that they did not like any of the Ridley proposals but that they could reluctantly accept a moratorium, or freeze. Only Adrian Monk opposed the motion.

Of course this was a failure for London. The hopeless freeze concept had only been included in the Ridley package to make leaseback look more attractive. In Buenos Aires the British Ambassador, Anthony Williams, fussed around the Argentine Foreign Office, apologising for Islanders' hostility and trying to patch up relations. The Argentines issued a statement dismissing the importance of Islanders' opinions. They would, they said, only negotiate with Britain.

There were more talks scheduled for New York in late February and Councillors Adrian Monk and Stewart Wallace were chosen by their colleagues to attend. It was a dismal meeting and it was announced on 24 February that the Argentines had thrown out the freeze concept.

That was no surprise. Of more interest was the desperate personal appeal by the leader of the Argentine delegation to the two Islanders. Recognising that they hobbled British policy, Wallace and Monk were told that Argentina would give them all the material comforts and special status that they wanted in exchange for some symbolic gesture over sovereignty. Any mealy-mouthed mumbo-jumbo would do so long as the Argentines could hold a piece of paper up to their people saying that the 1833 score had been settled. It was clear that leaseback would have been seized enthusiastically by the Argentines. The countdown to war might have been stopped there and then, but the councillors had no mandate to make even the slightest concession, even if they had wanted to do so.

Back in the Islands, they were grilled on local radio. BBC South America correspondent Harold Briley was visiting and he asked outright if there had been any threat of force. Stuart Wallace answered:

> There was no overt threat of any sort. There was simply the implication that 'you are being silly. You can't possibly go it alone when you are so far away from the country you regard as

the mother country. Now be reasonable and have an agreement with us.'

They talked about how much patience the Argentines have had with us, and how any stability we have here now is due to their involvement here and the provision of certain services which have cost them money and political capital.

There were to be no more talks that year and with local elections planned for September, much of the steam had gone out of the present councillors. Life in Stanley was gloomier than usual, but calm.

Writing in his memoir 'My Falkland Days', Rex Hunt described the air of unrealistic optimism that still pervaded the Foreign Office in London. While on leave in Britain, he attended a meeting with Nicholas Ridley, the British Ambassador to Argentina and other senior officials, at which the prevalent view was that Islanders should still be pressed to make concessions to the Argentines. It was reported that Argentina was well disposed towards the leaseback idea and that they were 'reasonably relaxed' about the progress of negotiations. However, Argentine diplomats had said their military compatriots were less patient.

Rex Hunt listened, amazed, as the diplomats disregarded all the evidence that must have been gathered by Ridley and subsequently by a senior Foreign Office official who visited Stanley to quietly confirm opinion. The tack was to change slightly. Rather than emphasising the supposed benefits of friendship with Argentina, Islanders should be educated about the dangers of hostility to change. It was suggested that Islander confidence could also be secured with offers of resettlement in the UK for those who could not accept leaseback, promises of more distribution of farming land and economic development initiatives.

To his credit, Rex – who clearly risked confirming he had gone native – repeated the message that had been reiterated many times: *Islanders were not going to buy any of this.* "There was an air of un-reality in the meeting, far removed from the realities of the situation in the Falklands," he wrote.

Pouring cold water on the the Foreign Office dogma might have had some impact. Rex recalled that by the end of the meeting it had simply been decided to play for time with Argentina, and persuade the new Falklands Council, when elected, to allow talks to continue.

In July the hawkish Argentine Foreign Minister, Nicanor Costa Mendez, passed a note to the British Embassy, which, with hindsight, seems pregnant with threat. The British Ambassador was told that Argentine patience was being severely strained by the slow progress of talks:

The time has come for these negotiations to be effective. It is not possible to postpone [substantive talks] without territorial integrity and national dignity being affected.

Ominously, there was an understated reminder that the air and fuel services could be withdrawn if there was no progress. These veiled threats were precisely what many Islanders had feared since the Communications Agreement was signed in 1972.

Emigration continued against a grim economic backdrop. Sheep farming was going through a bad phase. In April one farm laid off its entire work force. The population dropped to almost 1,800.

As if that was not enough, there was growing evidence, clear to some Islanders, that the Argentines were planning an endgame. One did not have to be a professional spy to read the signs. And yet London seemed to be ignoring them.

Major Gareth Noott arrived in the Falklands in March of 1981 with a platoon of Royal Marines to take over the Islands' defence as the latest Naval Party 8901. He was not entirely new to the Falklands, having visited Stanley several times aboard HMS *Endurance* when he commanded the small Marine detachment on the ice patrol ship back in 1969.

The 34-year-old officer, temporarily promoted from Captain for the posting, was not happy that he had left his wife and two young daughters, but anticipated an uneventful and reasonably pleasant year spent renewing his acquaintance with the Falkland Islands.

Naval party 8901's brief was to form a 'tripwire,' a Cold War defence concept that required the commitment of minimal men and assets. The device was supposed to be high profile, credible and well understood by the potential enemy. Any attack on the thin line of defenders would activate the tripwire, triggering an overwhelming strike on the aggressor.

Noott was aware, of course, that the only boots even remotely likely to stumble over his wire would be made of the finest Argentine leather, but routine pre-departure briefings had not given him any reason to believe that there was a serious risk of this – at least not on his watch. He recalled that the intelligence assessment prior to his departure from Britain and throughout most of his time in the Falklands had been that the Argentines would not consider invasion until they had settled their dispute with Chile over the Beagle Channel, and such a settlement did not appear imminent. "My briefing," he recalled, "suggested that there might be a lot of shouting, but nothing would happen."

Even when his replacement, Major Mike Norman, arrived with his team, twelve months later, virtually on the eve of invasion, the intelligence had not changed much. Noott recalled that Norman told him, "We'll spend the winter settling in, getting sorted out, and come the summer what we can expect is a blockade situation."

The Naval Party 8901 of 1981 spent the year much as its predecessors had done, training, maintaining the rundown Moody Brook barracks and socialising. As Noott explained, the challenge was to keep his young, fit and energetic men gainfully employed:

> The main thing was to stop the Marines from going mad and drinking themselves to death. It could have been a problem if you didn't give them something to do.
>
> We had a very basic system. There were three sections, and one would be tasked to maintenance, while another section was training, and the third section was patrolling out in camp. They rotated weekly. The main task of those at camp was to visit the settlements and to be seen to be around. It was all about keeping up morale, so that the Islanders felt they were being protected.

Priority for the commanding officer was to develop a training plan for the year, and in this Gary Noott was fortunate to have one of the toughest Marine NCOs in the Corps. Corporal Geordie Gill had married a local girl during a previous Falklands' tour and was delighted to return to his second home. A qualified sniper (who later took a heavy toll on the Argentines), Geordie was as gung-ho as they come. When he suggested to his boss that he could keep the Marines busy practising hostage rescue operations with live ammunition, Gary Noott was delighted. It confirmed that, as far as training went, the Islands had real advantages.

> Under Geordie's very capable management – in other words no one actually got killed – each of the sections were trained up to carry out live firing hostage rescue in a timber and canvas simulated building. It was all about bursting in, firing a few shots and chucking a few grenades around. Obviously there were no live hostages, but there was plenty of scope for fuck-ups!
>
> Geordie asked me if I wanted to come along and watch, and I said no! All I needed was for him to come back to me at the end of the day and tell me that no one had been killed or injured.
>
> If anybody in UK had heard what I was doing, I would have been court martialled on the spot. It was a risk, but in the Falklands you had the latitude to do that.

16

Noott enjoyed a genteel social life, slipping comfortably into the senior social strata of colonial Stanley. It was a small clique consisting of the Governor and his wife Mavis, Chief Secretary Dick Baker and his wife Connie, Director of Public Works John Broderick, and the recently arrived new Chief of Police, Ronnie Lamb. The Chief Medical Officer Daniel Haines and his doctor wife Hilary and a few other administrators completed the circle. The male domination was relieved by the presence of senior nurses from the hospital, what Noott called 'the spare birds list'. He remembered social protocol as rigid:

I said to Mavis Hunt once that I was thinking of having a curry lunch up at the mess on Sunday and would she and Rex be happy to come? She said, "Yes Gary, delighted. There's only one problem: the OC RM comes to lunch at Government House on Sundays."

Nevertheless, he knew some locals, and he detected a sadness about Stanley which was evidence of its decline.

It was something I discovered from Jack Sollis [the local skipper of *Forrest*, the small coaster that carried the Marines around the islands]. He told me that in years gone by there had been a butcher, a baker and a candlestick maker. They had all gone. Everything was dying from the centre, while on the outside everything appeared to be OK.

The junior ranks of the Marines spent their free time in Stanley's few rough and raucous pubs and at the Saturday night dances in the Town Hall. When the bars and the Town Hall closed, duty drivers were usually waiting with a truck so that they and their girlfriends and drinking partners could retreat to the bar at Moody Brook, which did not have to adhere to normal licensing hours.

Noott was inclined to let the Marines amuse themselves as they saw fit, as long as they remained able to train and do their work. By nature he was not one to worry about petty rules. Many of the soldiers grew their hair longer than the regulation length and abundant moustaches drooped fashionably below upper lips. Some men even began wearing single earrings, in the style of the local men, although most excess hair and jewellery came off on the rare occasions when the Marines joined Falkland Islands Defence Force to parade through Stanley and salute their Commander in Chief, Rex Hunt.

Noott insists the lax discipline did not matter. "Yeah, I suppose their hair was a bit long," he said. "So was mine. I allowed a degree of idiosyncrasy."

The Islanders and Rex Hunt did too, although questions were asked when, some seven months after the Marines' arrival, Captain Nick Barker of HMS *Endurance* inspected Naval Party 8901. Even then, however, Noott did not place much importance on the issue:

> I think there were probably some comments in his report, but I wasn't going to lose much sleep. As far as I was concerned the Marines got something of value out of the Falklands. If people wanted to criticise their hair and so on, well, let them.

Most years the Bootnecks, as the locals called them, married a clutch of local girls, taking them back to the UK. The drain on the female population was not good for the Islands and seemed to hasten the day when the community would be unviable. But to the girls the young soldiers were exotic and a good catch. Marrying a Marine was also a way out of the Falklands for those who (like most Islanders) had no automatic right to live and work in Britain. There were far more men than women in Stanley and, as the Marines' OC recalled, "when the girls got fed up they would ring the bell and everyone changed."

He found the political signals coming out of London disturbing. Both Marines and Islanders were angered by Whitehall plans to weaken the tripwire defence. For a while in 1981 it appeared that on-off plans to replace the dilapidated Moody Brook Barracks with a modern complex in Stanley were going ahead. Gary Noott had even seen the blueprints. But suddenly they were again cancelled, this time with the kind of emphasis that rang of finality.

Then the bombshell: after the 1981/82 southern summer, HMS *Endurance*, the Falklands' guard ship, was to be scrapped. There would be no replacement.

The senior Marine tried to allay local fears by saying that there would be more frequent visits from ships of the 'grey funnel line' – conventional destroyers and frigates. But this did little to reduce the sense of abandonment. More importantly, a very strong signal had been sent to the Argentines. Correctly or otherwise, Buenos Aires interpreted the Falklands' defence cuts as proof positive that Britain had lost interest in its colony.

These were depressing developments for the Marines, but maintaining the tripwire would soon be the responsibility of others: they were counting the weeks until the end of their tour and they could then put it all behind them.

The Marines concentrated on their training, especially Corporal

Gill's thrill-a-minute live firing hostage rescue simulator. Perhaps because they remained so busy, or perhaps because the Marines were used to having military intelligence supplied from sources further up the military chain of command, they did not notice the increasingly blatant signs that suggested Argentina was preparing to invade.

Chapter Two

Warning Signals

Much of the day-to-day management of the Falklands was left to Dick Baker, the Chief Secretary and Rex Hunt's right hand man. Through his routine daily contacts the affable Colonial Office man was picking up some odd signals. He and his wife, Connie, had served many years in the small Pacific territories, always paying careful attention to 'the coconut radio'. Here in the Falklands there was the 'diddle-dee telegraph' (after the prolific shrub that covers the Islands), and it too provided a mix of patchy evidence and rumour that could only be ignored at one's peril.

Twenty years on from the Franks Report, which claimed no one, least of all ministers in London, could have anticipated an invasion, the Bakers still shook their heads in disbelief. They found Lord Franks' conclusions ridiculous, even insulting to those who were on the ground. Both are certain that from evidence they gathered during the last six months of peace, there was justification for the British Government to take notice and head off the coming crisis. Dick Baker was not coy. "Not only could people have foreseen it, a lot of us *did*," he said. "The tragedy was that no one in London seemed to want to know, or to react to the signals."

They also felt that ordinary Islanders were being kept in the dark. Plenty of them were developing uneasy feelings, but they did not have as many pieces of the jigsaw as Dick Baker and Rex Hunt. Had they been told of the growing risk, even a few days before the invasion, an evacuation of Stanley children could have been arranged. It had been done in two world wars when Stanley was under threat and it could have been done again. However it was considered that any such talk would be scaremongering, and Dick was not encouraged to publicise his fears.

Remarkably, it seemed that some of the evidence was being deliberately leaked from Argentina and could only be interpreted as a warning. In October 1981 a senior expatriate officer in the Public Works spent a few weeks being treated at the British hospital in Buenos Aires. When he returned to Stanley on the Argentine LADE aircraft he was a very worried man indeed and made his way immediately to Dick Baker's house. He told the Chief Secretary, "I've been hearing these terrible things at the British Hospital. They say they are definitely going to invade at the end of March."

Later that year the wife of Councillor Adrian Monk, the hard-liner who had said all of the Ridley proposals "stink," also came back from Buenos Aires and hot-footed it to the Bakers' door. Norah Monk had been visiting an old friend in Buenos Aires, a rich Anglo-Argentine socialite called Eleanor Salmon, who entertained the movers and shakers of the capital. They included senior members of the ruling military junta. Eleanor Salmon had told Norah Monk that the Islands would be invaded. She had it on good authority and was even able to give an approximate date. She had pleaded with her friend to continue on to Britain rather than go back to the Falklands.

Argentina and Britain were planning their next round of talks for New York in January 1982. They would also be attended by two Falkland councillors. Could the junta have been feeding such stories to Falklands' residents, knowing that they would get back to officials and councillors? Perhaps Norah Monk's husband Adrian and his ilk were being told that they had one more chance to be reasonable – or else.

As he did whenever a sliver of useful information was picked up, Dick told Rex Hunt of these reports, and he assumed Rex passed the information on to London. He doubted, though, that they were being taken seriously. "We were constantly making reports of one sort or another," he said. "But no doubt they would have been regarded by London as local tittle-tattle."

Rex Hunt confirmed that all such reports "went on the secret line to London." He agreed that they were worrying, but none of them gave any hint of the vital missing fact: "We did not know *when* they were going to invade."

Some of Dick's reports had shades of a John Buchan thriller. Often there was little tangible evidence to back up the reports that came in from around the Islands, but they could not be ignored. He remembered a typical suggestion of intrigue coming from Iain Stewart, the manager of the local Cable and Wireless station, and his wife Hulda, who had been enjoying their Christmas 1981 holidays on remote New Island on the far west.

Twice Iain phoned me. He felt he could talk to me, and said, 'Look, we don't want to be scaremongering, but we kept on

21

hearing these aeroplane noises. We didn't see them, but they seemed to be close. It sounds like a Beaver [aircraft used by the local air service] when the prop is in coarse pitch.'

These reports came from other islands too, and we thought with hindsight that they were probably the sounds of helicopters from Argentine warships doing reconnaissance.

Then there were reports from Weddell Island of lights seen at sea and evidence of people coming ashore; farm gates left open and damaged fences, that kind of thing.

Hard evidence of Argentine skulduggery emerged when Air Service pilot Eddie Anderson spotted an Argentine oil rig support ship, the *Yehuin*, in a secluded bay. HMS *Endurance* steamed off to investigate and was told by the Argentine captain that he was simply sheltering from heavy weather. *Endurance* had not noticed the heavy weather but, consistent with the British kid-glove policy, *Yehuin* was allowed to motor away. It seemed obvious that the ship was intelligence gathering, and perhaps testing *Endurance*'s ability to react. After the invasion, *Yehuin* turned up in Stanley under Argentine naval control.

By the late summer Dick Baker believed that all the evidence he had passed on suggested that something big was afoot. In particular, he thought a major military exercise that the Argentines had said they were planning was to be a sham.

He assured himself that the intelligence people must be aware of what was going on, but he was still troubled. "Why did nothing happen about it?" he wondered later. "That is the great mystery to me."

He had a good point. Although there were at least two spies at the British Embassy in Buenos Aires, they were hardly covert. One was a military attaché whose interest in all things military would have been assumed by the Argentines, and the other was a civilian, Mark Heathcote, who worked for MI6, the Secret Intelligence Service. In his book *At Her Majesty's Secret Service*, the intelligence specialist Nigel West says that Heathcote was 'declared' to the Argentines, meaning they knew why he was in Buenos Aires. It would, consequently, have been easy to insulate him from any informants or activities that might have shed light on 'Malvinas' plans.

To be fair to the Argentines, they had sustained remarkable secrecy in Buenos Aires, and Nigel West writes that not even the CIA agents there had any idea what was going on. If the Americans had picked anything up vis-à-vis the Falklands, no doubt they would have passed the information on to Heathcote.

In any case, the professionals seemed ambivalent. Stephen Love

22

visited the Falklands twice; on the last occasion, shortly before Christmas 1981, when Dick Baker's antennae were twitching wildly. Dick described Love as "a caricature Colonel Blimp" who appeared to enjoy the party circuit rather too much. Nevertheless he told Love about his suspicions. "I said several such things to him, but you never knew to what extent he was taking it in or mentally discounting it."

Mark Heathcote also visited in 1981. Protocol dictated that Rex Hunt dealt with him, and any detailed conversations between the two remained confidential. But in his post-war report Lord Franks absolved Heathcote of blame, claiming that the agent's attentions were spread too thinly around a very large part of South America.

Dick Baker increasingly felt that his efforts to sound alarm bells in London were wasted. He had some dark suspicions: either his reports were being dismissed as alarmist tittle-tattle or, more worryingly, there was a deliberate policy to ignore the signals and weather the storm of an invasion in the hope that, when the outrage subsided, Britain would be rid of a troublesome colony. He recalled: "We used to joke that we were expendable. If a few of us expatriates had a hard time or even got killed, but the Falkland question had been settled, that would have been an adequate price to pay."

By February the Argentines had become quite brazen in their sabre-rattling and intelligence gathering. There were unexplained nocturnal flights over Stanley. Those who heard the aircraft or saw the lights in the small hours believed that they were military Hercules planes. Twice they dropped flares as they flew over Stanley Airport. The flares may have been signals to LADE staff who would have confirmed the accuracy of their navigation.

The Argentine Air Force operated a small flight of Lear Jets, equipped for photo reconnaissance and beacon calibration. They had flown to Stanley at infrequent intervals during the late 1970s to test the airport's navigational aids. But now the fast jets began behaving mysteriously.

On one occasion HMS *Endurance* lay at anchor in Stanley harbour, from where her tiny Wasp helicopters ferried supplies to the Marines at Moody Brook. Suddenly a Lear Jet sped from west to east down Stanley Harbour, making one pass over *Endurance* before flying back to the west. Neither the route nor the height were normal for a beacon calibrating flight, and were far more consistent with a mission to photograph *Endurance*.

Remarkably, no one on board the ship spotted the aircraft. Government House had also missed it, as Connie Baker found out when she visited Rex Hunt's wife, Mavis, later in the day. "Do you know, Connie," said Mavis, "Nanny really must have been drinking the gin at lunchtime because she says she saw a Lear Jet go past."

"She did," responded Connie Baker, "because I saw it go past too. It just flew straight over *Endurance*."

Normally the head of LADE, Vice Comodoro Hector Gilobert, would have advised Dick Baker when a calibration flight was due, but this time there was no warning. The debonair and friendly Argentine was coming to the end of his time in Stanley. He and Dick had enjoyed a warm friendship, but now the Chief Secretary was chilly and demanded an explanation.

In his halting English, Gilobert insisted that he had known nothing of the flight and Baker believed him. But after checking with the mainland, the Argentine called back to confirm lamely that there had been an unexpected "calibrating flight". Perhaps knowing that his explanation was not credible, he seemed embarrassed.

Dick again raised his suspicions with Rex Hunt and hoped that the information would be passed on to London. He remembered being sure that Rex shared his fears, but thought the Governor did not want to talk about them.

The Lear Jet crew appeared to be up to their tricks again a few weeks later when there was another flight during which it loitered over the Stanley area. Gerald Cheek, then the Director of Civil Aviation, said that LADE had advised him of the incoming flight. Gilobert's posting to Stanley was ending, and his replacement, Vice Comodoro Gamin, had officially taken over. But before he settled down in LADE's imposing Stanley house, Gamin had been shuttling to and from Argentina. Now he was on his way back to Stanley, but the pilot reported an undercarriage problem, prohibiting a landing, and flew off again. Later the same day, the aircraft returned with Gamin, and this time it landed. However when the duty customs officer, Fraser Wallace, walked across the tarmac to greet the Lear Jet, the door was opened, Gamin left very quickly, the door was slammed shut again and the pilot began an immediate take off. Gerald Cheek recalled, "It was all rather suspicious, as what looked like a camera pod was fitted to the underside of the fuselage."

In the last week of February 1982 diplomacy breathed its last gasp, although most thought that the Argentines could be conned along for some time yet. Years earlier, Foreign Office minister Ted Rowlands had described British policy vis-à-vis the Falklands and Argentina as "kicking the ball into the long grass". Tim Blake, a farmer and councillor who participated in the talks, explained it: "When you met you kicked the ball around the pitch for a while and then with a bit of luck, you kicked it into the long grass and it would take a bit of time to find it. It was the method we had been using ever since 1971."

Tim Blake and Councillor John Cheek, who had been newly elected to the Legislative Council in October 1981, travelled to New York, where they joined British and Argentine diplomats. They were to report back to their colleagues on any proposal that either party might put forward, before returning to another round of long-grass-kicking one month later.

The councillors returned to Stanley on 2 March, exactly one month before the invasion, and reported confidentially to their colleagues on Executive and Legislative Councils (Exco and Legco). Even before their LADE plane touched down in Stanley the Argentine popular press was shrieking outrage at the 'failure' of the talks and quoting bellicose words from the military government. Even the *Buenos Aires Herald* (never a lapdog of the military government) soberly reported a source in the government, believed to be the Foreign Minister, Nicanor Costa Mendez, saying that Argentina was preparing to break off diplomatic relations with Britain unless there was a successful outcome very soon. He refused to discount the possibility of military action:

> No diplomat can talk about the use of force. A decision of this nature is taken without any prior notice. We are willing, very firmly, to go as far as need be if the archipelago is not returned as soon as possible.

Islanders were rattled and demanded to know what had gone on in New York. Unfortunately for Blake and Cheek, they had been sworn to secrecy and were unable to tell their constituents anything. In the information void, a legend developed about this meeting. Locals believed that Argentina had issued an ultimatum, about which they should have been informed.

Almost two decades after the meeting Tim Blake felt free to talk openly. Considering the growing tension, the meeting was, said Blake, inconclusive and not particularly tense:

> At the end of day one we were going to continue discussing ways of co-operation, and ways forward. All we had to do after that was draft a communiqué. But they had obviously conveyed to BA what they thought had been agreed, and were told to go back and start again. So we covered exactly the same ground on day two.
>
> Then we drafted a communiqué, saying that we would aim to progress the relationship, and that we respected each others'

position on the sovereignty dispute. It was another 'long grass' situation.

We had no inkling that they were losing patience. It was odd. To this day I don't believe that the people in New York were aware of the level of planning in BA.

The idea that we were [made] aware that they were going to invade is something that people have invented.

Some councillors meeting in Executive Council favoured breaking the confidentiality clause and openly discussing the parlous state of diplomacy with ordinary Islanders. But Governor Rex Hunt insisted that confidentiality could not be broken. There were other meetings during the next few weeks, but no public explanation.

Penguin News was outraged:

The meetings have been shrouded in secrecy to a degree that would not exist in most other democratic countries. Such secrecy is tantamount to irresponsibility. While Legco and Exco plus every petty Foreign Office agent in Stanley are in on the big secret, we, whose way of life is up against the wall, are left un-informed and wondering.

But somehow the old taboo remained and the 'I-word' was still not being mentioned. No one was systematically assessing the threat of invasion and talking about it, even though the clock was ticking.

It seems likely that in the disappointing wake of the New York talks, the junta gave the final green light to planning and preparations for an invasion. The intelligence gathering activity was stepped up.

By far the most audacious of the Argentine Air Force's stunts was the landing of a Hercules transport on Stanley's tiny runway. Such large aircraft had visited before, when the Argentines flew in building material for the LADE chief's home. But the 6 March landing was carried out with a clearly spurious excuse.

With hindsight, Dick Baker saw the flight and the landing as either a spying mission or a rehearsal for an Entebbe-style raid. It was a quiet Sunday afternoon and the pilot had radioed Stanley claiming his Hercules, supposedly on a routine mail dropping flight to an Antarctic base, was leaking fuel. He needed to land immediately. When Vice Comodoro Hector Gilobert disturbed the Baker household asking for permission, Dick did not refuse it, but decided he would drive to Stanley Airport to have a look at the aircraft.

Dick watched with growing concern as a few dozen obviously senior officers disembarked. They were not the sort of men to go on supply flights, but they *were* the kind of invasion planners who would love to have a good look around Stanley. The Chief Secretary smelt a rat and the stench became stronger when one of the airport's technical staff told him that there was no firm evidence of a fuel leak. [Rex Hunt disputes, this, however, saying that he had been informed that the aircraft was obviously leaking fuel as it taxied in.]

Gilobert packed the officers and crew into LADE vehicles and took them for a tour of Stanley and its environs, possibly slipping in a visit to the little penguin colony which just happened to be located in the bay where Argentine amphibious troop carriers rolled ashore some three weeks later.

Argentina's plans for invasion were well advanced by early 1982, but were to have been carried out at least a month after the actual invasion date and possibly as late as September or October, during the southern spring. But when the British Antarctic Survey (BAS) scientists in South Georgia, some 750 miles south-east of the Falklands, reported on 20 March that an Argentine military transport ship had unloaded men and materials at nearby Leith Harbour the situation began to spiral out of control. Suddenly there was an opportunity to bring the invasion forward.

After consultation with London, Rex Hunt asked the BAS men to order the Argentines to reboard their vessel and depart. Although they had obtained commercial rights to dismantle the station from the British owners, Kristian Salveson, they had ignored British immigration procedure.

The British Embassy in Buenos Aires registered an official protest and Buenos Aires duly ordered the ship to leave Leith. The BAS observers in the mountains above the old whaling station reported, however, that a handful of men had remained. And they had raised the Argentine flag.

HMS *Endurance* was in Stanley on 20 March, her crew enjoying a 'run ashore' with the Marines of Naval Party 8901. There was the usual competition for the charms of Stanley's girls at a Saturday night hop. At about midnight the music was interrupted and the DJ announced that all *Endurance*'s sailors and the tiny onboard Marine force were to report back to the ship. Clearly something was up.

Endurance was to have left the next day for Montevideo, where the new detachment of Marines was to be picked up. Those plans were scrapped and before dawn *Endurance* weighed anchor and headed for South Georgia.

There was frustration in Stanley and relations with the few Argentines living there became fraught. The LADE air service was continuing, but on the night of Saturday 20th a few local youths, fuelled with bravado and beer from the dance, broke into Vice Comodoro Gilobert's office and daubed 'tit for tat, you buggers' across a desk. They draped a Union Flag over the Argentine flag before leaving. The office was not seriously damaged. Two days later an outside wall of the LADE office was spray-painted with the words 'UK OK'.

It was relatively harmless stuff, but Vice Comodoro Gamin, who had just replaced Hector Gilobert, was worried. The LADE Fokkers never scheduled overnight stops at Stanley, but on this occasion one of the aircraft had developed a fault and needed to remain on the tarmac. He insisted that Gary Noott's Marines guard it around the clock. This was not too much bother to Noott, as, unknown to Gamin, the Marines had been staking out the airport. Ironically, they had been guarding against Argentine action, but turning this around to guard an Argentine asset against mischievous locals was straightforward enough. "We had been on a shorter state of alert for a couple of weeks," recalled Acting Sergeant Geordie Gill. "For a few days before the invasion we had a section [about seven men] in the airport terminal building every night. A few guys kept watch while the rest of us slept and were ready to move at very short notice."

Buenos Aires newspapers loved the antics in Stanley. They reported a mob attack on the LADE office, during which the Argentine flag had been torn down from a staff outside the building and burned. No such flagstaff existed. There were further fictional accounts of assaults on Argentines living in Stanley.

It would have been funny, but the raiders of the LADE office had played into the hands of the propaganda merchants, helping them to escalate the crisis. Rex Hunt went on local radio appealing to the hotheads for calm.

The Royal Marines stranded in Montevideo when *Endurance* was directed to South Georgia were rescued by the British Antarctic Survey's ship, RRS *John Biscoe*. The bright red ship, an angular and elderly little steamer of a design that harked back to the 1940s, was in Stanley, having completed her seasonal programme of work in the Antarctic. Rex Hunt asked the skipper to head for Montevideo, cram the 41 Marines aboard, and bring them back to Stanley.

All members of the new NP8901 were volunteers, mainly from 42 and 45 Commando. A few troops had travelled to the Falklands some weeks earlier to prepare the hand-over, but most of the fresh force flew out of Britain with the soon-to-be Falklands CO, an old friend of Gary Noott's, Major Mike Norman.

Before leaving Britain Norman was briefed about the evolving political situation, but given virtually no up-to-date information about the Argentines' military assets, capability or intentions. In particular, the intelligence officers told him nothing about Argentina's amphibious capability. This, according to Norman, was to become a serious issue:

> When we made our final decision as to which of the two beaches we would defend, we chose the one that we thought was a good amphibious option, based on our knowledge of landing craft. Had we known that the Argentines didn't have landing craft but had amphibious personnel carriers, then we would have selected the other beach, which was long and shallow.

This was particularly unnecessary ignorance, as Norman found out about a year later when he lectured on the defence of Stanley to a military audience. At the end of the presentation, a Colonel Sidwell stood up to speak:

> I'm surprised that you didn't know about their Amtracks [amphibious personnel carriers], because when I visited Argentina before the war, they showed them to me and said, 'These are what we are going to use when we invade the Malvinas.' I came back and reported all that to our headquarters.

Mike Norman was shocked:

> The Argentines were telling Colonel Sidwell, 'You'll see these again.' Amtrack is not a very sophisticated vehicle. If we had had decent anti-tank capability, they would have been fairly ineffective.

The political brief was equally succinct. An intelligence official said there was little doubt that the Argentines would now tighten the economic screw on the Islands. Fuel supplies might be withdrawn and the air service might be cut off, leaving Stanley isolated. The agent's final summary was casually imparted, as if he cared little:

> Life for you and your detachment, and all the Falkland Islanders, will get very uncomfortable in the next six months. They could always, of course, take the military option, but I don't think they'll do that. However they are a very unpredictable race.

During a briefing from SAS staff Mike Norman asked how re-inforcements might be despatched to the Islands in a crisis. The officer maintained a straight face: "We'll parachute them in from Concorde."

During the four-day trip south from Montevideo *John Biscoe* received a visit from the Argentine Air Force. Clearly Argentine eyes and ears in Stanley were aware of the ship's mission. A few hundred miles off the Argentine coast a Hercules buzzed the *John Biscoe* repeatedly. The plane was so close that Falklanders among the crew had to be restrained from turning the ship's fire hoses on it. Until then Norman had not appreciated the hatred that so many Islanders felt towards the Argentines.

On the evening of Monday 29 March, three days before the invasion, Gary Noott and his slightly depleted force (ten of his forty men had embarked on *Endurance* for the South Georgia mission) welcomed their replacements and began the normal hand-over procedure. It was a mundane process of checking stores and accounts, and briefings.

There was some pressure to get this housekeeping done as everyone still assumed *Endurance* would soon be back in Stanley, embarking the departing Marines for their trip home.

That first night in Stanley Gary Noott and Mike Norman sat up late sharing a bottle of something strong and chatting. They shared no sense of alarm, but Noott told Norman about the many suspicious Argentine flights, in particular the bold Hercules landing. He still feared an Entebbe-style raid and was convinced that a relatively small number of men pouring from the back of a Hercules or two could make a successful assault on the town. He told Norman about the airport guard section and said that he had taken the extra precaution of having a quick-reaction section on round-the-clock standby at Moody Brook. Now that reinforcements were here, he planned to stand that down.

Apart from those precautions, everything in Stanley appeared to Norman to be unremarkable:

> I don't think anybody thought that there was going to be military action. Every night that week, apart from the night of the invasion, there was either a drinks and buffet party or a dinner party that I had to attend.

The two officers explored the town. Noott was surprised to meet Hector Gilobert by the LADE office. The Argentine was supposed to be back on the mainland, having handed over to his replacement.

Gilobert explained that he had come back to help sort out the LADE accounts.

They joked that he could also lend a hand with the Moody Brook accounts if he had the time to spare, as these had proved to be troublesome. The three men laughed heartily and went on their way.

The next surprise meeting was with a small band of journalists living at the *Upland Goose Hotel* on Stanley's seafront. Simon Winchester from the *Sunday Times* seemed to be the natural leader of a team that included reporters for the *Sun* and the *Daily Mail*.

The two majors were quizzed about what was going on and the journalists were taken aback by Norman's response:

'You'd better come up to Moody Brook for tea and tell us what *you* think is going on. Because we don't know if anything is going on.' We said, 'Should we be getting worried now that you three have arrived?'

On Wednesday afternoon, 31 March, the mood changed. The Marines' secure link with Britain was through their Commander in Chief, Rex Hunt, at Government House. He had received a message which was as confusing as it was disturbing. American intelligence had picked up a radio signal indicating that some action around the Falklands was imminent and they had passed it to London.

Hunt called the two senior Marines to his office and told them in his typically understated style that an Argentine submarine would carry out a 'surfaced overt' reconnaissance of the beaches around Stanley over the next day or two. The Marines were to 'look out for it and observe'. Unless the invaders came ashore with all guns blazing, they were to 'arrest them peacefully'.

A submarine mission made perfect sense if an invasion was on the cards: sending special forces ashore to survey landing beaches is a normal tactic. But why 'surfaced overt?' Mike Norman summed it up:

I said to Gary, 'If they want to carry out a reconnaissance with a view to invading, they are not going to stick a sub on the surface in Stanley Harbour or Port William so we can all see it.'

The Marines studied a large-scale map of the area and identified a few likely targets for the Argentine sub. They put a 24-hour observation post on Sapper Hill to the south-west of Stanley, which gave a good view of beaches to the south, placed another lookout at Cape Pembroke Lighthouse and reintroduced the rapid reaction section at Moody Brook.

31

They had looked at the defence plan briefly the day after the arrival of the new party, but the meeting with Governor Hunt made Norman, as he put it, "sufficiently worried" to ask Noott to walk through it, showing him the terrain that might be involved in an attack. Conscious that the expanded Marine force did not have enough weapons to go around, they also despatched a few men to borrow rifles from the Falkland Islands Defence Force and zero them on the range. Early the next day, Thursday, the men set off with a few Marines to check possible landing sites and defensive positions.

Gary Noott had spent part of the previous winter revising his predecessor's defence plan and the latest version had only been approved by Rex Hunt a few weeks earlier. It was reviewed by the OC every year during the long winter months as little more than an academic exercise.

The plan's emphasis was on defending the Governor as the living symbol of British rule. Noott recalled that the Marines' original plan was to position food and ammunition dumps around the Islands (in fact they were never laid) so that the Governor and at least one group of Marines could flee into the camp and remain there until help arrived. (Rex Hunt later said he had only agreed to the idea of laying dumps and as many Marines as possible escaping into the camp, but it was never envisaged that he would go with them. This was certainly consistent with his decision to stay at Government House, regardless of the circumstances, later.)

Fighting within Stanley certainly did not come into the plan. There would be initial violent opposition to any landing, ensuring that a 'peaceful annexation' could not be claimed.

Noott and Norman decided that one of the two beaches in York Bay, a quarter of a mile north of Stanley Airport, would be the most likely location for a large-scale landing. They decided to make a stand in York Bay and, if that failed, conduct a fighting withdrawal to Stanley. Norman believed that, at the very least, his men could slow the Argentines:

> The general idea was to have sections positioned at strategic points along the road. They would open fire with everything they'd got, making the Argentines stop, deploy their troops, and cause maximum casualties.
>
> As soon as they started returning fire, the Marines were to pull back through the next section, with covering fire if necessary. The Argentines would get themselves together, start advancing, only to be engaged again as soon as they came into range. This would continue until the final position at Lookout Rocks, where Lt Bill

Trollope would organise all the sections into a standing troop position before retreating to Government House. There was to be no fighting in the streets of Stanley.

We were trying to cause maximum casualties, to get them to stop and think. Perhaps then somebody, somewhere, would start negotiating.

Armed only with rifles, general purpose machine guns (GPMGs), 66mm anti-tank and two 84mm Karl Gustav anti-tank weapons, the Marines would be in place over the most likely beach, on Canopus Hill overlooking the Airport, at a bottleneck on the Airport Road called the Canache, and at a few other points along the road into Stanley.

Defending the correct beach would be crucial and here the disastrous lack of tactical intelligence became an issue. The Marines were specialists in amphibious warfare, and easily established that one of York Bay's two beaches, separated by a rocky point, would be suitable for a landing. But which one depended on the Argentines' equipment.

The Marines *wrongly* assumed that the invaders would use conventional landing craft, more suited to the steeply shelving east beach. Instead the invaders rolled in over the west beach, which was gently sloping and ideal for their Amtrack amphibious vehicles.

Stanley Airport was also viewed with concern. An invading force was most likely to land troop transports on the runway, possibly in the Entebbe-style raid that Noott believed they had rehearsed, or in support of a seaborne landing. The runway should be cratered but the Marines did not have enough explosives to make a significant impact on the asphalt. They would have to be satisfied with placing large objects on the runway.

The modified and more aggressive plan was the best the Marines could come up with, but Mike Norman was realistic:

I'd been asked by my young Marines when we were doing our pre-embarkation training, 'What's the best thing we can do if an Argentinian invasion force lands? How many do you think they would send?'

I said, 'If we were to attack an island with a defending force of 41, then the minimum invasion force would be a brigade. The best thing we can do is go fishing for the day!'

Their rushed survey complete, the team paid a visit to the lighthouse keepers at Cape Pembroke and the few Marines there who were scanning the horizon for a submarine. It was there, at 15.00, that they

33

received a message radioed from Moody Brook. Rex Hunt had received an encrypted 'secret/flash' telegram from London and he needed to see them urgently.

It took the men 45 minutes to drive across the rough terrain of Cape Pembroke and along the road to Government House. The Governor met them in his office with a strange requirement of protocol. Because Mike Norman was the senior major by just two months, and officially the new OC of NP8901, the signals intelligence (sigint) he now had could only be shared with him. Noott had to leave. It must have seemed a slight, but it made little difference as a few minutes later Norman gave his colleague chapter and verse:

Rex Hunt said, 'We've got another sigint. I'll read it to you: "We have apparently reliable evidence that an Argentine task force will gather off Cape Pembroke early tomorrow morning, 2nd April. You will wish to make your dispositions accordingly".'

I looked at Hunt, and Rex said, 'The silly buggers! We've been calling their bluff for 25 years and we are the ones who are going to catch it.'

This was not the first time Rex Hunt had been facing an overwhelming attack, and he was unflustered. On the staff of the British Embassy in Vietnam, he had experienced the Viet Cong's merciless Tet Offensive and the chaotic withdrawal from Saigon. "He was very calm," recalled Mike Norman. "He is not short of courage."

As Gary Noott paced up and down outside the office, Mike Norman turned his attention to practical matters. "We've got a lot to do now," he said to Rex Hunt. "I'll come back and tell you when we are ready."

First priority was to get the Marines back to Moody Brook. The departing party were being put up in the spare rooms of friends around the town, and most were enjoying a final few days with girlfriends. Ten hydrographers left behind by *Endurance* were also to drop their maps and instruments and get to Moody Brook ASAP.

Geordie Gill had first been posted to the Falklands in 1967. He loved the place and was virtually a local. He had returned voluntarily for three tours since and was married to a local girl, Sonia (although they were separated). His two daughters lived in the town. He had a very privileged billet with his relative by marriage Chuck Clifton, the landlord of the popular *Globe* bar. Geordie recalled:

We had just had a session at the *Globe*, and I had gone up to my room to get ready for lunch. There was a knock at the door and it was the duty driver, who said he'd been told to come to collect

34

me, and take me around to help him pick up all the lads from my detachment, and get them back to the Brook.

Back at the Brook and while the lads were getting off the truck, I went to my boss and asked what was happening. 'This had better not be another drill,' I said, 'because the lads are a bit fed up.'

He said, 'It's not. I'll tell you but don't tell the others until I can brief them.' He explained what was going on, and then he said, 'Get in there and close the bar.'

That was probably the most dangerous thing I did, because as soon as they'd got off the truck the lads had headed for the bar. The new detachment were in there already, and I had to tell the barman to close up. He said, 'Is it serious?'

I said, 'Put it this way: you don't want the lads drunk.'

Nidge Buckett (who would later receive the British Empire Medal for her work during the occupation) knew the Marine detachment well, and she and her husband, Ron, were putting up several of the young men. One of those staying in the Buckett household had missed Geordie's roundup, so Nidge volunteered to drive him to Moody Brook herself. She recalled seeing a camp that was clearly tense and preparing for something. She drove in, dropped her lodger off, and seeing the sergeant-major, started chatting with him. Uncharacteristically, the sergeant-major gave her the brush-off, saying he was too busy to talk. Nidge shrugged her shoulders and drove off back to Stanley. But a few minutes later the truth dawned on her, and she jammed on the brakes. "I thought, Oh shit! They're coming. I realised what I had seen. It was organised chaos. They were moving, and they were moving purposefully."

Mike Norman was certainly purposeful. He recalled the briefing he gave his force when all the grumbling about the bar's premature closure had ceased, and the men were assembled quietly:

I said, 'All those that thought you were going home, we've got new plans for you. The Argentinians will be here tomorrow, and it is very likely they will invade. We will now start getting the defence plan ready. Tomorrow is the day you'll really earn your pay.'

Then we gave them their priorities of work. They were still out preparing positions at last light.

We loaded all the barbed wire we had onto a truck and took it down to York Bay, where we put it all on the *wrong* beach. We hadn't enough to do two beaches, and barbed wire was the extent of our defensive stores.

Mike Norman, just four days into his Falklands posting, was in command of a force of Marines and a handful of co-opted sailors which, although double its usual strength, was horribly small.

While preparing a final set of orders, he found he had to consult Gary Noott almost constantly and, eventually, he suggested that it would make sense for Noott to take over command. They had been good friends for years and there was no competition between them. Norman remembers a mature and sensible response from Noott:

'No, you command. If there's any problem, just call me in, as we are doing now.'

So we agreed to stay as we were and I ploughed through his contingency plan. Meanwhile Gary was outside burning and destroying cryptos [secret signals] and any classified files.

The same was going on at Government House.

Geordie Gill recalled that the mood among the Marines was calm. "It's what we were there for," he said. "It's what we had trained for and everybody wanted to prove themselves."

He did not consider the impending invasion much of a surprise. The briefing before the 2001 deployment had recognised the increased tension. "I had felt that the deployment that year was a bit more serious," Geordie said.

He was, though, annoyed because through most of the year he had been responsible for his own section, but temporary promotion to sergeant meant that he now had to take on HQ duties. As a qualified sniper, this was not where he wanted to be. Nevertheless, he got on with his duties without question, leading the team of men who were putting barbed wire on the anticipated York Bay landing point. There, this confirmed tough guy experienced a moment of almost spiritual calm. As Geordie explained:

It was coming up to dusk as we were putting the barbed wire out, and it was one of the absolutely fantastic Falklands sunsets. The sky was blood red and everybody stopped what they were doing on the beach to look at it. I've talked to a couple since, and we were all thinking the same thing: if this is going to be the last one that we see, then at least it's a good 'un.

Thursday was a normal working day in the Government Secretariat. Dick Baker had been fielding routine business and enquiries from the reporters led by Simon Winchester. He had made an arrangement to

36

see them for a relaxed chat after work, but as he was thinking about leaving the office for the day Rex Hunt called saying he was to attend a meeting at Government House at 16.30, "You will know what for," he said.

Similar calls had gone out to the other heads of government departments: the Treasurer, Harold Rowlands; Chief of Police, Ronnie Lamb; Senior Medical Officer, Daniel Haines; Harbour Master, Les Halliday; Acting Director of Public Works, Harry Bonner; Gerald Cheek of Civil Aviation; Phil Summers, Commanding Officer of the Defence Force. The list went on.

A worried group gathered in the lounge of Government House. Rex Hunt told them that all the diplomatic stalling had failed and they had some final departmental duties to perform before the Argentines arrived. The police were to call out special constables; the Public Works was to place heavy vehicles and whatever other obstacles they could find on the airport runway. The Air Service was to ferry its little *Islander* aircraft to the racecourse for possible reconnaissance flights. The hospital was to prepare for the worst; and the Defence Force was to mobilise. They should, however, all make their preparations quietly: the news would be announced to the general public a few hours later.

Probably all who were there worried about the prospects for the Defence Force. They were all part-time soldiers who trained more for ceremonial duties than actual warfare. Superintendent of Education John Fowler asked that some plan be made to ensure that the Islands' young men were not slaughtered. Their commanding officer indicated that he would see to this.

It was, recalled Dick Baker, "a very strange meeting". His senior local civil servant, Harold Rowlands, sat stony-faced, and afterwards "shambled off" looking demoralised. There was little discussion and no sense of panic. It was as if everyone had secretly known what was coming. The taboo had, at last, been broken.

Dick Baker stayed on after the other men left. Rex Hunt was not sure about the legal procedure for declaring a state of emergency and Baker was to check this out with the government's senior legal officer, Harold Bennett.

The Chief Secretary was also told that he would lead a team to arrest the handful of Argentines who were living in Stanley, principally the two Argentine military officers employed by LADE, Vice Comodoros Gilobert and Gamin, and the team of workers who were building a new depot for Gas del Estado, the state-owned company which supplied gas to the Islands. Government House had received a third message saying that London now had "reason to suspect there may be an inside element to this invasion". The gas men looked like a fifth column.

Around Stanley that afternoon there was plenty of talk about increasing tension around South Georgia, but little fear of invasion. The situation even had potential for a laugh or two. At the Government's rather grandly named Plant and Transport Authority depot, the mechanics broke the monotony of fixing Land Rovers by giving David Colville, the fiercely anti-Argentine Editor of the *Falkland Islands Times* a 'scoop'.

Senior mechanic Rudy Clarke persuaded a young Chilean immigrant on his staff to phone the *Times* editor and impersonate a journalist calling from Argentina.

Effecting an even thicker accent than usual, the Chilean completely fooled Colville with a bravura performance: "How do your people feel about our planned visit to Stanley? We will soon liberate you all from British imperialism."

The editor insisted that Falkland Islanders did not *want* to be 'visited'. Eventually he slammed down the phone, and scurried up Ross Road to advise the stressed Dick Baker and as many councillors as he could contact that they had better get ready for 'liberation'.

Back in his office, Colville received another phone call from the mechanics. This time he was reminded of the date: April Fools' Day.

At 7.30 that evening the joke did not seem at all funny. Then Rex Hunt went live on the Falkland Islands Broadcasting Station to tell Islanders the grim truth.

To the last he was going to avoid alarming them and the radio station backed him up by keeping to their normal schedule. Special requests (music for the ill and elderly), the for-sale and wanted notices, and 'Sing Something Simple' would go ahead come hell, high water or invasion.

The Governor's historic announcement had a slow-burn effect. His listeners became gradually more horrified.

I have an important announcement to make about the state of affairs between the British and Argentine Governments over the Falkland Islands dispute.

We have now sought an immediate emergency meeting of the Security Council on the grounds that there could be a situation which threatens international peace and security. I don't yet know whether it has been possible to arrange a meeting today, but our spokesman has been asked to make the following specific points. The Secretary General has today summoned the British and Argentine Permanent representatives to express his deep concern over the situation in the South Atlantic and has urged restraint on both sides. It is right that the Security Council should endorse and back up his approach.

We, for our part, have continued to make every possible effort to resolve the current problems by diplomatic means. The British Ambassador in Buenos Aires yesterday delivered a further message to the Argentine government urging a negotiated settlement to current problems, and offering to send a senior emissary to Buenos Aires. The Argentine Foreign Minister had today responded to this approach in negative terms. He had declined to discuss further the problems occasioned by the illegal presence of Argentine nationals on South Georgia, and he had specifically stated that he no longer wished to use diplomatic channels to discuss the situation in South Georgia.

In addition to the Foreign Minister's unwillingness to pursue diplomatic exchanges, there is mounting evidence that the Argentine armed forces are preparing to invade the Falkland Islands. In these circumstances it is essential that the Security Council urge that there should be no resort to armed force and that diplomatic negotiations should be resumed.

In these circumstances, I think it is necessary to take certain precautionary measures here in Stanley. I have alerted the Royal Marines and I now ask for all serving members or active members of the Falkland Islands Defence Force to report to the Drill Hall as soon as possible. They will be on guard tonight at key points in the town. Schools will be closed tomorrow. The radio station will stay open until further notice. If the Security Council's urging to keep the peace is not heeded by the Argentine Government, I expect to have to declare a state of emergency, perhaps before dawn tomorrow.

I shall come on the air again as soon as I have anything to report. But in the meantime I would urge you all to remain calm, and to keep off the streets. In particular, do not go along the Airport Road. Stay indoors, and please do not add to the troubles of the security services by making demonstrations or damaging Argentine property. This would play into their hands and simply provide them with the excuse they need to invade us.

As Rex Hunt's voice faded, a stunned silence descended on every house in the Islands. People could hardly believe what they had heard. It was broken by the chirpy voice of continuity announcer Michael

39

Smallwood: "Remember what it says on the first page of the Hitchhikers' Guide to the Galaxy, folks: don't panic!"

At 11 o'clock on Thursday evening, when the Marines had prepared their defences and eaten a hot meal, Mike Norman gathered them together for a final briefing. He fielded a few questions first. One wag piped up: "I don't suppose, sir, there's any chance of settling this with a game of football, is there?" (In better times *Endurance* had played soccer against the Argentine Navy during courtesy visits to Buenos Aires.)

Another young Marine was fresh from Northern Ireland and wanted to know if he should give the Argentines a verbal warning before opening fire. Norman said there should be no such courtesy.

For hours Norman had been worrying about how he could adequately explain what was about to happen and inspire the men to go out and fight against such overwhelming odds:

> It was probably the most difficult thing I've ever done: trying to give convincing orders to men who you knew had no chance of winning and were very likely going to die. They knew that too. They were not fools. And I was convinced that most of us would surely die.
>
> I just went for it and gave it in an upbeat fashion, telling a joke every now and then. I made a play on the fact that we were Royal Marines and proud of being an elite force, and this was a bunch of dagos coming; basically a hobo army with national servicemen that was used to bullying natives. Who the hell were they to think we were going to lie down and be run over? We had a good fighting tradition and we would give them a bloody nose.
>
> I remember my final words: 'Tomorrow, when it all happens, forget the Falkland Islands and forget the Royal Marines. Tomorrow you are fighting for yourself. We are going to be totally outnumbered, and each of you will be fighting for your own life.'
>
> They all burst into applause, saying, 'Let's get 'em! We're off!'

There would have been little point in trying to stop the rush for the armoury. The men were keen and for the first time the quartermaster was not being mean with kit. For once they ignored the 'Gucci' stuff – the coveted watches and leather gloves, grabbing instead rifles (the supply normally only adequate for forty-one men had been augmented with weapons borrowed from the Defence Force), rocket launchers, grenades and as much ammunition as they could carry.

There was a weapon of last resort for Rex Hunt. The Governor had asked Mike Norman to let him have a 9mm pistol, and the officer obliged.

The naval hydrographers were issued with Sterling sub-machine guns, taught how to load a magazine of 9mm ammunition and then unload it again in the right direction through the business end.

Considering the strong likelihood of sacrifice, it is remarkable that a former Marine who had settled in Stanley made his way back to the Brook to join his old comrades. Jim Fairfield had married a local girl and left the Marines a year or two before. But corps spirit is a strong thing, and he turned up asking for a uniform and a rifle. Norman and Noott happily attached him to a section.

Mike Norman stood by the main entrance to Moody Brook saying a few words to the sections of heavily laden men as they jumped into Land Rovers and trucks and headed for the hastily built defences above the beach, at the airport and along the Airport Road. He felt in awe of them:

> These men were being let off the leash. I saw each section off from Moody Brook with the same message: 'Do your job well – nothing stupid, mind. There's no need for medals.'

Gary Noott set off with Geordie Gill and a section of men to establish the HQ and operations room in Government House. It was, Geordie remembered, a terrible moment, and yet he was in no doubt about what he had to do.

> People you'd known for years were driving off into the darkness and you knew that you were probably never going to see them again.
>
> Being marines we always thought that the Navy would help us. But we were told we were on our own. I thought, 'There's going to be two troops' transports and five warships off the Islands by first light. They've got armour, they've got artillery, they've got mortars, they've got air cover. And we're going to fight them until we're overrun.' In every other conflict that I'd been in, before or since, you always knew there was a chance you could get hurt or killed. Every other time there was chance, but in this one we all more or less knew it was going to be us.
>
> You were worried for the Islanders, but you had to put that out of your mind and just do what we had to do. Ever since then I've felt guilty that my daughters Tanya and Alicia, were up on Pioneer Row, about 400 metres away from where I was going to be fighting, and there was nothing I could do to help them.

I felt it was something worth fighting for, and I'm pretty sure that most of the rest of the lads did too. It was our flag that was flying, the people were British and we were the only ones there to try and stop these people taking this away from them. And for me it was personal, I was fighting for my country *and* for my kids.

Chapter Three

Battle for Stanley

Bill Curtis was an idealistic Canadian. Worried that he and his family would die in the nuclear holocaust that looked entirely possible in the late 1970s, he and his family emigrated some 8,000 miles to the peaceful Falklands. There, he had barely completed the shell of his new house before his war-free dream was shattered.

Back home, Bill had worked in electronics and he now hit on a scheme to meddle with the LADE beacon on the ridge just outside Stanley. He drove to Moody Brook where the stressed Mike Norman made time to consider Bill's plan. The Canadian wanted some Marines to help him break into the beacon and shift the radio beam. With luck and a lazy pilot, an Argentine Hercules packed with troops would be directed past the Islands, into the deep Atlantic.

If ever there was a man to whom straws were desirable flotation aids it was Mike Norman, so he nodded his agreement and Bill Curtis was loaded into a Land Rover.

Driving through Stanley, those in the vehicle saw occasional little groups of civilians talking over gates and fences. They glanced up nervously as the Marines smashed Stanley's strict 20-mph speed limit. They passed the telephone exchange and saw the shadowy figures of the Defence Force on sentry duty, their rifles poking out from the gloom.

The weather was infuriatingly perfect, calm and almost balmy. When Bill said as much, there was a grim, grunted reply from the Marine behind the wheel: "Yeah. A great day to die."

A more normal April night might have delivered wind-blown stair rods of frigid rain that would have dampened the Argentines' enthusiasm for a fight. But whatever anybody would die of the next morning, it was not going to be hypothermia.

The men forced the door of the candy-striped installation, but were confronted by a mystifying array of wires and buzzing boxes. The beacon-tweaking caper was shelved in favour of random destruction.

This was not going to send the invaders hopelessly off course, and any military pilot worth his salt would not have to rely on a comforting navigational beam. The action was indicative, however, of the desperate measures being adopted that night.

By midnight the Marines had abandoned their barracks. Gary Noott and a handful of his men, including Geordie Gill and a few of the hydrographer sailors left behind by *Endurance,* had set up a head-quarters at Government House (known to all as GH). Rex Hunt's office was in a timber-built section of the building, so the Governor moved into his deputy's office in the original stone wing and Noott set up his operations centre in an adjacent room.

Geordie recalled hours of tension and sustained efforts to maintain spirits.

> You cracked jokes, but deep down you didn't want to let your mates know you were scared. It was the waiting. It's always the waiting that is the worst thing. I could see a lot of the lads looking at me because I was almost 35 and I'd been in the Marines a long time. I thought, 'If I show them that I'm scared (which I was – I've never been so scared in my life) it's going to make it worse. So I was putting an act on. I was saying, 'If you're scared, think how scared they are. We've only got to take on the Argentines, but they know they've got to fight Royal Marine Commandos, which is enough to scare anybody.' It was when I was on my own and had time to reflect that it came crashing back down.

Like all of the Marines, he was familiar with the Governor, who would sometimes referee their rugby matches and share a beer or two in their mess while watching videos of the big rugby games from back home. Geordie recalled that as the Marines waited and worried that night, Rex demonstrated his concern for them.

> I was at the east end of GH, with two other lads. We were all blacked out and I felt this tug on my sleeve. I looked around and there was Rex, in his suit, white shirt and tie. He said, 'Everything OK, Corporal Gill?'
>
> I thought, 'Yeah! We're just about to be hit by about 2,000 enemy soldiers and there are 60 of us. Couldn't be better!' But he was good news. I've got a lot of respect for him.

From GH, the HQ unit attempted to keep in touch with the dispersed sections, especially Mike Norman, who planned to be in direct command of the sections opposing the anticipated landing at York Bay. He had established a tactical HQ at Lookout Rocks near the Airport Road. Sections, mostly of six men led by an NCO, were on Canopus Hill above the airport; at Hookers Point, overlooking a major bottleneck; on a low ridge parallel with the Airport Road; by the (now vandalised) Argentine beacon, and on the Murray Heights overlooking the southern approaches to Stanley.

Two men were detached from the Canopus Hill section to establish a presence on York Bay. Another section was located at Navy Point, on the west side of the entrance to Stanley Harbour, just in case a landing craft helmsman foolishly attempted to arrive in style through the front door. Confirming the Argentines' wisdom in launching their initial attack from an unlikely quarter, just one man was located on Sapper Hill to the south-west of Stanley.

Meanwhile the Falkland Islands Defence Force (FIDF) was preparing for the invasion quite independently of the Marines. Their OC, Major Phil Summers, had tasked the approximately forty part-time militiamen to guard such key points as the telephone exchange, the radio station and the power station.

No one has ever questioned the courage of the young and poorly trained weekend warriors who turned out that night. Like the Marines, they waited and wondered if this would be their last night. But their role was seriously flawed. FIDF and Marine plans were not coordinated and, as the locals had no radios, communications were almost non-existent.

Mike Norman was disappointed that the FIDF were not placed under his control. "I was absolutely amazed that I wasn't allowed to task the FIDF," he said. "I had to *suggest* orders to the Governor."

Militarily this was irrational, but from every other angle it made a great deal of sense. To send the ill-trained FIDF into a battle it could not win and lose the flower of the Islands' youth would have been virtually criminal. In any case, it was the Marine force that constituted London's tripwire, not the FIDF.

But as far as the FIDF was concerned, they were going out that night to fight if necessary, and by doing so they exhibited as much bravery as the Marines. The professionals had borrowed most of the Defence Force's modern self-loading rifles, meaning that newer recruits and those who arrived late at the Drill Hall were issued with Short Magazine Lee Enfields, the famous 'smellies', the ancestors of which had been used in the trenches of the First World War. The FIDF models were post-Second World War, but they were still bolt-action single shot weapons.

There seemed, however, to be some consolation in the assumption that the armourer would, at long last, break into the hallowed stock of grenades. But Phil Summers was by day a civil servant at the Treasury and he had a parsimonious attitude to public property. His alleged reply to demands for the grenades is the stuff of local legend: "You can't use those," he said. "They're far too expensive!"

Private Fraser Wallace had joined the force only a few weeks before and had never fired a rifle. In the crowded Drill Hall he helped fill magazines with 7.62mm ammunition and when that chore was over he joined others guarding the approaches to the HQ. He recalled some very basic orders and a very frightening night:

> 'You see an Argentine, you shoot him,' I was told. 'That's the magazine, and that's the trigger.'
> I hadn't a clue! I had a vague idea which way to point it but that was as far as it went.
> Everything you heard was amplified about ten times. You weren't quite sure whether you were hearing things or if something really had happened. I was laying down by the gutter in the road and I heard shots. I was convinced the entire Argentine army were after me. They'd really come to get me!
> Phil Summers did his reassuring, fatherly act: 'It's all right son. We're all a bit nervous now. You're just hearing things.'

Gerald Cheek, then a senior NCO with the FIDF, recalled: "We were requested to phone in to HQ whenever possible, and when I made the routine call at 06.00 hours Phil Summers informed me that the Governor had said FIDF members were not to engage with the enemy under any circumstances, and they were to surrender when ordered to do so without offering any resistance."

It seems that by 06.00, most of the FIDF men had received this message and had decided to return to the Drill Hall.

Anthony Davies, known as 'Taff', was the only experienced soldier among them. Taff had been a Marine and met his wife Jackie when serving with Naval Party 8901 in the late 1970s. He left the Corps in 1979 and settled in Stanley. That night he felt he had to do something to help and became the FIDF's newest member. Taff recalled that, in spite of the lack of experience and the understandable nerves, the men were calm. He believed that they could have been used much more effectively, but could also see that the decision not to throw them into combat was correct: "We had 2,000 screaming Argies breathing down our necks. We got off very lightly that night, but the decision didn't make sense to us then."

The FIDF's separate chain of command led to serious confusion. The danger of 'blue-on-blue' or friendly fire incidents between

Marines and FIDF was huge. Mike Norman himself nearly opened up on the FIDF. He recalled that, unknown to the Marines, an FIDF team was in the middle of their defensive barrier.

> I was talking to Marine Patterson, and in my peripheral vision I saw movement. I whispered to Patterson, 'There's somebody coming up the road!'
>
> Patterson and I had the doors open and we were both trying to get our rifles from behind the seats and get the safety catches off. I thought, 'Streuth! The OC's going to be the first casualty and he doesn't even have a flaming rifle in his hand.'
>
> By this time we could see them clearly. Then I was amazed to hear Patterson, who'd been in the Falklands for a year, say, 'Hi Fred – or some other name. How are you?' He'd recognised one of his local mates. It was the FIDF.
>
> I put my rifle down, and said, 'Where are you going?' They said, 'We've got to be back at the Drill Hall by first light.'
>
> They don't know how close they came to being shot.

So far, so amusing. But the next FIDF-related confusion led to a serious error. About an hour before dawn the solitary Marine watching the south-westerly approaches to Stanley from Sapper Hill signalled that he had detected men approaching. These could only have been Argentine special forces, the Argentine Buzo Tactico commandos who were to attack the barracks at Moody Brook and Government House. However, earlier in the night, Mike Norman had asked Rex Hunt to task Phil Summers to move some FIDF men into a position on the rocks above the racecourse in case the Argentines attempted a heli-copter landing there. The men had moved into place quite promptly, but Norman did not know this. When he heard of the Argentine move-ments south of Sapper Hill he assumed this was the FIDF section belatedly moving to its new position.

The sighting should have given Norman just enough time to re-deploy men to block the approach of the Buzo Tactico and deny them the vital high ground above Government House. In the event there was no such counter-deployment and the assault on GH came as a complete surprise.

There had been a few moments of wry humour. Rex Hunt's chauf-feur and *major-domo* Don Bonner was deeply attached to his boss and Government House, where he had a grace-and-favour cottage. Don had borrowed Rex's 12-bore shotgun, staked out the flagstaff on the lawn and told Mike Norman that he planned to shoot "any Argy who tried to bring down the flag."

Norman found this amusing, but Don seemed serious. Fortunately for Don, no 'Argy' received a blast of buckshot. But Rex was touched by such loyalty. "I tried to send Don home because the Argentines were likely to treat my staff rather badly," he later recalled. "But as far as my recollection goes, Don was with me throughout the evening."

Another local civilian was involved in a far more serious duty. Jack Sollis was the captain of MV *Forrest*, the little government-owned coastal ship that the Marines used for their routine inter-island patrols. Jack was joined on the bridge by two of the hydrographer officers left behind by *Endurance*, Lieutenants Ball and Todhunter, and asked to take his ship on patrol in Port William, Stanley's outer harbour. There Jack and the naval officers would scan the horizon by radar, attempting to get an early warning of the approaching fleet.

About 80 feet long and unarmed, *Forrest* risked running into some very dangerous warships. The crew were well aware that if *Forrest* could spot the Argentine fleet, then the fleet could certainly spot *Forrest*.

The ship slipped its mooring shortly before midnight and made for the open sea. Jack made his first radar contact soon after 02.00. He radioed Mike Norman that at least one large ship – much bigger than any foreign fishing vessels that might be in the area – was about five miles off Mengeary Point, and approaching fast. A visual scan revealed no navigation lights. He then headed back to Stanley and *Forrest* was back at her jetty by 03.00.

Speaking on the radio from his tactical HQ, Mike Norman asked Jack Sollis to conduct a second patrol. Jack replied that he did not think this was a good idea. From where he was moored he could see the lights of an aircraft carrier to the east, beyond the Canache.

If he was right, this was alarming news. Mike Norman leaped into a Land Rover and drove to Hookers Point which provided a good viewpoint. He could see no such vessel, and concluded that Jack had seen the shadowy hulk of a grounded sailing ship, the *Lady Elizabeth*. In the clear night, a cluster of stars around the ship's masts might have resembled navigation lights. Back on the radio, he gently suggested to *Forrest*'s skipper that everyone was seeing things that night. The carrier was not there.

Jack Sollis was one of the Falklands' most experienced mariners and he was unlikely to mistake the hulk of a sailing ship for an aircraft carrier. Indeed, later in broad daylight, a Stanley resident with a good view of the outer harbour phoned the radio station to say that he could see a carrier in Port William. But Jack accepted that Mike Norman had a better vantage point and he put to sea again, this time taking the sensible precaution of dodging around the headlands and between Polish fishing ships moored in Port William.

At 05.15 the little ship radioed reports of two further contacts off Mengeary Point. The crew had spotted ships closing on them from the open sea to the east. Mike Norman realised that the position was becoming too dangerous and recalled *Forrest*. But the crew were not done. On the way back into Stanley they reported another two contacts near the expected York Bay beachhead and off Charles Point, sightings that were confirmed a few minutes later by the civilian staff of the blacked-out Cape Pembroke Lighthouse. Ten minutes later Jack reported that he could see smaller craft heading for York Bay.

Forrest's finest hour was almost her last. As she approached the Narrows, the entrance to Stanley Harbour, the section of Marines defending it were at a high state of alert. Psyched-up by the radio traffic which suggested half the Argentine fleet was in the area, they had flicked off safety catches and were aiming anti-tank missiles and a general purpose machine gun on the unlit ship. Wisely, the section leader, Corporal Yorke, called Mike Norman, requesting permission to open fire. Norman realised the supposed landing craft was *Forrest* and barked an order for the men to hold their fire.

Jack Sollis' entirely reasonable argument against taking on the aircraft carrier had been overheard by everyone on the network. Young section commanders are typically bad at radio communications. As Mike Norman put it, "They talk to you when they want to talk to you, not when you want to talk to them." But from that point on every operator was hanging on his transmit button.

Coups and battles had been covered before on live radio, but Patrick Watts, the manager of the government-owned Falkland Islands Broadcasting Station (FIBS), made broadcasting history with the first invasion phone-in.

Rex Hunt had a dedicated line to the FIBS studio and used it to update Islanders and issue whatever instructions he thought necessary. But before the day was out locals would be calling in with tactically useful reports of the Argentine advance. Eventually, even the invaders would use FIBS to get messages to Government House.

At about 03.00 Rex Hunt delivered the latest grim news. He told listeners that President Reagan had personally telephoned General Galtieri and urged restraint. Galtieri had cold-shouldered the most powerful man in the world. Unless Britain recognised Argentine sovereignty immediately he would do whatever was necessary.

Rex calmly announced that Galtieri's intransigence had forced him to take drastic action:

I have no alternative other than to declare a state of emergency with immediate effect under the Emergency Powers Ordinance of 1939. Under these emergency powers I can detain any person, authorise entry to any premises, acquire any property, and issue such orders as I see fit.

I must again warn people in Stanley to stay indoors. Anyone seen wandering on the streets will be arrested by the security forces.

I have no further news about the Argentine Navy task force, but may I just say that the morale of the Royal Marines and the Defence Force is terrific, and it makes me proud to be their Commander in Chief.

With the legal powers to justify his action, the Governor now ordered Chief Secretary Dick Baker to lead a small team of armed sailors rounding up the several dozen Argentine citizens living in Stanley. They included the new manager of LADE, Vice Comodoro Gamin, and his predecessor, the popular Vice Comodoro Hector Gilobert.

Dick and Hector were friends, but he had no idea why the Argentine had returned after handing over to Gamin in February. Would he lead an Argentine fifth column? Or perhaps he was there to act as a go-between in surrender negotiations. Perhaps he had even been telling Gary Noott and Mike Norman the truth: he *had* come back simply to sort out the LADE accounts. Whatever the reason, he was to be arrested.

Of more concern was the team of some two dozen youthful Argentine engineers and builders who were erecting a new depot for Gas del Estado. Some of them had been seen showing an unnatural interest in Stanley's dock facilities, and the latest troubling information to be received from American intelligence via London indicated that there would be an 'inside element' to the invasion.

Dick Baker, gentle, polite and supremely non-martial, led his party of armed hydrographers out to arrest the suspects. Not surprisingly, he remembered it well:

There were a few local people to arrest, and I remember being terribly apologetic to them, and saying, 'Because you are Argentine or married to an Argentine, or work for LADE we have got to take you into custody.' We put them in the refreshment room of the Town Hall, which was near the police station.

Then we went on to arrest the Gas del Estado people. When we got to the *Upland Goose Hotel*, they were all in their rooms. We were very careful about entering, so we did it the way they do in the best films: I stood to one side with an armed man on either side and knocked on the door.

The hotel owner's daughter, Alison King, spoke Spanish, so she interpreted. They all expressed disbelief and amazement. One even asked if he had to pay his bill before leaving. I said, 'No, I think we can worry about that afterwards.' No one showed any signs of belligerence, but none were unduly upset either.

Next on the list were the senior LADE officers. Travelling up Ross Road in a Marine truck at 06.05, Dick Baker heard the opening shots of the war being fired at Moody Brook, and rightly assumed the invasion had begun. It was not, however, on top of them yet. Still wondering whether Gilobert and Gamin might have been put in place to help, and also concerned that they might be armed and ready to fight, Dick decided to call in on Rex Hunt again to further discuss the issue.

Rex Hunt agreed that it was a mystery, but Dick was told to go ahead with the arrests and then make his way home to Connie and the girls. There would be nothing more he could do. It was 06.15 when the Chief Secretary left Government House by the west door. Virtually at the same moment the second prong of the special forces team began its attack. Dick Baker:

> As soon as I opened the door there was a fusillade of shots. I tried to get out a couple of times, and then decided I had better stay where I was. When I went back in to Rex's office he said, 'What the hell are you doing still here?'
>
> I said, 'I can't get out! They're firing on us! And I still haven't got Gamin and Gilobert!'
>
> I was stuck in GH, so I asked one of the sergeants what I could do to help and he said, 'Sit in that corner, sir, with your arse against the concrete and keep out of the fucking way. That's the best thing you can do!'

For Geordie Gill the fear and tension that had been building up during too many hours of waiting had vanished.

> When we heard them hit Moody Brook and we saw the flashes, it was fantastic. The waiting was over and now we could get down to doing our jobs. You just stopped being scared. OK, they might be going to kill us, we thought, but by Christ they'll know they've been in a fight. We weren't going to let down the other Marines back in the UK.

The vanguard of Argentine forces in Operation Rosario, the 'retaking of the Malvinas' were well-trained special forces of the Marine Amphibious Company. [According to author Nick van der Bijl writing in his book *Argentine Forces in the Falklands*, they were *not* men of the Buzo Tactico, as has often been claimed. A small force of Buzo Tactico – commando divers modelled on the famous American Navy Seals – did, however, assist with the later mechanised landing on York Bay.]

Some 90 men of the Marine Amphibious Company, armed with light weapons including British-made silenced Sterling sub-machine guns, landed from inflatable boats launched from the destroyer ARA *Santisima Trinidad* (a British-designed Type 42 ship), rather than from the submarine which Norman and Noott had been tasked to look out for.

Anyone with experience navigating small boats around the Falklands would have known that the coasts are surrounded by an almost continuous belt of thick kelp; seaweed with strands up to an inch thick that entangle propellers and choke outboard engines. The Argentines had no such knowledge, and their boats spluttered to a stop one after another. The current pushed the boats away from their targets and the soldiers cursed and cajoled their engines while paddling furiously. From the earliest stage, Operation Rosario was delayed and stressed.

Once on shore at Mullet Creek, a few miles south of Stanley, the group divided into two – one to pin down, kill or capture the Marines at Moody Brook, and the other to snatch Rex Hunt from Government House, which, it was hoped, would be undefended. The party bound for Moody Brook had the longer and more difficult hike. Sweating with the hard work of traversing extremely uneven moorland and the fields of boulders which bisected their route, the party was slipping badly behind schedule. The situation was exacerbated when one man fell and injured an ankle. He was left behind as the party fought to reach their objective before dawn.

As Hugh Bicheno notes in his book *Razor's Edge*, the 'decapitation' plan was dependent on surprise, and it was an early indication of the Argentines' inflexibility that the plan went ahead unchanged even though Argentine commanders must have known the timetable was slipping and the element of surprise had been lost.

The commandos undoubtedly planned to hit both targets simultaneously, but their timing was out and the abandoned barracks were attacked some ten minutes before Government House. Their attack was supposed to be a *coup de main*; so sudden, precise and overwhelming that the Marines would not have been adequately organised

52

to defend themselves or the Governor, and would have surrendered quickly in disarray. Given this intention, it would have been reasonable for the operation's planners to decree that there should be no loss of life if at all possible. They would have believed dead and injured Marines or Islanders would have complicated the diplomatic furore that was sure to follow Operation Rosario, but which they hoped to ride out.

Years afterwards, some Argentine accounts still maintain that the invaders maintained an effort to avoid loss of life, even after they were bogged down in a ferocious open battle against the Marines. No account of the fighting supports this.

Mike Norman, at his tactical HQ a little to the east of Stanley, remembered feeling a frisson of fear as he recognised the sound of live bullets and grenades at the Brook. Until then, he and Gary Noott had been expecting the Argentines to do the obvious: pour ashore in York Bay. He now realised that at least some had entered by the back door. He and his men were facing the wrong direction and Government House was going to be hit before the sections east of Stanley could make their planned fighting withdrawal, so the OC and his small staff immediately headed back to join the slim HQ section and the sailors defending GH. Simultaneously he ordered some of the five sections dug-in around the beach, the Airport and the Airport Road back to Stanley.

Section Five, above Stanley Airport, sped back to take up new positions around the Cable and Wireless station next to Government House. They covered the west entrance to the GH grounds.

Section One, led by Corporal Armour, was withdrawn from its position on Hookers Point covering the Airport Road. Their route back to GH took them into trouble. The men (members of the new Naval Party 8901 to whom the geography of Stanley was still a mystery) ran through the streets towards the west in the general direction of Government House but got lost.

Fortunately, they met up with Corporals Carr and Williams leading Section Six, which had been ordered back from the Murray Heights. Both NCOs were old Falklands hands and were able to give useful advice to the others. They moved ahead towards the football pitch that separated Government House from the ordinary homes of Stanley and were met with fire from a wooded area and ridge a few hundred yards south of GH. Carr and Williams radioed the contact to Mike Norman and were ordered to make their way to GH via the more accessible Ross Road on Stanley's seafront. Corporal Armour's Section One sprayed automatic fire into the trees as Section Six made a run for the seafront.

Having lost their own radio communications some time earlier, Armour's section then took a bold initiative. This account from Corporal Armour's official engagement report:

One Section pepper-potted down the road towards the wood where we knew Government House to be. Movement was slow as we had to crawl and monkey run until we reached the hospital. It was now daylight. From there the section fired and manoeuvred behind the nurses' home and across the football pitch until we reached a hedgerow. I informed Marine Parker to call out, 'Royal Marines!' as we approached the house. We were eventually heard by Corporal Pares, who told us where the enemy were. The section, under cover from Corporal Pares, then dashed into the house where we were deployed upstairs by Major Noott.

Things were getting confusing for Section Six on the seafront. Radioing their HQ for further orders, Gary Noott ordered them to 'go covert' near Sapper Hill, which, with their local knowledge, they were well equipped to do. But by now the Argentine special forces were spilling out into Stanley and getting anywhere near Sapper Hill meant street fighting.

Corporals Carr and Williams and their men ran the few hundred yards up Barrack Street past Joan Bound's Newsagency and the Co-Op general store, and tried to dash across the children's playground on St Mary's Walk. Here they came under rifle and machine-gun fire from four or five enemy sheltering in gardens. They returned the fire and withdrew. There were more attempts to reach the Sapper Hill area, but each time the men came under accurate fire from the gardens of civilian homes. Eventually the section came within sight of the wooded area and the low ridge from where they had taken fire earlier. There were movements in both areas, and the section laid down fire with its GPMG. They then leapt fences and ploughed through gardens near the *Malvina House Hotel*, to the jetty where *Forrest* was moored. Jack Sollis was asked if he would carry them across the harbour. Jack (quite rightly, according to Mike Norman) said no. With the sun now up and the enemy in Stanley, the bright red ship would be a fat target. Jack offered the ship's small inflatable boat instead, but all attempts to start the outboard motor failed and Section Six decided to stay put.

Mike Norman and his small team were back at GH within six or seven minutes of hearing the attack on Moody Brook. The CO ran to the ops room where Gary Noott and Rex Hunt were discussing the situation. As he did so, a frenzy of firing began outside the west entrance and Norman reversed his steps to find out what was going on:

I ran outside and shouted to our blokes, 'What are you firing at?' But it wasn't them. It was incoming fire. Then, as well as the firing, there were lots of very, very loud explosions.

Gary shouted out to me, 'What are they firing?'

I said, 'It sounds like bloody artillery to me. Or mortars.'

Noott was shouting from the west porch of GH, while Norman was sheltering behind (of all things) a rusting Norwegian harpoon gun that was now a weird garden ornament. On the other side of the harpoon was Lieutenant Todhunter, one of the naval officers who had been at sea with Jack Sollis earlier that night. Norman was in a safer position than Todhunter, and while he pondered whether he should swap sides with the less experienced man, it dawned on him what the exploding ordnance was: grenades. This, he said, was worrying: "If they were tossing grenades in, they were very close."

In fact these were stun grenades of the type used by the SAS to disorientate and confuse. The devices were working. Some Marines were so confused by the concussion that they got to their feet and had to be pulled back to safety by their comrades.

Geordie Gill was inside GH. His initial delight that battle had commenced was being tempered with the awareness that some parts of GH were not standing up well to attack.

I couldn't believe how much fire was coming into GH. It just about wrecked upstairs because it was mainly wooden, but downstairs was mainly built of Falkland stone, and that was good enough protection. But most of the windows were shot out.

Those who were able to do so scrambled towards the superior shelter of a stone wall separating Government House from the low ridge to the south. As they sheltered on the north side of the wall some Argentines were doing likewise on the south side. In places they were separated by only three or four metres. Still the attack continued, but by this time the Marines were returning fire and Argentine efforts to cross the wall were thwarted.

They were dressed in black but because dawn was now coming in, we could see these murky figures. One appeared on the wall in the gloom, and Corporal Sellen and Marine Timms shot him.

Two more were shot. They weren't dead but subsequently at least one did die.

The injured men were part of a 'snatch squad', bravely but dogmatically sticking to the plan that said they should be able to rush GH unopposed and capture Rex Hunt. Geordie Gill said it was like "the shoot-out at the OK Corral – the three of ours against six of theirs, about ten feet apart and blasting away from the hip."

The attackers pulled back. This was not how it was supposed to be. Firing died down, for a few minutes. Mike Norman recalled a nervous but fatalistic mood among his men:

> I was laying there, shaking from head to foot like a piece of jelly! I suspect all the others were the same. In those situations, you have to give yourself a talking to. I said to myself, 'You knew it was going to come to this. You told the lads it was going to come to this. Now get a grip, because if anybody climbs over that wall now, you are not going to be able to hit the wall let alone the target.'
>
> I shouted out to the Sergeant-Major, 'You OK Sarn't Major?' He said he was fine and asked how I was. Suddenly everybody started talking. In that strange time when it was all quiet the Marines were saying goodbye to each other; 'It's been good to know you,' that sort of thing.
>
> I actually said to Todhunter, 'Are you married?'
>
> He said, 'No. It's much easier for me.'

The CO briefly considered leading some of his men to attack the Argentines from the flank, but there was sniper fire from the high ground every time a Marine tried to improve his position. Amazingly, there were no hits, but the near misses were alarming. The bursts of firing alternated with shouted demands for surrender and abusive replies. Mike Norman:

> They were shouting in English: 'Stop fighting, Mr Hunt! Come out Mr Hunt! Tell your Marines to stop fighting!'
>
> This went on and on, and the Marines were getting fed up. Every now and again someone would shout back, 'Fuck off! We're not going to surrender. If you want us, come down and get us!'

Having already lost three men, the special forces team was not about to do that. They had been forced into a stalemate and now needed the support of the vastly superior main force then landing on York Bay. Their Amtrack amphibious armoured personnel carriers were armed with heavy machine guns and the troops within carried mortars. They could level GH if necessary. The plan to snatch Rex Hunt had failed and now the only choice was to keep the Marines pinned down and wait.

The surprise attack had, however, succeeded in fragmenting the Marines' defensive plan. The Marines had hoped to bring the main Argentine advance to a temporary halt, forcing them to talk. But with most of the men forced back to Government House, that plan was now hopeless.

The Marines might have slowed the main landing if they had chosen to defend the correct beach. Marines Wilcox and Milne, designated Section Five (A), had deployed to York Bay's eastern beach with one general-purpose machine gun. Almost nothing went right for the pair. The lights on one of their two motorbikes failed and two-way communications were lost when the transmitter on their radio set broke down.

Listening to the radio between 05.15 and 05.30 (but unable to make any calls), Wilcox and Milne heard Jack Sollis and the lighthouse staff report Argentine ships in Port William. A few minutes later they heard the rumbling of engines and spotted the silhouette of an amphibious landing ship. They watched, expecting the ship to stop off their beach and pour forth troops, but it steamed on past. They had picked the wrong site and there was no point in remaining there. Wilcox and Milne mounted their motorbikes and jolted their way back to join Five Section above the airport just before it was recalled to Government House. The main landing would now have to be opposed not on the beach, but on the road.

Lieutenant Bill Trollope had joined Section Two, which was armed with Carl Gustav 88mm anti-tank missiles (a more modern version of the Second World War bazooka) and 66mm disposable missile launchers dug in on a low ridge running from Hookers Point west towards Stanley. This was the only section that would hurt the main Argentine force.

The men listened to the attack on Moody Brook and Government House, heard Mike Norman's radio orders for most other sections to pull back to Stanley and waited, feeling increasingly lonely. Then, as a watery light began to illuminate the sea, beaches and moorland, they saw the Argentines.

Off to the east were two warships; a frigate and a corvette. Unseen was the tank landing ship *Cabo San Antonio* which had opened its bow doors while still some distance from the sandy beach of York Bay and disgorged the huge rumbling Amtrack amphibious armoured personnel carriers of the Second Marine Infantry Unit. They were now appearing on the ridge above York Bay and grinding their way with terrifying impunity towards the defenders. The heavily armoured vehicles carried a crew of three and about 20 troops. They were capable of 60 kilometres per hour on land, and from their armoured hulls sprouted heavy machine-gun turrets. So daunting were the Amtracks, that civilians would later describe them as tanks.

Trollope counted sixteen of the leviathans crawling over the ridge, all heading for the Airport Road. Each was packed with around twenty troops. It was time to consider their position. Sections which would have been closer to the enemy had already been withdrawn, meaning that he and his men did not need to give anyone covering fire. But by the same token, no other section was available to cover his little force. Trollope decided to withdraw immediately to a hastily prepared position on the very edge of Stanley, near the cluster of houses known as White City. The leading Amtracks were close behind. This from Trollope's post-battle report:

> Six armoured personnel carriers began advancing at speed down the Airport Road. The first APC was engaged at a range of about 200 to 250 metres. The first three [missiles], two 84mm and one 66mm, missed. Subsequently one 66mm, fired by Marine Gibbs, hit the passenger compartment and one 84mm (Marines Brown and Betts) hit the front. Both rounds exploded and no fire was received from that vehicle.
>
> The remaining five APCs which were about 600 to 700 metres away deployed their troops and opened fire. We engaged them with GPMG, SLR and sniper rifle (Sergeant Shepherd) for about a minute before we threw white phosphorus [a smoke screen] and leap-frogged back to the cover of the gardens. Incoming fire at that stage was fairly heavy, but mostly inaccurate.

The section's supply of anti-armour missiles had been expended and they could not delay the advance further. Trollope's men escaped at speed, vaulting fences and crashing through the gardens of terraced houses along Davis Street, as if in some hellish steeplechase.

Eileen Vidal, the government radio telephone operator and a single parent caring for a brood of children, was in one of the houses. At the height of the firefight, she dived behind a sofa with her children. An Argentine mortar round landed in the garden, and they heard the desperate shouts of the retreating Royal Marines as they vaulted fences and ran through their garden. This was quickly replaced by bursts of gunfire and the Spanish yells of the Argentines in hot pursuit.

The youngest child, Leona, was praying, but Eileen looked out the window long enough to see an Amtrack rumbling past. She looked directly into the eyes of the young Argentine manning the gun turret. "I was pretty quick dropping to the floor again," she recalled.

Trollope's Marines shook off the pursuing Argentines and the section went to ground at the west end of Stanley. They had run out of cover and it was obvious they could not reach the besieged Government House.

Their well-documented claim to have hit one APC with at least three missiles brings into question the Argentines' insistence that they lost only one man during the invasion, a Captain Giachino, who was one of the three Amphibious Commando Company men very visibly shot during the initial assault on Government House.

Armour-piercing missiles from the 88 and 66mm weapons were well capable of 'brewing up' the vehicle and no men, either crew or passengers, were seen escaping from it. Whether or not the Argentines lost men in this incident remains a moot point. They certainly never admitted it.

[Marine sharpshooters at Government House also claimed, credibly, to have killed more men than the single man the Argentines acknowledged. The Argentine death toll may have been embarrassingly high, and it is worth remembering that covering up death was not new to the junta; they had kidnapped, murdered and disposed of thousands of their own people – the 'disappeared' – over the preceding six years.]

There were no illusions about being able to hurt the Argentines badly enough to make them withdraw. Rex Hunt had been informed that the APCs were heading for Government House, and it was only a matter of time before the attacking Argentines were heavily reinforced. His dedicated line to FIBS had broken, but he called Patrick Watts by telephone and Patrick held the phone to his microphone:

Hunt: They infiltrated a party behind us. Once they got very close to us, but they've now withdrawn. It's only a matter of time before they regroup and come again. They have five armoured personnel vehicles on the way from the Canache that landed in York Bay. It's just a matter of time until they overrun us, but we'll see how long we can hang on anyway.
Watts: Sir, are you going to try and hang on and keep them back for as long as possible, or are you going to surrender?
Hunt: We are not surrendering, we are resisting. If someone is

prepared to come in and talk to me, I'll have them in, but I'm not going out to talk to them or to surrender to them. We're staying put here, but we are pinned down. We can't move.

Watts: They're obviously trying to get just Government House, are they?

Hunt: They are not doing any damage, I hope, to the rest of the town, but obviously when the armoured personnel vehicles come we'll have to give in because they can flatten the place.

Watts: Has anyone been injured, sir, or shot?

Hunt: We haven't had any casualties reported yet, thank goodness. I don't know how the sections are at the lighthouse and the airport, but here we're alright.

They must have 200 around us now. They've been throwing rifle grenades at us; I think there may be mortars, I don't know. They came along very quickly and very close, and then they retreated. Maybe they are waiting until the APCs come along as they think they'll lose less casualties that way. But I'm waiting for them to send somebody in to see me.

It's getting light and they have a much more commanding position. We can't move from here without being shot at because they are up above us, behind. So I'm afraid it's just a matter of time, but . . . well, we'll do what we can.

Alistair Grieves, a government laboratory technician who lived in the so-called 'White City' houses just a few yards from where Section Two was pumping anti-tank missiles into the lead Amtrack, called up with a report of the action:

Watts: Alistair, I understand you've seen some of the vehicles, have you?

Grieves: No, we haven't sighted vehicles, Pat, but there have been some really heavy bangs, the whole place is shaking, it's a bit nerve-racking to say the least. There's a lot of machine-gun fire and small-arms fire as well. I had a quick look out through the curtains and all I could see was smoke, so I honestly haven't a clue what's happening. But every time something big goes bang, it shakes up here.

Watts: And where are you giving this report from, Ally? Are you standing up, sitting down?

Grieves: I'm lying on the floor, boy!

Watts: Keep inside, keep your head down, and if you see them passing perhaps you can give us a call. Cheers.

Like Alistair Grieves, most citizens of Stanley understood the gravity of their situation only too well. But there were one or two for whom no damned Argies were going to interfere with the daily routine. Just before 08.00 Marine Turner, normally a clerk at Moody Brook, but now clutching a rifle in the bushes on the Ross Road side of Government House, noticed a civilian approaching at a brisk pace. With smoko satchel slung over one arm, the overall-clad man clearly had a purpose.

There was a slight lull in the fighting, but bullets were still zinging through the air every time a Marine put his head up. Turner shouted to the man that he should turn back and take cover immediately. But the local barely interrupted his pace. "It's alright for you lot," he shouted across the road indignantly, "but some of us have got to get to work."

The loyal employee continued down Ross Road and was eventually dragged into the Police Station by one of Ronnie Lamb's constables.

A few minutes later Rex Hunt was again being interviewed live on air. He was as pugnacious as ever, but the implied message for the Argentines, whom he clearly hoped were listening, was "Let's talk."

> Watts: How much longer do you think you can hold out, sir?
> Hunt: Oh, they've got 30mm cannon on these armoured personnel carriers, so one or two shots from them and we'd be finished, I'm afraid. But I'm hopeful that they'll send somebody in to talk.
> Watts: And you'll talk to them, will you, sir?
> Hunt: I'll talk to them, but I'm not walking out. I'm not surrendering to the bloody Argies, Patrick. Certainly not!
> Watts: Fantastic! Well done, sir! Goodbye.
>   Well, you heard the Governor. I never thought they'd do a thing like this, I can tell you. I told everyone they wouldn't. Anyway, the problem is that they are here.

As the sun rose, the tactical situation around GH briefly swung in the Marines' favour. Government House was overlooked by the ridge held by the Argentines but, whereas until now they had been shadowy figures, they were now making the basic error of allowing themselves to be seen against the skyline.

By around 08.00 an uneasy truce had come into effect. Defending the east end of GH with his sniper rifle, Geordie Gill decided to venture out and try to help the three Argentines who had been seriously injured in the initial attack, and whose groans and calls for help could be clearly heard. He recalled:

They were just poor sods like we were, doing a lousy job for their government, so I thought I'll get out and see if I can pull them in or at least give them some first aid. There was a bloke from the new detachment, Terry Pares I think, who covered me while I went onto the little lawn at the top of the drive. As I did so, I saw a section of these guys pepper-potting forward. You're not allowed to improve your positions during a truce. I took a look at these wounded guys, and realised it meant climbing over two fences to get to them. I thought, sorry . . .

I'd shouted in to the boss about the Argentines improving their position, and two heads appeared in a window of GH. They were Noott and Norman. I said, "They're up there and moving. They're getting closer, and if they move again I'm going to take them out."

I got told, "You can't. Don't shoot." I thought, "Nah! This isn't a way to run a war." Just then someone from up the hill fired a shot at me, so I hit the deck. Next thing, these heads appeared at the window again, and one said, "Corporal Gill, if you fire again, you'll be on a charge."

I thought, "Hang on! I'm going to be dead by dinner but they're threatening to put me on a charge." I pointed out in not too polite terms that it wasn't me who'd fired. These two heads looked at one another, and one of them asked if I could still see the Argentines. I said, "Yeah", and he said, "Well take 'em out." I thought, "This is Christmas."

My first two shots must have gone low. So I racked the sights up and the next time I saw the guy go down. His mate stuck his head out to see what had happened, and I got him. I was firing through a hole in the hedge, up on one knee over about 500 yards. And then Terry shouted that he could see one of them, and asked if he should take him. I said, "Yeah", so he opened up with about half a magazine from his SLR, and shouted, "I think I got him, I think I got him!" I saw this body fall down in my field of view on its back.

Then me and a machine-gunner had an interesting little time. He was well down beside a rock, but I saw the smoke from his muzzle.

I'm certain I accounted for two and I'm pretty certain of a third.

At 08.35, when another half-hearted cease-fire had come into effect, Gary Noott suggested that Mike Norman might advise Rex Hunt about the options that were still open to them. Norman recalled a bizarre meeting:

I went into the ops room. There was a huge oak table with a green baize cloth over it. I said, 'Where is he?' Rex was sitting underneath the oak table, which was the safest place to be. We had been walking around GH as if we were in a concrete bunker, but bullets were whizzing through it.

I was actually holding up some green baize and looking at Rex Hunt underneath the table. I told him that the Marines and the Governor could still break out and set up an alternative seat of government anywhere else on the island. We thought we could go across the road in front of Government House, drop down on the beach, beetle our way along to Moody Brook and then go up out the back of Moody Brook. We were fairly convinced that we could get away. But there was no way he was going to entertain it.

I said, if we didn't go for this alternative seat of Government we could continue to fight until we were overrun. Our defence would be determined, unrelenting but relatively short-lived. But we were quite prepared to do that if that is what he wanted us to do.

Rex Hunt had never intended to flee for the camp, and it had not been in the plan that he had previously agreed with Gary Noott. He reminded Mike Norman of this. His judgement was undoubtedly right. Leaving the Islanders would not look good. There would be scant places to seek shelter from the autumn weather and the searching Argentines. And the indignity of capture after a failed escape attempt would far exceed the indignity of whatever might occur over the coming few hours.

Fortunately, the Argentines had heard him talking to Patrick Watts at FIBS and now they too wanted to talk. The Argentine command began transmitting on a frequency that the Islanders were known to use. It is thought that one of the women operators at the telephone exchange heard the transmission, rang FIBS and told Patrick Watts to tune in as well. He did so and patched the Argentine caller into FIBS. At first the whistles, feedback and static made the transmission barely audible. But finally this – clearly scripted – message emerged in English:

This is a call to the British colonial government of the Islas Malvinas. In order to fulfil orders from the Argentine

Government, we are here with a [unintelligible] task force [unintelligible] remaining faithful to our [unintelligible] principles. For the purpose of avoiding bloodshed and property damage among the population, we hope that you will act prudently. Our concern is for the welfare and safety of the people of the Malvinas.

At GH Dick Baker and the Governor heard the transmission and thought that the voice sounded like Colonel Belcarce, an ex-military officer and diplomat who had been one of the architects of Argentina's Malvinas policy during the 1970s. He had visited the Islands many times and his local knowledge would have been very useful. According to Dick, their next radio message had a sinister edge to it. Clearly aware that the infantry attack had failed to achieve its task, the voice said that the heavily armed Amtracks were on land and approaching Stanley.

Rex turned to Mike Norman and asked what that meant. Mike said, 'It means we're stuffed, sir.'

It was a threat. We didn't know if they were going to act correctly or slaughter everyone. But the implication was that if he surrendered personally, no one would get hurt.

By this time we were getting messages from the other end of town to say that shells were going through houses. No one had been hurt, but nasty things were happening.

Rex decided we would try to reply to this message. He was not going to surrender, but was prepared to negotiate. But although we could hear them, we could not transmit on the same frequency, and we didn't know what other frequencies they normally used.

Somebody suggested that Gilobert or Gamin would know, so we phoned the LADE house, and sure enough, Gilobert answered. He was practically in tears. I could overhear this conversation. He was declaring that he had nothing to do with this and had no prior knowledge. He said if there was anything he could do to help he would be only too willing to do so.

Rex said, 'As it happens, Hector, there is. We need you at GH to help us tune this radio to the Argentine frequencies. I want you to get down here, if you will – and carry a white flag.'

As Hector stumbled in the west entrance there were a couple of loud reports. It was their troops firing on him – we had told our troops not to fire. He fell in the door looking whiter than the flag he was carrying. I think he was very brave to walk down to GH.

Hector Gilobert suggested the Marines try a few frequencies.

Rex Hunt was now determined to open a dialogue and, as Dick Baker recalled, this would mean someone venturing forth to make personal contact with the invaders once messages had been exchanged by radio.

> Rex was looking at me and saying 'Someone [pause] *someone*, has to go out there and stop those tanks. It needs to be someone who can talk to the commanding officers.'
>
> I knew it had to be me, because if Rex went out it would be construed as surrender, which was what he did not want.

A blind transmission was made on the frequencies that the Argentine had supplied. Everyone in the room hoped that the Argentines were listening as they were told that Gilobert and Dick Baker would leave GH with a white flag and make their way towards the Town Hall, where they were prepared to meet senior representatives of the Argentines. No reply was received, but at 08.45 Dick and his erstwhile Argentine friend left GH. Dick Baker recalled the longest walk of his life:

> We didn't have a white flag – they're not the sort of things they issue to Her Majesty's embassies and government houses. So Rex produced an umbrella and pulled down a white lace curtain to attach to it. His words to me were, 'Don't lose my umbrella, Dick. I paid the earth for it from Briggs in Piccadilly.'
>
> We staggered through the east door and the Argentines did fire on us, but were either trying to put the wind up us or were bloody bad shots.

Nobody was using the word yet, but surrender was the only option. However Mike Norman still had one trick up his sleeve. His Section Four covering the entrance to Stanley Harbour from Navy Point were equipped with a Zodiac inflatable boat and an outboard motor. Norman told the section commander, Corporal York, to 'thin out'. A small-scale guerrilla campaign, sustained until British troops could return, might be useful.

Recalling Norman's joke about the best thing to do if the Argentines invaded, Corporal York replied, "Right boss, we're going fishing." They booby-trapped their GPMG with a grenade (it subsequently exploded injuring or killing an Argentine) and jumped into the Zodiac for a hair-raising ride across Port William. In broad daylight, they dodged an Argentine frigate, hiding between the few Polish fishing vessels in port, and escaped. Their continued evasion became a morale booster for the Islanders.

Other units were ordered to hold their fire, stay where they were and await orders.

Within GH there was one final drama. Gary Noott took advantage of the lull in the fighting to check the building's defences. In a corridor leading to the kitchen, he heard voices above him. They were three Argentines who had infiltrated GH during the lull after the initial assault about two hours earlier. Summoning Geordie Gill to help, he went into the room that appeared to be directly beneath the voices. He recalled an unconventional firefight.

I was carrying an SMG [sub-machine gun]. On the SMG there are two firing positions, single shot or automatic. I planned to put it on automatic and fire a burst through the ceiling – it sharpens them up, maybe damages them a bit and they're less keen to play.

I put the lever forward, pulled the trigger and there was a bang. I hadn't put the lever far enough forward and it had only fired a single shot. At which point I thought, 'Oh shit!' I could imagine all sorts of shit coming the other way.

Geordie immediately helped out by putting a burst into the ceiling from the other end of the room. He recalled:

That got them moving again, and we were just starting to enjoy ourselves, when Noott said to me, tell them to come down with their hands up. I shouted 'Arriba los manos', and the reply was 'OK, OK!' They came around the corner and I must admit I've never been closer in my life to murder than I was at that time. At that point we thought we had lost one of our sections, but actually their radio had failed. I thought, 'Why should you lot live?' I was so close to squeezing that trigger. It seemed to take ages for me to make my mind up, but it couldn't have been more than a second. I'm so glad I didn't give in to it.

Noott noted ruefully that the satisfaction of capturing some Argentines was short-lived: "A little later we had to let them go again, and we were then *their* prisoners."

The Marines' surrender was, however, still a little way off. Dick Baker and Hector Gilobert were on their way down Ross Road to meet the Argentines and arrange a truce during which Rex and the Argentine commanders could negotiate. When they reached the Town Hall and Police Station area, Gilobert entered the Police Station and called FIBS. In his halting English he asked to go on the air. Patrick Watts was pleased to help, and Gilobert addressed his message, in Spanish, directly to the Argentine high command.

> *Soy el Vice Comodoro Gilobert. Quiero hablar con el comandante de las fuerzas* . . . I am with the Deputy Governor at the Police Station. We both want to speak to the commander of the forces. If you are listening, I propose that we meet in front of the Town Hall, in front of the Catholic Church. He should come with one man and a white flag. There is absolute guarantee of mutual respect.

A few minutes later, the Argentines radioed their reply, and, again, Patrick Watts relayed it:

> [We are] accepting your requirement, the officer commanding the force of disembarkment [sic] is coming up now to the Catholic Church, to the square near the Catholic Church to meet people that you have suggest [sic].

Dick remembered a horribly tense 20 minutes or so as they waited to meet the invaders.

> Then we saw this John Wayne type striding along with helmet on. The APCs were behind him and he had men on either side of him with white flags. He came and greeted Gilobert by name, offered his hand to me, and I, without thinking, took it.
>
> He uttered some banality like 'You are a very brave man, Mr Baker.' And then he said, 'Are you going to take me to meet Mr Hunt?'
>
> This was Admiral Busser who was in charge of the forces on land. The overall commander, General Osvaldo Garcia, was still at sea. Busser spoke excellent English.
>
> As we walked back to GH, the Argentines started to loose off at us. Busser made a megaphone of his hands and called out for them to stop, because we were under a flag of truce. He said, 'If you hear what I am saying, raise your right arms.'
>
> Slowly one raised an arm and then they all did it. He turned to me, and said, 'And they call this the age of electronic communications!' At least he was a man with a sense of humour.

Marine guards at the east entrance to GH – among them the redoubtable Geordie Gill – were not at all happy about letting the Argentine party past. Geordie recalled a tense stand-off as Busser's bold march to GH came to a halt.

> He had five or six of these special forces guys as an escort. Me and a couple of other guys went out to say Busser could come in, but they couldn't. One of these characters leaned over and tried to take the magazine off my SMG, which nearly got him a face full of nine-mil. From behind us all you could hear were the clicks of the safety catches coming off the rifles of our guys who were concealed among the trees lining the drive. His special forces were looking at each other, suddenly realising they were in a killing zone. Busser came in on his own and the special forces guys just stayed there and waited for him to come out. They were under quite a few weapons by that time.

Mike Norman recalled that the Argentine commander encountered a dignified scene as he entered the Governor's office at 09.15:

> Rex Hunt had brushed down his pinstriped suit and smartened his hair up. I stood on one side of the desk and Gary on the other side. Rex stood behind it. In came Busser. Before he could say anything, Rex Hunt said, 'This is British territory. You are not invited here. We don't want you here. I want you to go, and to take all your men with you now.'
> I looked across at Gary, and cocked an eyebrow thinking, 'Well we've tried everything else; perhaps this one is going to work.'
> Busser smiled and he said, 'I've got 800 men ashore, another 2,000 on the way. We don't want to kill any of these Marines. We thought that if we came in such numbers they would not fight. I want you to stop the action now before Marines are killed and civilians of Stanley are killed.'
> Rex Hunt paused for a minute and said, 'In that case, you don't give me any option.'
> He turned to me and said, 'Tell your men to lay down their arms.'
> So we broadcast to everybody that the fighting was over and they were to lay down their arms. They all signalled back confirming they had understood. We asked them where they were and Gary and I went around to supervise the surrender.

The FIDF were disarmed in their drill hall, where they had been since returning section by section a few hours earlier. One group had been intercepted by the Argentines not far from Government House. Lined up against a wall with weapons levelled against them, they briefly thought their time was up. But after a tense few minutes, they were escorted to the drill hall and, like the rest of the FIDF, eventually taken home under armed guard.

Some, perhaps most, of the Defence Force were unhappy about their early withdrawal and at least one section on guard to the south of the town had sent a runner back to the HQ questioning the order. They had, however, at least avoided the humiliating final act of the Marines' drama. On the road outside Government House, over-zealous Argentines forced the Marines to lie face down with arms outstretched. Argentine photographer Rafael Wollman snapped sensational pictures, which were splashed across front pages around the world. Later, the Marines were corralled in the grounds of Government House awaiting their deportation, lightly guarded by the men who had defeated them.

Nidge Buckett, who the previous day had delivered her Marine lodger back to Moody Brook, had been asked to deliver his clothes to Government House. She recalled that as she approached GH she saw the Marines and knew that her emotions were about to overcome her.

> I got out of the Land Rover and I knew I was going to cry. Then I heard one of the boys shout, 'Don't you fucking cry, Nidge.' I looked around, and I thought 'Fine!' I just dumped the stuff off and left. I didn't cry, because whoever it was really gave me a boost, and I thought I'm not crying in front of these people.

The images of British colonialism literally brought to its knees were deeply humiliating, and allowing such photographs to be taken was the Argentines' biggest mistake after their decision to invade. The pictures shocked and enraged the British so deeply that the Thatcher government had to restore the country's honour or fall.

In conversation with the Marine commanders the Argentines were smug. Mike Norman recalled that one English-speaking major was certain that Britain would accept the *fait accompli*:

> He said, 'We have provided a solution that your government and Mrs Thatcher are desperately looking for. I don't think there will be any reaction.'
>
> I said to him, 'You have completely misjudged the British people. They will not stand for this. We will be back.'

For the time being, however, Busser and his men were in control and self-satisfaction was their privilege. Later in the day Rex Hunt and

Dick Baker were taken to meet the overall Argentine commander General Osvaldo Garcia in the Town Hall. Rex was told that he, his staff, their families and the Marines (less the section that had 'gone fishing') were to be flown back to Britain, via Buenos Aires, that day. Rex asked that Dick be allowed to stay on for a little longer, and, surprisingly, Garcia agreed.

Mike Norman, Gary Noott and their men were delighted to be alive. No Marine had even been injured. After the humiliating surrender and the misguided photo opportunity, they found themselves being treated with some courtesy. Some men were taken back to Moody Brook and allowed to collect personal possessions. The old barracks had been devastated in what looked like a classic house-clearing operation: walls were riddled with bullets and scorched by white phosphorous grenades. Again, there was no sign that the Argentines did not intend to kill.

The sense of defeat spread quickly across the town. It was made all the more profound by the Argentine euphoria and the lack of any indication that Britain would be able to do anything to reverse the situation. The mood was tearful and gloomy.

Such was the lack of discipline among the Argentines at the radio station, that they did not notice as Patrick Watts succeeded in establishing one final link with Rex Hunt. Remarkably, the Argentines did not seem to notice his voice broadcasting across the Islands. Rex sounded tired and emotional as he paid tribute to the bravery of Hector Gilobert (a friend who was now officially an enemy) and Dick Baker. He told listeners that he had ordered Busser to withdraw forthwith, but Busser had replied saying that he was just following instructions. He had, however, gladly accepted medical help for his injured men. Rex ended his broadcast still sounding tired, but typically pugnacious.

> That's all I've got to say. I'm sorry it happened this way. It's probably the last message I'll be able to give you. But I wish you all the best of luck. And, rest assured, the British will be back.

Before the day was out Rex Hunt, most of his staff and their families and most of the Marines were aboard Argentine aircraft *en route* for Montevideo, where they were released into the care of British diplomats. The RAF despatched a VC10 transport to return them to Britain.

Just a few days before, the newly arrived Major Mike Norman and his detachment sergeant major, Colour-Sergeant Bill Muir, had been grumbling to each other about the relatively scruffy appearance of

Gary Noott's motley men. They were long-haired, abundantly moustached, wearing jewellery in the fashion of local men, and generally looking as if they had gone native. What's more, Noott didn't seem to mind.

Now it mattered not a bit. When the chips were down, all the Marines, newcomers and old Falklands hands, had fought hard and honourably.

In his post-action report the Sergeant-Major let his starchy mask slip. One can only imagine Bill Muir fighting the smile creasing one corner of his mouth as he penned the final paragraph of his report for Mike Norman. "At no time during the conflict," he wrote, "were earrings worn by any member of the Royal Marines."

Later, as senior officers backing Britain analysed the reports from the Falklands, some blimpish officer applied a generous amount of Tipp-Ex correction fluid to the NCO's little joke. Marines and earrings? What was this nonsense? Perhaps you had to be there.

Chapter Four

Waking up to Reality

Government House had fallen. The rambling but charming old complex of timber and stone, which had evolved with lean-tos and additions over the 140 years since Governor Moody laid the first stone, was of no practical value at all, but it was a potent enough symbol for men to die over. Now the Argentines planned to make it into a museum.

The Falkland Islands Broadcasting Station, an ugly corrugated iron building in the centre of Stanley, was, on the other hand, of immense practical value. The Argentines took it quickly and peacefully.

In the absence of a daily newspaper, FIBS (surely the most unfortunate of acronyms for a radio station) was a vital source of news. Owned and operated by the government, its broadcasters were usually quaintly deferential to the authorities, but, under the guidance of Broadcasting Officer Patrick Watts, its news and sports coverage was lively. Only FIBS could possibly make darts an interesting sport on radio.

Broadcasting across the Islands and by an antiquated cable system to simple speakers known as 'boxes' in Stanley homes, FIBS was the only means of disseminating information quickly. The twice weekly Newsmagazine, Calling the Falklands from the BBC World Service, the 7.30 Announcements, and the BBC World News were compulsory listening.

There had never been a more dramatic FIBS broadcast than the remarkable invasion phone-in. But when, early on the morning of 2 April, the Argentine troops entered the station with their dedicated broadcasting team, the radio drama simply entered another remarkable phase. The Argentines had prepared to use the station to emphasise the dawn of a new era and their authority. FIBS was the only way of communicating with the newest Argentine citizens. And it was the best way of controlling them.

Retaining Patrick Watts and his small team of part-time announcers made good sense. Apart from the practical need to broadcast in English, keeping familiar voices on the air would reinforce the Argentines' key, if dishonest, message that life could continue more or less as normal.

Patrick Watts was exhausted, but he still retained a sense of duty, drama and history. After his station was taken over he remained at the microphone. The soldiers informed Patrick that they were now in charge, but as they fussed around preparing taped communiqués, edicts and a scratchy recording of the Argentine National Anthem, he made a furtive phone call to Rex Hunt. Following his surrender, the Governor was calmly awaiting formal eviction from GH. With studio speakers turned down so that the Argentines could not hear him, the Broadcasting Officer asked his boss, live on air, whether he should continue transmitting under new masters. The Governor replied as if he was accepting another gin and tonic at a GH cocktail party.

Yes, please. I think for the sake of the Islands it is necessary for you to keep up the Falkland Islands Broadcasting Service.

I don't know how many hours you've been on the air, but I think you've done a tremendous job. I think you've reported everything very well, and keep it up, even with a gun in your back.

Patrick appeared to accept this. But, even with Rex Hunt's blessing, he was troubled and a few minutes later, apparently without any interference from the Argentines, he spoke emotionally to his listeners about the tough decision he faced. He appealed for their understanding, at times fighting back tears:

Up until one hour ago you were hearing this station as it was run, with the Governor in charge of the station and me in charge of broadcasting, a job which I have loved and enjoyed doing for you, and a job that I have done to the best of my ability. Now I have been told that I must obey the orders of the people who have taken over the station.

I have a difficult decision to make: I have to obey what they tell me, or I have to disobey what they tell me. To obey what they tell me is an easy way out. To disobey is not so easy because if I do then I have a gun pointed at my back.

I have two children in the Falkland Islands which I love very much. I do not want any harm to come to me or them. So please understand that I have to obey the orders that I am given, and the orders that I am given are coming down from two people from Argentina who insist that they are friends of the people in the Falklands.

We are told that we are to continue in the same way, but we have to broadcast the communiqués from the Argentine people. Let's make it quite clear that it is no longer the station that you knew, run on the same lines as previously. They are answering my phone calls and telling me what I must do. So I have to obey these instructions.

Whether the Falkland Islands Broadcasting Station will ever return to the situation it once knew, I don't know, but I sincerely hope it does, because it's a job that I loved and enjoyed doing for you, and I hope that I can continue to do this job somehow because for me the Falkland Islands is the greatest thing on earth. OK? Sorry if it seems rather sentimental, but that's the way I feel at the moment.

The radio had sustained the Islanders throughout the night. There had been no exhortations to violence, no impassioned condemnation of the invaders, and certainly no suggestion of fear. The tone had been subtly subversive and defiant but dignified, indicative of a community that might be beaten but did not intend to be bowed.

It was, however, now a vital tool of the new rulers. Pre-recorded announcements, formal and redolent with historic pomp, began. They were broadcast first in Spanish by a rigid military voice, which may have been that of General Osvaldo Garcia, the commander of the invasion force (they were certainly in his name), then in English by an unknown announcer with an Argentine accent.

The English voice sounded, at first, slightly embarrassed. When, for example, he translated an appeal for 'collaboration' with Argentine forces, the English speaker changed it to 'cooperation'. Perhaps he knew that while cooperation might sometimes be reasonable, collaboration is the most despised of actions in an occupied community.

Whoever wrote and voiced the first communiqué from the Argentine Government of the Islas Malvinas was making history:

A partir del dia de la fecha 2 Abril de 1982 inicia su transmission LRA Radio Islas Malvinas para toda la Republica Argentina. Se escuchara a continuacion, el himno nacional Argentina . . .

From here after, April 2 1982, begins its transmission LRA Islas Malvinas Broadcasting Station for the whole of the Argentine Republic. We shall listen now [to] the Argentine National Anthem.

A dirge-like hymn scratched and crackled for minute after interminable minute. The radio station and the Islands themselves had been renamed and in future Islanders should pay respect to a strange new anthem. The authoritarian reality of the new government had been firmly underlined.

The new broadcasters were just getting into their stride. The 'edicts' and 'communiqués' came thick and fast, first in Spanish and then in a strange, stilted English.

> Argentine Republic, communiqué number one: the commander of the Malvinas operation theatre performing his duties as ordered by the Argentine government materialises here after the historic continuity of Argentine sovereignty over the Islas Malvinas. At this highly important moment for all of us, it is my pleasure to greet the people of the Malvinas and exhort you to cooperate with the new authorities by complying with all of the instructions that will be given through oral and written communiqués, in order to facilitate the normal life of the entire population.
>
> (Signed) Osvaldo Jorge Garcia, General de Division, Commandante del Teatro de Operaciones, Malvinas.

With barely a break for solemn music, the voices were back:

> Communiqué number two: relief of authorities. From hereafter the colonial and military authorities of the British Government are effectively released of their charges and shall be sent back to their country today with their families and personal effects. Furthermore it is hereby made known that General of Division Osvaldo Jorge Garcia on behalf of the Argentine Government is taking power of the government of the Malvinas Islands, Georgia del Sur and Sandwich del Sur.

By communiqué number three, euphemisms like 'personal misfortunes' and 'inconveniences' barely masked a more sinister theme.

> Instructions for the population: as a consequence of all the action taken and in order to ensure the safety of the population, all people are to remain at their homes until further notice. New instructions will be issued. The population must bear in mind that in order to ensure the fulfilment of these instructions military troops shall arrest all people found outside their home. To avoid inconveniences and personal misfortune, people are to abide by the following:

75

First: should some serious problem arise and people wish to make it known to the military authorities, a white piece of cloth is to be placed outside the door. Military patrols will visit the house so as to be informed and provide a solution.

Second: all schools, shops, stores, banks, pubs and clubs are to remain closed until further notice.

Third: all infringements shall be treated according to what is stated in edict number one.

Fourth: all further instructions shall be released to the local broadcasting station which will remain in permanent operation.

The reference to 'infringements' being treated according to edict number one was confusing, as there appeared to be no explicit threat of punishment in the first communiqué. Perhaps the pertinent phrase had been considered too authoritarian in tone, and had been removed. But Patrick interpreted the veiled threat sensibly: "If you don't obey what they tell you to do, then there may be a bit of trouble," he warned his listeners. He explained that he now had to obey the orders of one 'Francisco', and he interjected once or twice between edicts, attempting to explain them, and occasionally getting Francisco to do the same. At one stage he seemed to be deliberately confusing the Argentine with the banality of local life. If people couldn't go outside, asked Patrick, how were they going to feed their dogs? Francisco patiently repeated the instructions. Again Patrick interrupted. Yes, but how are they going to get their peat for their stoves? How can they feed and milk their cows? The Argentine was clearly exasperated but stuck to the letter of the edict: *"the peoples they must put a white flag in the windows . . ."*

Locals continued to phone the station. One listener in the camp congratulated FIBS on its broadcast. Clearly, he had found it hugely interesting, almost as good as the popular Christmas horse racing coverage.

There were reassuring messages from or about families living in the east end of Stanley, whose houses had been blasted with automatic and mortar fire. The occupants were safe, but some had lain on the floor, while sunlight glared through gaping holes in the roof and bullet-riddled water pipes spouted water.

Following on from the dictatorial tone of edict three, the next communiqué, dealing with Islanders' rights, seemed laughable.

Guarantees: the Governor of the Islas Malvinas, Georgia del Sur and Sandwich del Sur, notifies the population that, faithfully upholding the principles stated in the national constitution and in accordance with the customs and traditions of the Argentine people, he guarantees the continuity of the way of life of the people of the Islands, freedom of worship, respect for private property, freedom of labour, freedom to enter, leave or remain on the Islands, improvement of the population's standard of life, normal supply situation, health assistance, normal function of essential public service.

Furthermore, the population is exhorted to continue normally with their activities, with the support of the Argentine government, in an atmosphere of peace, order and harmony.

Suggestions that Islanders would benefit from the Argentine constitution were deeply disingenuous. The military had ridden roughshod over their own constitution, taking power illegally in Buenos Aires before torturing and murdering thousands of people who dared to oppose them. They were weasel words and few people, if any, believed them. In any case, amid all the 'freedoms' there was no mention of political freedom, and although Falklands democracy had not been perfect, Islanders had been enjoying increasing autonomy before the invasion.

There was, however, a good reason to insist that the locals remained indoors. The town was crammed with troops who were intoxicated with victory and still searching for the missing Marines or any Defence Force members who might be intent on resistance. Twitchy fingers rested on triggers.

As they demanded entrance to houses, the troops generally behaved correctly; some were even polite. But not always. Neil Hewitt, then just 11 years old, remembered his family being summarily ordered from their home on Davis Street:

We heard these tremendous bangs on the back door and there were shouts for us to come out. We had to go out and sit in the yard, and this Argentine was there with a machine gun trained on us. My brother only had underclothing on, and my stepfather was stripping off giving him his clothes. The machine-gun barrel looked about two feet wide from where I was sitting, and Mum thought we were going to be shot.

On Dairy Paddock Road, on the south side of the town, Mike and Trudy Butcher realised that it made sense to obey the new martial law. The couple peered cautiously from their windows and were surprised to see troops in a cheerful mood. Mike recalled:

It was the only time I ever saw them laughing during that whole 70-odd days. The armoured personnel carrier crews were resting that afternoon in the Dairy Paddock, sitting there thoroughly enjoying themselves and laughing, quite happy that the war was over.

Out on the farms, parents of children attending school in Stanley were deeply worried. In fact their children were fine. The Superintendent of Education, John Fowler, had made sure that extra staff stayed in the boys' and girls' hostels overnight and that the children kept their heads down. As soon as possible after the surrender, he began making plans for their evacuation to camp.

It was wise to do so, as there was no sign that the two schools and the camp children's hostels were safe. Briefly, things had not looked good at Stanley House, where the boys lived. Robert Wilkinson, who was 11 years old, remembered his first encounter with the invaders:

They made us line up on the front lawn and one guy came charging out from the trees with all the gear. I think most of us boys were interested in the weapons they were carrying. Another pair of troops came up the garden path. The older guy was an officer of some sort. I got the impression he was quite a nice guy because as he walked past I remember him patting one of the boys on the head and smiling; reassuring us, I guess. Then they went through and searched the house.

Just as Vice Comodoro Hector Gilobert had helped to negotiate a cease-fire, another Argentine helped with the evacuation of camp children. One of the resident Spanish teachers helped John Fowler to negotiate safe exit for a caravan of Land Rovers laden with children.

Using the Government radio telephone service, but watched over by an Argentine officer, John Fowler asked farmers across the Islands to help with the exodus by providing transport and hospitality. Early on Saturday, invasion day plus one, the Superintendent of Education, dressed incongruously in a suit and polished shoes, jumped into one of the eighteen Land Rovers, packed with fifty-two youngsters, and gave the signal to go. With white flags fluttering from each vehicle (as required by the new authorities) the convoy left Stanley.

Pat Whitney and hostel house parent Lorraine McGill were in the lead vehicle. As they passed the junior school they noticed the playground was swarming with armed Argentines and a machine gun had been mounted on the roof. Getting the camp children back to their parents seemed like a better idea than ever. Lorraine was travelling with her own children, Jane and Roy, and was keen to rejoin her husband, Robin, who was running the family farm on Carcass Island.

Pat too was concerned about his family. His 11-year-old son Kurt was in the back of the Land Rover and he quietly asked Lorraine if she would take the child on to Carcass Island. The normally brusque and rough man said, "Look, whatever happens, I know you'll look after him for me; you'll do your best." She agreed.

At the western exit from Stanley they saw an Argentine armoured personnel carrier and a few soldiers apparently trying to stop them. Pat muttered, "To hell with that!" and put his foot to the floor. Vehicle after vehicle followed, enveloping the Argentines in gritty dust.

At Fitzroy the convoy of children was met warmly by the manager, Ron Binnie, and an elderly couple, John and Lizzie Lee, who threw their house open to the children.

Some adults, including John Fowler, turned back to Stanley, passing their passengers on to drivers from Fitzroy. The perfect weather of invasion day had been replaced with heavy rain and the drivers slipped and slid their way across roadless East Falkland for about five hours. Eventually they saw a line of vehicles coming towards them from Darwin and Goose Green. People were pulling together to get the children home.

The youngsters were given meals and warm beds across Darwin and Goose Green, and the adults settled down to discuss their plight. There was agreement that the Darwin area would soon be occupied. Above all, they wondered whether Britain could really mount a task force to retake the Falklands. They had heard Margaret Thatcher promise this, but could it really be done?

Many children left the convoy as their parents met them and took them back to the homesteads of East Falkland. But a core of 'Westers' needed to cross Falkland Sound. This was where the little ship *Penelope* and its skipper, Finlay Ferguson, came in. *Penelope*, a barrel-hulled auxiliary schooner, had been moving sheep around Speedwell Island, but now Falkland Islands Company manager Brook Hardcastle asked the skipper to replace his sheep with children and carry them to Port Howard on West Falkland.

Penelope was perfumed with diesel, sheep manure and whatever the cook, Ivan Fairley, happened to be frying in a pan of mutton dripping in the galley – probably penguin eggs. For the children this voyage was an adventure, but Lorraine recalled being nervous:

We were halfway across the Sound, when we realised there were aircraft coming towards us – and we weren't flying a white flag. One of the children, Susie Nightingale, had some of her things stuffed into a white pillowcase so we emptied them out and Finlay hoisted Susie's pillowcase up the mast. The planes obviously saw us, and flew off, but it made us very aware of our vulnerability.

At Port Howard more grateful parents fussed around their children. New Land Rovers took Lorraine and the remaining children on to Hill Cove, where Sally Blake met them with welcome news: the BBC had reported that the first ships of the task force were departing from Britain. Help was on its way.

One more night with the Blakes at Hill Cove and then a pair of tiny boats from Saunders Island arrived to take the last evacuees on to the most remote Island farms of the west. As they landed on the beach at Carcass Island, Lorraine, Roy, Jane and their new friend Kurt were greeted by a hugely relieved Rob McGill. Over the coming weeks they would watch Argentine fighter-bombers scream past at almost zero feet, delivering their ordnance to the Royal Navy in San Carlos Harbour, and they would provide shelter and sustenance to an SAS patrol. But they would not see another Argentine face.

Dick Baker found himself in a very strange position. From the high drama of arresting potential Argentine fifth columnists, passing ammunition to the defending Marines at Government House and helping to negotiate a cease-fire, he was now back in the office staring at an in-tray. He had to blink hard to believe it.

Things that had previously kept him busy five days a week seemed very trivial. Rex Hunt had, however, been keen that the Islanders should have a reassuring representative of London with them for as long as possible and he was doing a good job just by being there. Strong local leadership might have been preferable, but councillors appeared to see themselves as representatives rather than leaders; a perception that the British had been happy to encourage. But Dick was as benign and decent a representative of Whitehall as anyone could hope for and his presence was reassuring. He hoped that he would remain until the British returned, but that seemed unlikely.

Dick and Connie Baker had said emotional goodbyes to Rex Hunt and his family, other Foreign Office colleagues, their friend Gary Noott and the rest of the captured Marines. They were all loaded into vehicles for the short journey to Stanley Airport, where Argentine aircraft waited to carry them to Buenos Aires and thence to Britain.

When things get difficult the British organise a meeting and, if possible, a committee. Which, when the dust had settled a day or so later, was exactly what Dick Baker did. Word was secretly passed to the heads of government departments and some specialist expatriate government officers who had remained that they were to meet mid-morning the following Sunday at the hospital. If questioned they were to say they were visiting patients. It might help if they carried a small bunch of flowers. Dick hoped that the senior Argentines would be relaxing a little by that stage. They might even be attending mass at St Mary's, where Monsignor Daniel Spraggon would subject them to a thundering, politically loaded sermon.

About 20 key figures turned up, including the Financial Secretary and most senior local civil servant, Harold Rowlands. John Fowler, who had successfully arranged the evacuation of camp children from Stanley, was there, as was Veterinary Officer Steve Whitley and the Senior Medical Officer, Daniel Haines.

The day room of the hospital's geriatric wing had rarely, if ever, seen such lively conversation. Dick recalled an immediate conflict between the firebrands who were in favour of non-cooperation and gung-ho resistance, and those who believed that a workable relationship with the Argentines had to be established:

> We had to do a bit of restraining with Steve Whitley because he was all for going out and sabotaging things, and sticking knives in a few Argentines. As Chairman, I said 'Look, Steve, we have to play this a bit cool because so far it seems to me they have been very correct. But if we start doing things like that they may march out a few wives and children and shoot them.'
>
> So we agreed the best thing was to make things as difficult as possible for the Argentines while maintaining the services that we needed – an example was the way many government vehicles suddenly became unserviceable.
>
> We decided to encourage anyone who wanted to do so to join the police as a special constable. That way they could walk around Stanley under the cover of a basic uniform, and people would be able to come to us with any problems. We knew the Argies would accept this, because they worried there was going to be all sorts of civil disruption.

There were a few other secret meetings at the hospital over the nine days before Dick Baker was finally deported, but the main principles of local government under enemy occupation were established that first Sunday. Civil servants, especially those maintaining vital services, would follow their own consciences. They could work with the Argentines to the degree necessary to maintain the community.

One other significant matter was discussed at a later meeting. The

Senior Medical Officer, Dr Daniel Haines, one of the more colourful characters of the occupation, whom the Argentines later exiled to remote Fox Bay with other potential 'trouble makers', decided that the civilians should demand to be evacuated from the war zone *en masse*. He produced a highly controversial draft letter to the British Foreign Secretary, requesting that *all* civilians, not just expatriate British Civil Servants, be evacuated from the Islands before any fighting commenced.

There was spirited discussion for and against the letter, but eventually cautious agreement that such a request could be made. There were fewer civil servants at this later meeting, and some of those who agreed to it felt uneasy. But later, if civilians were killed, they might find it difficult to explain why they had turned down a suggestion that might have saved lives. Most assumed that the letter was unlikely to reach Britain. In fact it seems almost certain that Dr Haines did get the letter to the UK with a departing Briton (the Argentines maintained their weekly LADE service for several weeks, and those who could afford to obtain passages on the increasingly congested planes, were free to do so). The text read:

> On behalf of the civilian British population of the Falkland Islands, we, the undersigned civil servants and administrators, request that a protecting power be appointed to help arrange the temporary evacuation of the civilian population of these islands under the terms of the Geneva Convention. We further request the immediate dispatch to Port Stanley of an observer from that power.

When word of the petition filtered out, many Islanders were furious. It seemed to many like the patronising action of expatriate officers who did not share their deep bond with the Islands. Locals did not intend to abandon their homes. They knew that, once out of the Islands, a deal would be hammered out through the United Nations, and if they ever returned it would be to a place that had changed utterly.

In Whitehall the request for evacuation must have been viewed with extreme concern. The invasion had been a terrible slap-in-the-face for the Conservative government. Their inept management of Falklands issues in the months leading up to 2 April was at least partly to blame, but now they needed a victory of almost Churchillian standards if they were to weather the storm. Without people to liberate, swift military action, as opposed to diplomacy and compromise, would be hard to justify. The letter was ignored.

The squad of special constables did not last long. Many were expatriate Britons who took the opportunity to leave on the Argentine air service. Others realised that there was little to be achieved, and by staying in uniform they came uncomfortably close to collaboration with the Argentines. But for a while Sulivan House, the Bakers' elegant grace and favour home, became their *de facto* headquarters.

Terry Peck, a councillor since the previous October and the one-time Chief of Police, had left the force after allegations of brutality a year or so earlier. But he had joined up again as a lowly special. He, in particular, took up Dick Baker's time with intelligence reports.

Both men liked the fact that policing in the Falklands had been a relatively informal affair, largely free of procedural red tape. This was village policing: a cuff around the ear was the usual punishment for mischievous boys and sometimes a more belligerent drunk. Dick and Terry forlornly hoped to maintain this style rather than see it replaced by anything the military police might favour.

So when Terry Peck told Dick Baker that there was a 'nasty domestic' situation to be seen to, Dick agreed that they should handle it their way. He recalled, however, that the incident got out of hand and the local methods began to resemble something of which an Argentine secret policeman might approve.

There was a well-known bloke who regularly used to get drunk and beat up his wife. Terry said she'd run away leaving her baby. 'We need to get to the baby, but he won't let us in.'

So we hatched a plan. We'd visit this chap, convince him to open the door, then we would wrestle him to the ground and Dr Daniel Haines would inject him with a tranquilliser. Then we'd take the baby to the hospital.

We rehearsed it carefully, and all went well until he opened the door. Then Terry just stepped up to the bloke, who was about twice his size, and thumped him. We grabbed him, and pumped the tranquilliser into him.

That didn't work, so we gave him another one. Daniel said later that it took twice the normal amount. We tucked him up in bed and left with the baby, which hadn't been harmed. This was typical of the mad things that were going on.

Many Stanley folk left the town to live with friends and families on the farms, where they assumed – sometimes quite wrongly – there would be less danger. Others, however, coped by continuing to live as normally as possible. A few shops remained open, particularly the two supermarkets. And some civil servants trickled back to their offices. Working alongside the Argentine administrators might be misinterpreted as acceptance of the regime, but ignoring the vital needs of the community would make life even more difficult. This, said Dick Baker, was a moral, and sometimes practical decision that each person faced alone:

> All the civil servants were concerned and confused. Getting paid was an issue because people had families to think about. Harold Rowlands, the Treasurer, decided he had to remain in his office, but when he was told he had to change everything into pesos, he said something like, 'I'm too old to deal with all the noughts'; in other words, 'I'm not going to do it.' The Education Department refused to teach because they were told they would have to work to an Argentine curriculum.

Harold Rowlands' skeleton Treasury and Savings Bank staff, Peter Biggs, Anna King, Robert King and Tracy Peck, wanted to keep savings, bank ledgers, and local currency in safe hands.

The Treasury was stuck in the 1950s. Computers had not yet replaced manual adding machines and ledgers were four-inch-thick volumes dating back to the Second World War. In the later days of the occupation the staff in their Dickensian office would be balancing these ledgers as Harriers attacked key positions less than a mile away. On at least one occasion the Secretariat was raked with rifle fire as the clerks worked.

Most Islanders had their savings invested in the bank and many clamoured to withdraw their money. But the staff explained that not enough cash was kept in the bank's vault and withdrawals were limited to £50 a day. Customers were assured, though, that, whatever happened, their savings would be secure. Not everyone was happy about this, as Tracy Peck, then a 17-year-old clerk, recalled:

> A lot of people believed their money was there in a little box, so we got some rude remarks. One awful man called me a traitor and said 'Whose side are you on anyway?' It really upset me. I used to go home every Friday and think, 'Oh well, it'll be all over by Monday.'

Later in the occupation the Argentine military pay office, which occupied the now redundant offices of the Education Department, worked with the Treasury to run a surprisingly honest compensation system for Islanders whose property had been damaged or looted. There was a sliding scale of payments: so many pesos for a stolen chicken, or slaughtered cow; so much for a broken window; and negotiable amounts for everything from flattened fences to stolen Land Rovers.

The compensation system was, at times, so efficient that one man claimed for two bunkers dug by troops on his land. The rate of £20.00 per hole was agreed and paid. (Later he took delight in passing the money on to the South Atlantic Fund, which helped wounded British Falklands veterans and their families.)

The scheme began to fail towards the end when Stanley was under artillery siege and air attack, but by then both Argentines and locals were more preoccupied with staying alive than processing claims.

Local staff also maintained a minimal presence in the Government Legal Department. Here Fran Biggs, a girl in her early twenties, learned to get on with an Argentine Army lawyer, a colonel who, she recalled, was decent.

> He would say to me, 'Don't worry, everything will be fine. The British will have the place back within a couple of months. I can't help being sent here. I don't want to, but I've got to do it.'

The real heroes were the men of the Public Works Department who ran Stanley's electricity and water supplies. Power station staff, under Ted Carey, and the water purification and distribution crew, under Dennis Plaice, quickly realised that if they refused to work for the Argentines the town's life support systems would be taken over by inept soldiers and would soon fail. The first to suffer would be the Islanders.

The Power Station crew had a dubious privilege. They would be collected from their homes and driven to work in Argentine Army vehicles, but once there they were closely guarded. For the first week, the routine was particularly harsh, as one of Ted Carey's senior power staff, Les Harris (who spoke Spanish fluently) recalled: "Every morning we were put against the wall by a chap with a gun, while another searched us. It wasn't a nice feeling going to work."

Gradually the guards got to know the staff and relaxed. The locals took advantage of their familiarity and developed a truculent attitude. Nevertheless, Les Harris thought Ted Carey had gone too far when he gave Colonel Manuel Dorrego, the engineer in charge of the Public Works Department, a mouthful of cheek:

> We weren't meant to get together in groups of more than two. One day this Colonel came up and found six or seven of us in the workshop. He blew his top with the sergeant who was guarding

us and told him that so many people together could sabotage something.

I stepped in and said, 'Look if we wanted to sabotage this place we can do it anytime we want to, but we have to think of our people.'

Then Ted stood up and said, 'Look here Napoleon, what's your name?'

'I am Colonel Dorrego.'

Ted said, 'Good, because a few Marines will be looking for you when this is over.'

That really boosted us, but I thought we were in for it. He backed off, but he was so angry that the sergeant was sent to the defences in the hills around Stanley. He sent another one to guard us, but we'd had the first one thinking our way, and couldn't get on with the new one. So I actually went down to see Colonel Dorrego and said, 'This new chap doesn't know the working of the machinery.' It was a lot of lies, but we got our sergeant back.

For those with desk jobs, the guiding principle was, "Do as much as possible to help our own people; as little as possible to help the Argentines." Late starts and early departures were the rule, and the working day became gradually shorter.

Time at the Secretariat was used as imaginatively as possible. Soon after the invasion government solicitor Ray Checkley approached Dick Baker with a copy of the Geneva Conventions. He suggested that they might photocopy and distribute relevant pages so that Islanders would be aware of their rights. Getting copies out to the farming settlements would not be easy but it was worth a try.

The men rightly assumed that the Argentines would not want a population of amateur human rights lawyers, and so they agreed to copy the paragraphs and distribute them in secret.

Rex Browning, a senior member of the Secretariat staff, was roped in to help and they decided to do the work the following Sunday when most of the good Catholic Argentines would again be receiving a verbal cocktail of pious guidance and political abuse from Monsignor Daniel Spraggon.

Come the day, Rex stood guard at the entrance to the Secretariat, ostensibly chatting to the young sentries in the Spanish he had learned years earlier at the British School in Uruguay. Dick and Ray began the mammoth photocopying task upstairs. The printed papers were just beginning to pile up nicely when Rex bellowed up the stairs, "Look out, someone's coming!" Dick recalled that they scrambled in vain to hide the documents.

Who should it bloody be but the Argentine wing commander who was their legal beagle. He was an English speaker, and I knew him quite well, as did Ray.

'Unusual for you to be working on a Sunday morning,' he said. 'Oh, I see! Yes, this is very naughty, isn't it? I'm afraid I'll have to confiscate all these copies.'

So the Geneva Conventions were never distributed, which was unfortunate because some of the 1949 agreement's principles as they applied to interned people were blatantly ignored in the weeks to come, in particular at Goose Green. There the entire population of the settlement was locked up for weeks in a building that was not marked as a centre for civilian detainees. Sanitation was inadequate; there was insufficient bedding and no separate accommodation for women. Furthermore, the prisoners were not provided with shelters in spite of the frequent air and artillery attacks. A few amateur human rights lawyers might have been useful.

Chapter Five

Good Argie, Bad Argie

By far the most sinister and dangerous individual on the Argentine side during the early days was one Major Patricio Dowling. Speaking fluent English and boastful of his Irish origins and sympathy for the IRA, Dowling headed the military police intelligence unit.

Dowling arrived with the invasion forces carrying dossiers on many Islanders and with the intention of introducing them to state control military style.

His first target was Rex Hunt. In his memoir, *My Falkland Days*, Rex recalled that shortly after the surrender on 2 April, Dowling strode into Government House, intent on prising from the Governor whatever diplomatic secrets he held. Rex recounted this in his memoir:

> He spoke excellent English and he described himself as Irish-Argentine, although his demeanour suggested classical Prussian. He flourished a list of names and demanded to know what I had done with my missing Marines [those who had escaped Stanley and headed for the North Camp, and those who had embarked on *Endurance* and awaited the Argentines' arrival at South Georgia]. I was shocked to see that he had a complete roll call of both outgoing and incoming detachments. He must have brought it with him from Buenos Aires.
>
> I naturally feigned ignorance. 'I only know the officers,' I said, thinking of Argentine attitudes to their men. 'I don't bother about the other men.' This seemed to satisfy him. He folded the list primly and put it in his pocket with a confident 'We shall find them.'

Dowling later took great pleasure in escorting Rex and Mavis Hunt, and their son Tony, to Stanley Airport, where they were to join the other British diplomats and the captured Royal Marines being deported. All were being flown to Comodoro Rivadavia and then on to Montevideo. Having been unable to get the combinations for the safes at Government House (all important documents had, in any case, been destroyed) the Argentine spent two hours going through every item of the Governor's luggage. As the Governor took off the ceremonial uniform that he had insisted on wearing as he drove through Stanley saying farewell to Islanders, Dowling searched every pocket and fold. Rex donned a more sensible business suit, and that too was checked. Dowling found nothing, although Tony managed to smuggle out *Sunday Times* reporter Simon Winchester's hand-written copy.

Dowling quickly moved on to evict Police Chief Ronnie Lamb and set up the unit's headquarters in Stanley's police station. To Islanders he personified that which they most feared about Argentina: the government terror machine which had spent the previous six years torturing and murdering citizens who dared to oppose or even think ill of the extreme right-wing regime. No one will ever know for sure how many innocent Argentines disappeared in what the military junta itself described as the 'dirty war,' but, 25 years on, Argentines were still traumatised by the injustices perpetrated on them.

Blue-eyed, slim and tall, Patricio Dowling cut a neat figure in his well-pressed fatigues. He often carried a British self-loading rifle, a trophy from the defeated Royal Marines. Usually in the company of two or three armed flunkies, he swaggered. Sometimes he was violent; other times he threatened. At all times he exuded a sense of danger.

Dowling walked into the *Upland Goose* and demanded rooms. The owner, the notoriously spiky Desmond King, had suffered at the hand of the Nazis when he was in the RAF during the siege of Malta and he liked such people no more now than he did then.

He responded with the obvious lie that there was no room in his inn and Dowling and his men had better look elsewhere. Dowling said that if half of the hotel was not made available immediately he would take over the entire establishment. King could cooperate or lose the hotel. From that day on half of the hotel was occupied by the Argentines, mainly their priests, administrators and propaganda merchants.

This was not cooperation, and had he lost control of the hotel, a large group of Islanders would have been denied the shelter that the *Upland Goose* offered them in the later stages of the war. Many Islanders were protected and comforted by the thick stone walls of the hotel which was, fortunately for them, still in the hands of the Kings.

Dowling bunked over the shop at the Police Station, but continued to eat at the *Goose* from time to time, no doubt despising the mutton and potatoes staple, but enjoying the experience of being waited on by

Falklanders. He did not realise that Des King's daughter Alison spoke Spanish. One evening, as she placed a plate of mutton unceremoniously in front of the police chief and an unknown colleague, she heard Dowling discussing (in his words) the 'final solution' to the 'problem' of the Malvinas: 'getting rid of the Islanders'. She was sure that the conversation had not been laid on for her benefit and that he was referring to tactics that could have been described as ethnic cleansing.

The intelligence chief had told Rex Hunt that he would find the Marines who had escaped Stanley and this became his first and most urgent task. After telling Mike Norman that they were 'going fishing', the six Marines had made for the farms of the north camp. Forty-eight hours later, tired, hungry and soaked, they knocked on the door of Long Island farmhouse, where they knew they could find a welcome.

Neil and Glenda Watson and their three children, Lisa, Paul and Ben, greeted the men early on Sunday 4 April. Neil had been a sergeant in the Defence Force and he understood the grim options open to the Marines:

> Three of the younger guys thought they could go back out to the hills, and we discussed how we could supply them with food.
>
> Come midday, we listened to the BBC news and they said that the task force was being despatched but probably wouldn't be in the area for a month. So then the older guy said, 'Look! We can't live out there for a month. They'll have helicopters. They'll have dogs. We'd never get away with it. We're going to have to surrender.'
>
> We all agreed that the people around here in the north camp would get more harassment from the Argentines if they knew there were six Royal Marines hiding in the area. They were not happy having to surrender but there was no other option.

Neil agreed to contact the Argentines. He telephoned the home of Vice Comodoro Hector Gilobert. Gilobert was Argentine first and foremost, but, as he had shown during the invasion, he felt a strong sympathy for the Islanders after living with them for some two years. Neil remembers a slightly bizarre conversation that revealed Gilobert's decency:

> Gilobert immediately said, 'How are they?'
> I said, 'Oh, they're fine.'
> He said 'OK, well would you mind keeping them for the night?'

I said, 'I'd love to have them for the night!' So I got a bottle of whisky out and we made the best of a bad situation.

But Dowling, who was all the things that Gilobert was not, heard the news and the phone soon rang again to tell the Watsons that troops would be there within the hour. Neil again:

All hell broke loose. We buried their rifles, grenades and some rocket launchers near the beach, then came back home just in time.

The Argies put up a good performance. They had two Pucara [ground attack aircraft] flying over the house to provide top cover and put three helicopters on the green. They took the guys out and tied them up just outside the house. It was a bit unpleasant really. The Marines just said, 'We'll be back.'

Next thing the door was completely kicked in and two Argies entered. One was an air force officer, I think, who had a 45mm automatic pistol, and the other guy, the one who'd booted the door in, was Dowling. He was carrying a rifle.

'Up against the wall,' he said. We did as we were told. You don't argue with SLRs and 45s. They were perspiring and *very* uptight. They obviously didn't know what to expect.

Lisa, our daughter, just sat there on the sofa sucking her thumb. She never moved. Dowling pointed his weapon at her and he repeated, 'Stand up there!'

Lisa said, 'No!'

We were appealing to Lisa, '*Please* stand up here!' We thought he was going to shoot her. He was so tense and uptight that it was dangerous.

He kept pointing the rifle at her, and she kept saying, 'No!' Eventually he actually gave in and Lisa just sat there with her thumb in her mouth.

We lied to Dowling that the Marines had left their weapons in the hills, and he swallowed the story, hook, line and sinker.

We had an Irish tea towel on the wall, and he said, 'Are your ancestors Irish?'

I said, 'No. Are yours? North or South?'

He got angry then: 'South of course! How long has your family been in the Islands?'

I told him they came here in 1840 and he said, 'That makes you more of an Argentine than I am.'

'Not fucking likely,' I said.

Dowling left the Watsons deeply concerned about the dangers that might lie ahead under Argentine occupation.

Next the secret policeman was to find and deport Councillor Bill Luxton, who was the Islands' most famous and vitriolic critic of Argentina (he was only slightly less hard on the British Foreign Office).

Luxton, a wealthy farmer, and his wife, Pat, had flown into Stanley in their Cessna light aircraft the day before the invasion and been trapped there. As the dust settled on the Saturday they decided to head home for Chartres on West Falkland, but, aware that a strange plane flying low over the Falklands might be shot down by the twitchy Argentines, Bill approached them for permission to fly. By unfortunate chance he ran into Dowling at the Town Hall. Bill recalled that the officer was hostile and immediately turned down the request. "Stay out of trouble," he was told.

Dowling probably assumed that the refusal and veiled warning would keep the Luxtons in their Stanley home. Instead the family loaded their Land Rover and tagged onto a group leaving for the assumed safety of the camp. At North Arm, after seven or eight hours' cross-country driving, they met with the local coastal freighter *Monsunen* and persuaded the captain to carry them across Falkland Sound to Fox Bay. From there they borrowed a vehicle and drove the thirty or so miles back to their farm.

About a week passed before Dowling made his move to arrest the Luxtons. He was furious when he realised they had fled. His intelligence on the family could not have been good because Dowling's helicopter-borne search began not at Chartres, but at Port San Carlos. There he resorted to crude violence. The local men were corralled on the green and ordered to lie face-down on the ground before being interrogated. It must have been a terrifying experience. The men were questioned aggressively about the whereabouts of Bill Luxton, but they knew nothing. When farm manager Allan Miller attempted to intervene Dowling promptly hit him hard in the stomach with the butt of a rifle, knocking the tall, beefy man to the ground.

Like the Watsons, the people of Port San Carlos were left with the residue of fear that was Dowling's calling card. A short time later his helicopter swooped in on Chartres. This time they found the Luxtons. Bill recalled what happened:

> About 20 of their special forces jumped out and surrounded the house. Dowling was very, very angry because we had given him the slip. He told us we could pack one change of clothes, and then they took us into Stanley.
>
> Dowling had a menace about him. I think he was just a cold-

blooded killer. I'd like to have frightened him as much as he frightened me. They sat us in the open door of this helicopter flying at 50 feet across Falkland Sound, and one knew that they had a habit of pushing people out of aeroplanes over the River Plate. When we left for Argentina, I had fairly low expectations of surviving.

In Stanley I was told we were to be deported. I was absolutely livid, but there was just nothing we could do. They had made up their minds that they were going to kick us out.

When we took off from Stanley Airport our son Stephen was sitting between us, and I have to say that Pat and I were both howling our eyes out with rage and everything else. Stephen said, 'Come on you two, stop it because we'll be back.'

There were two positive spin-offs from the Luxtons' deportation. First, while flying over the Falklands and being driven to Stanley Airport, they were able to collect useful information. A few days later at Gatwick Airport an SAS team debriefed them thoroughly, taking particular interest in the Argentine troop dispositions and their equipment.

Second, Bill spent the next few months talking to journalists from Britain and around the world, giving vivid first-hand accounts of the Argentine invasion and pointing to his own deportation as an example of behaviour that could not be allowed to continue. Seeing Luxton's name in the news must have been a constant irritation for the Argentines. In any case, they shipped no one else out of the Islands, preferring isolated internal exile for other 'trouble makers'.

One of Dick Baker's duties was to establish which British contract officers, mainly teachers, nurses, doctors, engineers and other specialists, were prepared to remain in the Islands. Those who occupied important symbolic positions, such as Whitehall-appointed Government staff and the chief of Police, had no choice – they were deported anyway. But the Argentines hoped that other skilled workers could be persuaded to stay on to help them run the Islands.

Dick agreed to tell the expatriate officers that those who wished to return to Britain could do so by the regular weekly air service (which remained operational until Stanley Airport was bombed at the end of the month). But if they remained their original conditions of employment would be respected and might even be improved.

Dick felt strongly that the officers should listen to their own consciences. Most could not be expected to place themselves in such danger. After all, few of them were there for the love of it. They had been enjoying a relatively easy life with good pay, generous leave allowances, government houses, and bonuses to make up for the short-comings of Island life. They had not signed up to work in a war zone.

With a few notable exceptions the teachers and most others wanted to go home as soon as possible. Some wags joked that LADE now stood for "Last Aircraft Departing for England," and some ordinary Falkland Islanders viewed the exodus with wry smiles. They had tolerated a sometimes superior class of expatriate Briton for years. Ordinary Islanders might be less educated, poorer and not quite good enough to drink gin and tonic at Government House, but at least they were staying put and standing together in adversity.

Others defended the expats. The Falklands were not their home, so why should they put their lives on the line? And continuing to work under the Argentine administration might well be seen as collaboration. Furthermore, it was well known that some of the fleeing expats passed on useful intelligence to the Ministry of Defence.

Whatever the rights and wrongs, the relationship between locals and expatriate British was different after the war, when most of those who had left in April returned. Little was said, but the Islanders' old subservient attitude had gone forever and few of the returning expats stayed for long.

There was, however, a moral obligation for the handful of contract doctors and nurses to stay, and they did not ignore this, working with dedication throughout the occupation.

A few other contract staff and their families remained for no other reason than their deep sense of solidarity with the locals. They were, most notably, the Superintendent of Education John Fowler and his teacher wife Veronica; the Government's senior mechanic, ex-soldier Ron Buckett and his wife, Nidge; and the only veterinary surgeon, Steve Whitley, and his wife Sue, a teacher. Some of these people would pay a very high price for their loyalty and Islanders would not forget it.

One other teacher decided to stay. Having completed his government contract and fallen in love with the Islands, Phillip Middleton was searching for a role that would keep him there. Following the invasion, he found one. With the two schools occupied by Argentine soldiers, Phil began conducting classes at home for a handful of O-level pupils. Classes ran for only a few hours a day, but it kept both pupils and teacher happily active.

When not teaching, Phil Middleton would work with Steve Whitley, the vet, to secure the abandoned property of those government officers who had left hurriedly. Furniture and clothes were piled into garages and sheds, while the contents of deep-freezes and liquor cabinets were distributed among remaining families. It seemed that even some invasion clouds had silver linings.

The house clearers were normally just a step or two ahead of the Argentine Army who considered the abandoned government homes to be fair game. The Argentines generally saw Phil, Steve and their colleagues as harmless. But in fact they were indulging in some dangerous mischief, the kind that would have lifted Patricio Dowling into an even higher state of apoplexy. Phillip Middleton:

> Steve had his 'magic scissors,' a gelding tool, that he used to cut the army telephone wires.
>
> We'd stop and Steve would get out. It was always Steve who did it, mainly because he had the big castrating scissors. He'd just drop down and cut the wires. My job would be to keep watch and make sure no one was watching us. Then we'd go on.
>
> Every time we went into a house that we knew the Argentines were about to take over we would walk around and make sure it was all right. Snip, snip!

The house-clearing missions were also a cover for photographing Argentine defences. Phil Middleton:

> I remember sitting in the front seat of the Land Rover, and suddenly this lens would appear over my shoulder or under my armpit. Steve would be in the back taking pictures.

Steve was by no means the only person with a concealed camera, but he was one of the boldest. Terry Peck walked the town with a Russian telephoto camera concealed in a length of drainpipe. Locals who saw him thought this was odd, but then these were very odd times. Argentines must have assumed that Islanders often wandered the streets clutching large pieces of plumbing. His pictures of anti-aircraft missile sites were smuggled out and later reappeared in the hands of Army and Air Force intelligence officers.

No one indulging in this low-key sabotage and spying knew exactly what risks they faced, but there were enough hastily daubed military signs around to make it clear that such subversive activity was banned. Anyway, with Dowling's gang at large, it was probably better not to think about it too much.

Nineteen years later, the then Argentine Governor, General Menendez, was asked about the penalties that might have been applied to any local accused of sabotage, espionage or using banned radio transmitters to pass intelligence to the British. He answered that they would have been considered spies and their punishment would have been appropriate.

This may have been an exaggeration, but there would certainly have been harsh treatment. Menendez himself had a reputation as a no-holds-barred anti-guerrilla commander during the 1970s.

Occupation was at best demeaning, at worst terrifying. Islanders were under the heel of a foreign dictatorship, which had so far generally behaved with moderation, but in whose armoury summary arrest, terror and even murder were known weapons.

Patricio Dowling's name was already being uttered with fear, his team was known to have dossiers on Islanders, and arbitrary house searches, arrests and questioning were becoming common. One of many such incidents illustrated the police state culture that Dowling and others were attempting to introduce. Walking along Ross Road, the author's father noticed government meteorologist Jimmy Stephenson being marched into the police station at gunpoint. "If I don't come out," shouted the angry and alarmed weather man, "tell them my only crime was that I showed too much interest."

It seemed that, as the British screw tightened on the Falklands, things could only get worse. Hard-liners, perhaps led by Dowling, would become far more dangerous.

Into this volatile environment stepped an Argentine of humanity and bravery who did a great deal to protect Islanders from the excesses of his compatriots. Comodoro Carlos Bloomer Reeve did not arrive with the invasion force, but stepped off an air force transport plane at Stanley Airport almost a week later. The wiry, normally easy-smiling, man was grim and emotional. He barely recognised the little airport now, littered as it was with camouflaged aircraft and bristling with guns. But, six years before, he had managed the Argentine LADE air service from here, working closely with Islanders he considered friends.

Bloomer, as most people in Stanley knew him during happier times, had been posted to the Falklands in 1975 and 1976. The air service had been introduced following the 1972 Anglo-Argentine Communications Agreement.

The air force officer and his family lived happily in Stanley, accommodated in a bungalow supplied by the local government. Running LADE's most remote outpost had not been too demanding. There was normally only one flight a week by Fokker F27 turbo-prop aircraft and, as the senior Argentine representative, he enjoyed a social life that, though redolent of British colonialism, was quaint and fun.

Like most other visitors, he and his family enjoyed the lifestyle, the wildlife that thronged the beautiful coastline and the general feel of being a healthy distance from the rest of the troubled world.

Bloomer's family had come from Scotland a generation or two earlier and he spoke fluent English in a slightly adenoidal tone. He would chat with the shopkeepers and the locals he met on the streets, and his children attended the school. There was nothing ostentatious about the man. Although later LADE chiefs would drive large Ford Falcon city cruisers, Bloomer preferred to negotiate Stanley's pot-holed roads in a little Citroen 2CV.

He and his wife Mora became very good friends with the senior Catholic priest, Monsignor Daniel Spraggon – a friendship that was to help both sides during the occupation. They were also close friends with the government's senior meteorologist, Danny Borland, a Scot who was distantly related to Mora. Bloomer Reeve employed a few local people as clerks and baggage handlers, and was known as a good boss.

He was the acceptable face of Argentina and, in spite of themselves, the Islanders liked him. Somebody in Argentina cleverly realised this and knew that he would sugar the pill of Argentine rule. But it was hardly kind to Bloomer. As he recalled, he had to cope with conflicting loyalties and friendships that must have appeared betrayed:

> There were big emotions. I was afraid to find the friends I had left. I was really rather uncomfortable about it. I was not coming as a conqueror, but I was coming to administer the life of the people with whom I had lived.

Bloomer Reeve had not been told about the invasion until three days before the landings. Serving as Air Attaché in Bonn, Germany, he had been summoned back to Buenos Aires on the spurious excuse that he was to discuss a contract with the German aviation company Dornier. He was shocked when, upon arrival at Ezeiza Airport, a brigadier told him that the Islands were going to be invaded on 1 April (the plan was delayed by 24 hours). He had two days to organise an interim government that would take over from the invasion force.

But fighting for the Islands was stupid. Bloomer Reeve, who had always placed great store in diplomacy, knew it, and felt the Argentine government was too impatient:

> We were winning the war with the Islanders *without* the war! We were doing very well. Had we gone on with what we were doing, in 15, 25 or 30 years, the Islands would have reached an agreement for double nationality and integration with the continent.

But orders are orders, and once you are in the job, you have to do your best, or leave the service. I thought we could do a good job.

I called my wife from the Malvinas to say I was there. It was a shock for her. Our children still had friends in the Islands. It was pretty difficult.

It helped Bloomer Reeve to justify his involvement in what he knew to be a misguided adventure to think that he could, at least, do something about the iniquities of the British colonial system. He had enjoyed living in Stanley in the 1970s, but felt the Islanders were exploited and deprived. Nearly all senior government jobs were held by expatriate Britons; London was not investing in the Islands' poor infrastructure, and even such basic services as medicine and education were under-resourced. To cap it all, Islanders were effectively second-class British citizens denied the right to live and work in their mother country. If he had anything to do with it, they would be given more control over their own lives and their standard of living could be improved. He would, at least, begin the process.

Creating a new government system in such a short time was out of the question, so Bloomer Reeve decided to leave the framework of the British administration in place, refilling posts if necessary. There would be Argentines of course – he himself would fill Dick Baker's slot as General Secretary to Governor Menendez – but he hoped that eventually locals would hold all key posts. It was a forlorn hope, of course, but he had to believe in what he was doing.

As his right-hand man, responsible for education, medicine and social matters, Bloomer Reeve had Naval Captain Barry Melbourne Hussey, another fluent English speaker, who was known in the Navy as 'El Ingles'. Hussey counted among his English relatives the film actress Olivia Hussey, who played Juliet in the 1968 film of *Romeo and Juliet*. As a man of humane principles, Bloomer Reeve believed he too would work to help the Islanders.

Other members of Bloomer Reeve's team were appointed to run telecommunications (based at the Cable and Wireless Station) and, crucially, the Public Works Department. An army engineer, Lieutenant Colonel Manuel Dorrego, filled the latter post.

Serving under General Mario Benjamin Menendez, the first Argentine Governor for 149 years, the interim military government was to stay in the Falklands for at least forty days. Bloomer Reeve believed that by then the system should be operating smoothly and he and his team would return to the mainland, probably to be replaced by civilians. Likewise, most of the occupation forces would be withdrawn, leaving just one Army regiment, a naval contingent and a small air force base.

With hindsight, such a plan seems absurdly unrealistic, but when Bloomer Reeve, Hussey and the other administrators landed in the Falklands early in April a diplomatic settlement and some kind of political compromise seemed more likely than war. In any case they were determined to do the best job possible. Dorrego, for example, was arranging a shipment of trucks and earth-moving plant to the Islands to start a road-building programme. Hussey had arranged for Argentine volunteer doctors and dentists to augment the British staff at the King Edward Memorial Hospital.

Dick Baker recalled that when Bloomer Reeve knocked on the door of his office and introduced himself, he did so courteously and with no trace of triumphalism:

> He said, 'You can imagine how embarrassed I am to be here.'
> I said, 'Knowing the post that you had here before and how many Islanders you knew, and that your children went to school here, you *must* be embarrassed. But, like all of us, you have a job to do.'
> He said, 'I'm grateful for you taking that attitude.'

Such was the respect shown that Dick was not even thrown out of his office. He remembered the strange relationship that developed between the two men until 14 April when, as the last official British representative in the Islands, he was finally sent home.

> Bloomer Reeve was very helpful, but we maintained a fairly distant relationship. I was told I had no actual authority any more, but he was quite happy to use me as a go-between with the rest of the civil service and any other Islanders.
> Bloomer Reeve would appear in my office from time to time to discuss things, or tell me what the General was going to say on the radio; edicts, such as 'from now on you will all drive on the right-hand side'.
> They were planning to ban people from listening to the BBC World Service, but I laughed, and said to Bloomer Reeve, 'You won't be able to manage this, as out at camp they need to listen to the radio to receive your edicts, and if they have radios they will listen to the BBC whatever you say.'
> He grinned wryly, and said, 'Yes, but I've got to go through the motions of doing this!'

A discussion about the police force revealed Bloomer Reeve's complex views and emotions. Terry Peck had been well known to Bloomer Reeve as the Chief of Police during his previous, happier, time in the Falklands. Now Terry was only an emergency special constable and seemed to be spending much of his time wandering around the town with a drainpipe. Bloomer Reeve was thinking of offering him his old job back. Dick Baker recalled the bizarre conversation:

> Bloomer Reeve said, 'I just want your man-to-man advice. There is one obvious candidate for Chief of Police. You will know who I am thinking of. But he can be very difficult. It occurs to me that if we make him Chief of Police, you would never get rid of him if you come back.'
>
> I thought, 'Bloody hell! First they're saying they'll never give up the Islands, now he's saying we may come back.' I thought it was very interesting that Bloomer Reeve in his heart of hearts never thought Argentina was always going to be there.

The Argentine seemed to enjoy his talks with Dick Baker, and Dick sometimes considered such meetings amusing. Bloomer Reeve's transparent acting was endearing:

> Once he had to give me a lecture. We sat there in the armchairs in my office, and he said, 'I understand that your Margaret Thatcher is sending a task force to retake the islands.'
>
> I said, 'Yes, so I hear.'
>
> He said, 'You'll never do it, of course. You haven't got enough manpower. All the military handbooks will tell you that in order to retake an island you need three times the manpower of those who are holding it. Maybe more. And you simply haven't got that many people.'
>
> I said, 'We'll see!'
>
> He knew and I knew that he was reading me this lecture so that I would pass it back along the line. I did pass it back along the line – in the guise of a joke.
>
> I know Bloomer Reeve helped a lot. I'm convinced his heart was in the right place.

Dick had hoped the Argentines would allow him to stay indefinitely. He'd been in other sticky positions in the Pacific colonies and neither he nor Connie were afraid to face whatever would occur over the coming weeks. Furthermore, he genuinely felt his place was with the

Islanders. He recalled the moment when he was told that he was going home.

Bloomer Reeve came in one morning and said he had some not very good news. 'The General' (he always used to call him that rather than the Governor, because he knew it would upset me) 'has decreed that you will leave with your wife and family. That's the bad news. The good news is that you can choose, within reason, when that is.'

I thought that was useful because it was at the time when the US Secretary of State Al Haig was shuttling to and fro. I thought that if Haig does his stuff, who knows, we might call some kind of truce. If so, I would be there. So I said could we make it the following Tuesday?

He came back the next day and said sorry, the General won't allow that. It has to be sooner. He made it clear to me that there was no appeal against this.

General Menendez had been briefed before leaving Argentina that the Islanders were to be considered fellow Argentine citizens and, within the parameters of military law, treated well. He seemed to accept this, but it was well known that a hard core of young officers, the most obvious of whom was Patricio Dowling, did not. Fresh from fighting the 'dirty war,' they despised the Islanders and believed they should be left in no doubt about who was in charge. This constant tension was a defining characteristic of the occupation.

Nicolas Kasanzew, an Argentine journalist on the Islands who allied himself with puppy-like loyalty to the hard-line faction, probably represented their view accurately when he wrote:

The Kelpers [Islanders] were our arch-enemies. From the first moment, I felt they were going to be fifth columnists. I was not mistaken. They are basically shepherds; primitive in their way of life. In their character and their appearance, they are hybrids. Their attitude towards Argentina was absolutely negative. Kelpers, like the English, respect nothing except force.

The General had little time to worry about the welfare of the locals. As well as heading the government he had to organise and command the defence of the Islands, a prospect that must have caused him many sleepless nights. He was, therefore, happy to delegate the day-to-day business of governing the Islanders to his General Secretary.

Bloomer Reeve had realised quickly that one of his greatest challenges would be containing anti-Islander feelings. He decided to exemplify the correct attitude to locals and protect them as much as possible.

His friend and colleague Barry Hussey had already demonstrated the same intent. Accompanying Dowling on a helicopter patrol, he watched, horrified, as the major assaulted a farmer. Outranking the military policeman, he gave him a verbal dressing-down: "Who do you think these people are that you can treat them this way?", he demanded of the sullen major.

Bloomer Reeve knew Dowling's type and did not care for them. He commented that just because a person works in intelligence, it does not mean he is clever. And such operatives are invariably arrogant. "They know too much, they are sure they know even more, and normally consider you perfectly useless," explained Bloomer. "Dowling considered every Islander an enemy. Many NCOs and some young officers thought the same, but most of them didn't have the power. However this man was the Chief of Police – *he had the power*."

Bloomer Reeve summoned Dowling to his office and, as he recalled it with understatement, ordered the officer to be 'more cordial' to local people. With some severity, Bloomer reminded the army man that he had to obey the orders of a senior officer, even one wearing an air force uniform. However, the sullen response was not convincing and so, in a hastily convened meeting with General Menendez, Bloomer Reeve asked the Governor to endorse his plan to ship Dowling back to the mainland. Menendez accepted his General Secretary's judgement and three days later Patricio Dowling was on an aircraft flying back to Argentina. He did not return and many Islanders were the safer for that.

Ordering the Bakers to leave did not give Bloomer Reeve as much pleasure. He told Dick and Connie that he, Barry Hussey and several other senior officers would move into their home, Sulivan House. In a gesture that the Bakers considered touching and revealing, Bloomer Reeve promised to look after their property. Connie recalled that it was almost as if he knew the Bakers would be back:

He said, 'All the time I am in this house, I will guarantee the safety of your property.'

When we got back months later we found they had packed many of our things under the stairs. They had rolled up the stair carpets and looked after the cats. Nobody had taken any souvenirs. Some bullets had damaged the car and the garage, but that wasn't their fault. It was amazing.

Leaving the Falklands was painful for the Bakers, not only because they were the last representatives of London, but because they were leaving friends to an uncertain future. "Apart from family bereavements, it was the most depressing day of my life," said Dick.

A sad little group had gathered at the LADE office to say goodbye to the Bakers. They boarded an army vehicle, the windows of which had been blacked out so they could see nothing of Stanley's defences on the way to the airport. Stanley's junior catholic priest, Father Austin Mongahan, bade them a tearful farewell. He was another who, although able to leave, had opted to stay on and share whatever trials his parishioners faced.

Connie too was tearful. It was, she said, like leaving a sinking ship:

> We knew that people had relied to a very large extent on us being there. As long as Dick was there with myself and the children, there was still some contact with the way things used to be.

The final link had gone. Islanders now faced their future alone. Many Stanley folk had become refugees on the farms, some unwittingly awaiting further trials of occupation and battle. Others were standing by their duties in Stanley.

But it was a considerable consolation that, although they had lost the popular Dick Baker, they had also seen the last of the man who might have been their nemesis, Patricio Dowling.

And, if they only knew it, Islanders had also gained a few powerful friends. Granted, they were Argentines, but they were men who proved that fundamental decency could survive when all other strands of civilised behaviour were unravelling.

Chapter Six

Surviving the Siege

During the occupation HL Bound, known to everyone by his boyhood nickname of 'Nap', wrote a series of highly observant letters to his friends in Britain. He even sent one distinctly tart note to an Argentine friend, with whom in the past he had always avoided political arguments. To his friend Bernardo Mayer in Buenos Aires he wrote that he was tiring of the new names being given to Stanley and other parts of the Islands by the invaders, but thought that "Puerto Argentino might soon be renamed Puerto Britannia".

Most of his letters were posted normally at the Stanley Post Office, which postmaster Bill Etheridge continued to operate with a skeleton staff and under the guidance of a new 'colleague', a Senor Caballeros of the Argentine postal authority, ENCOTEL. Caballeros was no fan of the military, did not approve of the invasion and respected his new colleague Bill. "When all this is over," he told the Islander, "you must come and visit me and we'll have happier times."

Between them the men got most mail through, but during the latter stages of the conflict the air and sea blockade was so effective that it was a futile task. A visiting official from the International Committee of the Red Cross carried out Nap Bound's final occupation letter.

On the 14th April, a few days after Dick Baker had been sent home and the British fleet was still steaming south, he wrote of an evolving situation in Stanley that was worrying but, so far, tolerable. In his letters he abbreviated Argentina and the Argentines to 'A'.

It would be foolish for me to say that everyone is well and happy here. But in spite of it all I can truthfully say that people and property are being treated with respect, though several properties on Callaghan Road and the extreme south end of Brisbane Road, Villiers Street and Dean Street have been evacuated by command of the army.

Stores are open as usual but military personnel are not permitted to enter them. I would estimate that about 60 per cent of the inhabitants of Stanley are now resident somewhere in the camp. At the moment most of the up to 10,000 military are not seen much in Stanley as they are busily engaged digging in around the beaches and mountains in preparation for the expected siege.

The occupying troops themselves are going through a terrible time merely to survive. Most of them have little or no protection from the climate and have often been seen begging for food. It is said that their midday meal consists of a green apple and a small bread loaf. Many of them seem to be not much more than children.

As you can imagine, the place is bristling with guns and heavy military equipment, but most of this is concentrated round the airport and, I suppose, at strategic points around the beaches. They have assured the population that lives and property in Stanley will not be put at risk, as there is no intention of allowing Stanley to become a battlefield.

They have moved massive quantities of men and equipment in by air, and now I believe they are concentrating more on food. In any case, we are still getting all sorts and shapes of aircraft buzzing in and out.

We are constantly reminded of who is in control. We have been ordered to drive on the right-hand side of the road, and of course the Argentine flag flies from every available mast. One amusing thing happened. The flag they hoisted in front of the Secretariat was the biggest they could find. The following day it blew a gale and snapped the flagpole in two. A bad omen for them.

As you will see from the stamp on this letter, the Post Office was quickly transformed, and for the first few days letters bearing FI stamps were cancelled with a line or two drawn by ballpoint pen and an Argentine cancellation mark was placed on the envelope. Now they have their own stamps which must be used on all mail.

The A peso is now used freely and can be exchanged at the Treasury at the rate of 20,000 to the pound. Many shops would not accept pesos but now they are required to do so.

All 2-metre-band sets [radio transceivers] and guns have been called in, and although we are still able to send telegrams, we cannot make or receive overseas telephone calls.

Morale in Stanley is remarkably high, though there are obvious signs of tension as the British fleet draws nearer. My own feeling is that perhaps enough sanity will remain to prevent an all-out onslaught.

Today we are expecting the arrival of the Anglican Bishop in Buenos Aires, Bishop Cutts, who is said to be bringing with him no less than 100 Anglo-Argentines for the express purpose of convincing us how much better off we are under Argentine rule. My God! I wonder what sort of reception they will receive.

Whatever the outcome of this dreadful situation, it is obvious that our Islands can never be the same again. Now that the celebrations are fading in BA they must be asking themselves, 'Whatever have we done?'

Nap Bound was right to wonder about the visiting Anglo-Argentines. The party was much less than 100-strong and when the Argentines organised a public meeting in the Post Office (the only large public building still free of Argentine troops), there was no sign of Bishop Cutts. Lucky for him. Unable to direct their anger directly at the military, the Argentine civilians received the full impact of the Islanders' wrath. Nap wrote:

> I cannot begin to list all the plums they were offering as a means of improving our life here, but they even went as far as suggesting that the As would build a completely new town somewhere else in the Islands. We would then be free to live our lives out in Stanley, but of course, with all the new benefits.
>
> People were so angry that at one stage it almost broke into open violence and all you could hear were cries of *'Get out, and stay out!'*
>
> It is unfortunate that they were Anglo-Argentines, as these people have always been held with a high degree of suspicion. Most people here consider that they are only there as long as their pockets are full.

Canadian immigrant Bill Curtis, who had attempted to redirect the Argentine aircraft beacon on the night of the invasion, produced the showstopper at the Post Office meeting. With great stage presence, he enunciated his words distinctly, pausing for dramatic effect. But his voice rose rapidly to a crescendo:

> Me and my family left Canada because we didn't like the way the country was being militarised. We got to the Falklands and found somewhere we could settle peacefully. [Dramatic pause] And then you turkeys turned up. *Now piss off!*

There was wild applause and their alarmed minders ushered the Argentines out. Several of the visiting women were in tears. The mission had been a complete failure and the party was promptly flown back to the mainland.

Bill Curtis' anger was understandable, but in fact, as a foreigner, he had been receiving more considerate treatment from the Argentines than he might have expected.

The Canadian Embassy in Buenos Aires was concerned about the plight of its only citizens in the war zone. Somehow they made contact by phone, and urged the Canadians to leave while it was possible to do so. A friend who had come with them to help build their home did, but Bill and his wife Barbara said they were staying put. They may have figured there was not a lot of point; the threat of annihilation seemed to be following them around. With the cooperation of Bloomer Reeve, they agreed to stay in contact with the Canadian Embassy, phoning every week or so to confirm they were safe.

Carlos Bloomer Reeve also made it possible for the larger American community to keep in touch with their Buenos Aires embassy. Most of the Americans were members of the Bahai faith. John Leonard was the oldest American there; he had come to the Islands as a Bahai 'pioneer' in the mid-1950s when his time as a navigator in US Air force bombers in the Pacific was still a fresh memory. Now a believer in the peaceful unity of nations, he was shocked that this most isolated corner of the world had been violently invaded. "I went through 15 months in the South Pacific Islands," he recalled, "and I can never remember a time when I was as terrified as I was during the invasion."

In a radio conversation with John, the American diplomats advised the 26-strong community to leave. Their passages home would be paid for. Bloomer Reeve authorised a meeting of those Americans living in Stanley and also distributed a written circular to the few who lived on the isolated farms. The response from the Bahais was, recalled John Leonard, unanimous:

'We don't want to leave the Falklands unless everybody has the option to do so.'

When I got back and I told Bloomer Reeve about their reaction, I could almost see him scratching his head and thinking, 'What's the matter with them?'

I went back on the radio-phone to tell the Consul that some people were just not interested in leaving. He sort of indicated that we had rocks in our heads.

After further consultation, several non-Bahais did agree to leave. The puzzled consul wished his remaining people well and said he admired their courage. Bloomer Reeve agreed to keep an avenue of communication open with the American Embassy and from then on John Leonard would contact him regularly regarding the welfare of the American community.

John Leonard was another who became convinced that Bloomer Reeve and Hussey were sometimes all that stood between the Islanders – Americans included – and serious hardship. He said:

> It would be impossible to overrate them. In so many circumstances Bloomer Reeve, in particular, proved to be very helpful. At one time the military were running out of meat and they decided they'd kill the dairy cows. Of course that would have cut off the milk supply to Stanley people. So Bloomer Reeve negotiated with the aggressor – some unknown in the Argentine forces – and it was agreed the dairy cows should be spared, at least for the time being.

With the dangerous Major Patricio Dowling forcibly repatriated by Bloomer Reeve, the Military Police became a rather more benign force. They still presided over summary interrogations, searched diligently for the source of illicit radio transmissions (see chapter eight), weapons and infiltrated British special forces. And there was little doubt that they would have dealt strictly with any local found breaking their code of military law. But the MPs, now often under the control of a Captain Romano, were just as likely to be tough on Argentine soldiers who were caught stealing, begging for food or looting abandoned homes.

The latter offences were committed in spite of the signs crafted by Government printer Joe King and signed by General Menendez, prohibiting entry by soldiers. Bloomer Reeve insisted afterwards that all soldiers caught looting faced courts martial and were sent back to the mainland. Considering the situation, this punishment may not have been a very effective deterrent.

Stanley could only function if key people continued to run the Public Works Department (PWD). Although the occupiers benefited from their services, the engineers, mechanics and technicians made it clear that they were working for their own people and they drew the line at work that was purely for the benefit of the military.

Ron Buckett, the head of the Plant and Transport Authority – a grand title for the PWD's motley collection of Land Rovers, cars, tractors, trucks and excavators – conveyed this message to Colonel

Dorrego, the new PWD boss, in no uncertain terms. Initially Ron and his staff of mechanics distributed Land Rovers to locals wanting to leave Stanley for the farms. Other vehicles they secretly disabled, while a few were kept in good running order for the hospital and power and water staff.

Ron, a one-time Army warrant officer, recalled that it was not long before the mechanics were ordered to work on Argentine military vehicles and requisitioned civilian Land Rovers.

Two of the men were being pressured by the military, but they said no, they weren't going to repair vehicles that the Argies used. So I said, 'Fine! Take all your tools out of the garage (which weren't theirs) and go home. Don't come into work.'

The same afternoon Colonel Dorrego informed me that the men had to go back to work and bring their tools with them. I said, 'They don't want to work with Argentines, they won't work on Argentine vehicles, and I'm not telling them to go back.'

He said, 'You know, I can have you shot for this.'

I said, 'Fine, that's your choice. You're in charge at the moment but the situation will remain the same. They're not going back and I'm not telling them to go back.'

Ron Buckett knew that Dorrego would not carry out his threat, and believed that the Colonel was not a bad man, just a professional soldier who had picked a short straw:

He didn't really want to be in that position but he was trying to make the best of it. He expected us to carry on as normal with him as the figurehead, and he couldn't really understand why we *couldn't* carry on normally.

Ron remained at his desk, considering what needed to be done to prepare the civilian community for the coming conflict and amusing himself by making out bills to the Argentine Army. In the first month he invoiced them £14,000 for rent of earth-moving equipment. Dorrego played the game, saying he would see to it, but no money changed hands.

The quietly dignified opposition of most Islanders contrasted with the actions of just two local men who sided blatantly with the Argentines.

The action of one of these men came as no surprise. Businessman Reynold Reid had come to the Falklands in the 1950s from Chile, and raised families from two marriages. Reynold was accepted locally, but generally with caution. He had never tried to hide his support for the Argentines or his bitter derision of the British, and when the Communications Agreement of the 1970s generated opportunities for trade he embraced them enthusiastically. There was nothing wrong with this, of course: his business activities were legitimate, and locals happily bought his imports from Argentina. But his enthusiasm for the new era of enforced closeness with Argentina, further soured his reputation, and no one was surprised when, on the day of the invasion, he was seen giving advice to the invading soldiers.

It is unlikely, though, that Reynold Reid was of great value to the occupiers. He was not influential in the community. What the Argentines desired more than anything else were pedigree Islanders who had propaganda value, were respected and who might persuade their compatriots to give the Argentines a chance. Alex Betts, a young and clever local, came close to fitting that bill. A fourth generation Falkland Islander, Alex had been drifting ideologically for some years, and was one of a small group who questioned the legitimacy of both British colonial rule and the Argentine claim. At the time of the invasion he was one of the very few local people employed by the Argentine state enterprises which had a presence in Stanley. He also had an Argentine fiancée, a young woman who was working as a domestic at the LADE manager's house.

In the days before 1982 he would certainly have protested violently had anyone suggested he was pro-Argentine. He would have said he was only pro-Falklands. His story illustrates the fact, not often acknowledged, that the relationship some locals endured with London was ambiguous. Not all were blindly loyal when they saw the mother country perpetuating a class system that kept British administrators and wealthy landowners in the top social, political and business strata, and ordinary Islanders as an under-class, without even the right to live in Britain. Alex felt all of this acutely. He had an impoverished childhood, and his formal education ended when he was just 14. He spent the next 15 years working on farms. But he wanted better things and began a distance-learning course that eventually qualified him as a bookkeeper. With his family, he moved into Stanley, where the children would receive a better education, and where he could find accounting and administrative work.

The young man was respected for his intelligence and initiative. He learned Spanish and, in an era when the locals entertained themselves with concerts and dances, he played guitar and sang. Anyone looking for a hint about the way his views were changing simply had to listen to his interpretation of Woody Guthrie's powerful anthem for the deprived and exploited. Alex, backed by friends on guitars and drums, tailored the words to *This Land is Your Land* to the Falklands. He was saying the Falklands don't belong to Argentines or British, but to ordinary Islanders.

But somewhere along the line, his loyalty was sidetracked towards Argentina. Perhaps he saw this as the only practical way to get his revenge on London. Perhaps he was seduced by the celebrity he could enjoy as a 'Malvinese' who dared to be different. And perhaps the charms of an Argentine woman helped him down that road.

Whatever his rationale, Alex Betts burned his bridges very efficiently when he continued working for LADE and Gas del Estado (the Argentine gas company) after the invasion, and openly fraternised with the occupiers. Eventually he and his fiancée even moved in with Gas del Estado staff. The extent to which he helped the Argentines is not clear. He may have been of more use in the months preceding the invasion as an accurate barometer of locals' attitudes. However he was certainly valuable as a propaganda tool. Having an Islander to articulate support for the invaders – and Alex *was* articulate – must have been very useful indeed.

It did not, however, matter how much material help either Alex Betts or Reynold Reid gave the invaders. Their fraternisation with the enemy was bad enough. Islanders labelled them treacherous and ostracised them. At some stage both men probably appreciated the gravity of their situation, but there could be no turning back, and in the end it was inevitable that they would flee to Argentina.

At the radio station, now LRU Radio Islas Malvinas and an instrument of the military government, broadcasting settled into a bland routine. There was music (tangos for the Argentines relayed from Comodoro Rivadavia on the Argentine coast, and country and western for the locals), commentaries on Argentine football and 'news' that was often no more than propaganda.

The diet was seasoned with occasional announcements from the military government and tub-thumping addresses by General Menendez exhorting his troops to fight 'por la patria' to the last man.

Norman Powell, an English-speaking Argentine broadcaster, had arrived soon after the invasion and ran the studios. Patrick Watts, broadcasting hero of the invasion, stayed on, constantly negotiating with his new boss to salvage as much dignity as possible for his emasculated little station. A handful of local part-time announcers supported him, including Michael Smallwood who had memorably underlined Rex Hunt's eve-of-invasion speech with the advice, "Don't panic!"

Normal communications around the Islands were virtually impossible, and the radio station fulfilled a useful role relaying personal messages. The sometimes poignant words illustrated the loneliness felt by everyone and the nagging fears for the safety of family and friends who had been separated by the crisis. Just a few of the messages read by Michael Smallwood one evening in late April:

> To Heather at Salvador: Blackout no fun talking to myself. Might see you sooner than I thought, given half a chance.
> To Mrs J Blakely: Leaving 5 May. All I have left is yours. Thanks for all you've done for me. Regards to all, Doug.

Doug's message was over-optimistic: by 5 May Stanley Airport had been bombed and a blockade was securely in place. No civilians were leaving the Falklands.

Broadcasting became increasingly difficult and irrelevant as transmitters were switched off or broke down. First, medium wave transmissions ceased permanently, and then short wave transmissions went the same way. Eventually, only the ancient cable system remained to distribute the station's output around Stanley.

The BBC World Service, particularly the Islanders' own programme *Calling the Falklands* (increased from weekly to nightly during the crisis) was far more important. The BBC's objective reporting, including brave despatches from Harold Briley in Buenos Aires and Brian Hanrahan and Robert Fox with the task force, was essential listening.

The Argentines didn't agree and jammed *Calling the Falklands* with increasing efficiency. The mellow voice of presenter Peter King, ending each broadcast with his inspirational catch phrase "Heads down, hearts high," would be drowned out by a sound like a chain saw at full throttle. The BBC realised its service was being jammed when its reporters landed with the troops at San Carlos and reported the fact back to London. An additional frequency was quickly introduced, and the Argentines were never able to jam it.

There was competition from a new medium: television. Before April 1982 there had been a few video players and TVs in the Islands, but no local station. Argentine telecommunications experts installed a transmitter within days of the invasion, shoe-horning a studio into the old FIBS building. Canal Siete was ready to entertain and misinform.

A shipment of TVs was flown in and sold to locals on an absurdly easy hire purchase basis. A number of the most visceral critics of Argentina rather sheepishly gave in to the temptation of TV, but justified this by saying that they knew the payments would never be completed.

1. The Argentine Hercules aircraft which landed at Stanley Airport some weeks before the invasion. A fuel leak was claimed, but Dick Baker and the Marines believed it was a rehearsal for an invasion or an Entebbe-style raid. *(G.L. Bound)*

2. Confident and cheerful, the main force of Argentines march into Stanley following the fall of Government House. *(G.L. Bound)*

3. An Argentine amphibious Amtrak armoured personnel carrier manoeuvres through Stanley ready to end the stand-off at Government House. *(G.L. Bound)*

4. Captain Jack Sollis *(left)* on the bridge of MV *Forrest* some time before the invasion. Also in the picture *(middle)* the ship's engineer Nutt Goodwin and Major Hooper, a Royal Marine.

5. A captured Royal Marines section is marched towards Ross Road covered by at
   least one member of the Argentine Buzo Tactico. In the background Dr Alison
   Bleaney and her husband Mike can be seen entering the King Edward Memorial
   Hospital. *(Royal Marines Museum)*

6. The manager of the Falkland Islands Broadcasting Station, Patrick Watts, at the
   station's controls. He broadcast throughout the invasion. *(Peter King)*

7. Government House photographed from the hospital. The Argentine flag flies. Behind can be seen the ridge of Mount Tumbledown. *(Peter King)*

8. The King Edward Memorial Hospital. The red crosses were painted on the roof when it became clear that British air attacks were likely. *(Peter King)*

9. Ross Road, Stanley. Armed Argentines circulate while a local woman looks on. Crates of ammunition are stacked against the public gymnasium, which had been transformed into a barracks. *(G.L. Bound)*

10. The Argentine flag flies over the roofs of Stanley. *(G.L. Bound)*

11. Argentine Panhard armoured cars were not suitable for crossing the roadless Falklands moorland, but did patrol the streets of Stanley. *(G.L. Bound)*

12. Despite attacks on Stanley Airport, Pucara ground attack aircraft were a potent threat against British troops. To avoid Harriers, they often flew low over Stanley. The horizontal lines are power cables. *(G.L. Bound)*

13. Not all Pucara aircraft remained a threat. Many were destroyed during the initial attacks on Stanley Airport.

14. When the Argentine authorities began a campaign to keep Stanley clean, these posters were produced by locals and appeared around the town.

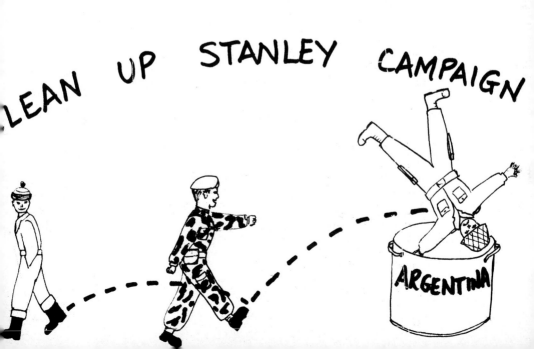

15. The community centre at Goose Green became a prison for the local residents. The Argentines allowed them to mark the roof to discourage British air attacks. *(G.L. Bound)*

16. Damage to a civilian home at Goose Green. *(Bob McLeod)*

17. Goose Green was a major Argentine air base. Following British air raids, most Pucara ground attack aircraft were destroyed. *(Bob McLeod)*

18. An Argentine soldier guarding a position near Moody Brook. The undeveloped film was found in a trench after the war. *(Robert King)*

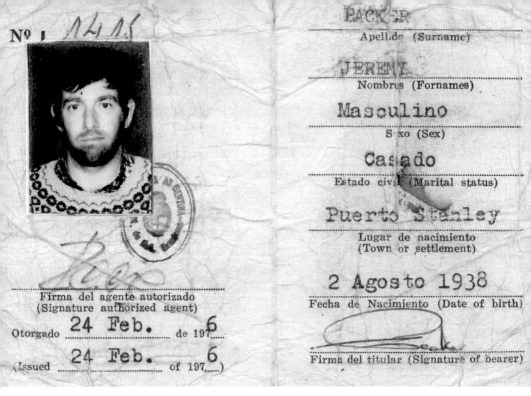

Nº 14115

PACKER
Apellido (Surname)

JEREMY
Nombres (Fornames)

Masculino
Sexo (Sex)

Casado
Estado civil (Marital status)

Puerto Stanley
Lugar de nacimiento
(Town or settlement)

2 Agosto 1938
Fecha de Nacimiento (Date of birth)

Firma del agente autorizado
(Signature authorized agent)

Otorgado 24 Feb. de 1976

(Issued 24 Feb. of 1976)

Firma del titular (Signature of bearer)

19. Forged identity card belonging to Terry Peck. He travelled under the name Jeremy Packer. *(Ailsa Heathman)*

20. An Argentine anti-aircraft missile site near the west entrance to Stanley. The photograph was taken by Terry Peck and smuggled back to intelligence authorities in London. *(T. J. Peck)*

21. Still in battle dress and armed with a self-loading rifle, Terry Peck stands on the slopes of Mount Longdon. *(T. J. Peck)*

22. Argentine installation on the south side of Stanley covertly photographed by Terry Peck. *(T. J. Peck)*

23. In the immediate aftermath of the war the Union Flag has been hoisted over the smouldering remains of a building. *(G.L. Bound)*

24. In the hope of divine protection, the Argentine owner of this rifle taped a picture of the Virgin and Child to the butt. *(G.L. Bound)*

25. Argentine soldiers were imprisoned in this shearing shed. *(G.L. Bound)*

26. Defeated and cold, Argentine troops retreat through Stanley on 14 June. *(G.L. Bound)*

27. Now lacking confidence and swagger, Argentine troops retreat along the same route they had followed on 2 April. *(G.L. Bound)*

28. Argentine officers under guard on 14 June. Standing on the right of the group is Carlos Bloomer Reeve. *(Mike Butcher)*

29. Smoke hangs over Stanley as British troops inspect the armoured cars and other detritus of the defeated Argentines. *(Peter King)*

30. Major Mike Norman *(second row from front, holding top right corner of flag)* with members of his company following their return to Stanley on 14 June. Although defeated during the 2 April invasion, most of the marines returned with the task force. *(Mike Norman)*

31. The Director of Civil Aviation Gerald Cheek returned to Stanley from imprisonment at Fox Bay to find that most civil aircraft had been destroyed. *(Peter King)*

32. The author inspects some of the thousands of weapons discarded by the defeated Argentine Army. *(G.L. Bound)*

33. Stanley's Police Station was almost destroyed by a missile fired from a helicopter. As it was the base for the Argentine military police and intelligence unit, locals did not mind. *(G.L. Bound)*

34. First Aid to a Stanley house. When the guns stopped firing, local people came out to patch up their homes. *(G.L. Bound)*

35. First Aid was not enough for some properties. This Stanley home was levelled by a direct hit from an artillery shell. The occupants had already abandoned the house. *(G.L. Bound)*

36. Several of Stanley's original buildings were destroyed. Here the old Globe Store still burns. *(Peter King)*

37. Rex Hunt *(left)* is greeted by the Royal Naval Commander of the Task Force, Admiral Sandy Woodward, following Hunt's return. Patrick Watts stands behind them, microphone ready. *(G.L. Bound)*

38. Dr. Alison Bleaney, who was instrumental in ceasefire negotiations in Stanley, poses with Rex Hunt and an unknown military doctor outside Government House. The picture was taken following Rex Hunt's return. *(Peter King)*

39. Dick Baker waves farewell to Stanley at the end of his post-war service in the Falklands. *(Peter King)*

40. General Jeremy Moore, Commander of Land Forces, bids farewell to Dick Baker. Rex Hunt films the event, while Councillors Bill Goss, Mary Jennings and Financial Secretary Harold Rowlands wait to shake hands with the General. *(Peter King)*

41. Carlos Bloomer Reeve, photographed 19 years on, in the Argentine Air Force Library in Buenos Aires. *(G.L. Bound)*

42. Barry Melbourne Hussey, Bloomer Reeve's deputy in 1982, had been promoted to Admiral by 2001 when this photo of him was taken outside the Argentine Naval Club in Buenos Aires. *(Juan Manuel Ipiña)*

MALVINAS

1982 - 2 de Abril - 2001

POR EL HONOR DE LOS MUERTOS...

¡A SANGRE Y FUEGO!

¡VOLVEREMOS!

P.N.O.S.P.

PARTIDO NUEVO ORDEN SOCIAL PATRIOTICO

TE (15) 5 663 7311

E-MAIL lealtadylucha@yahoo.com.ar

43. Some Argentines do not forget. On the 19th anniversary of the invasion these posters appeared around Buenos Aires. The photograph shows Royal Marines surrendering at Government House. The Spanish text reads: Malvinas: for the honour of the dead... to blood and fire! We will return. (*Juan Manuel Ipiña*)

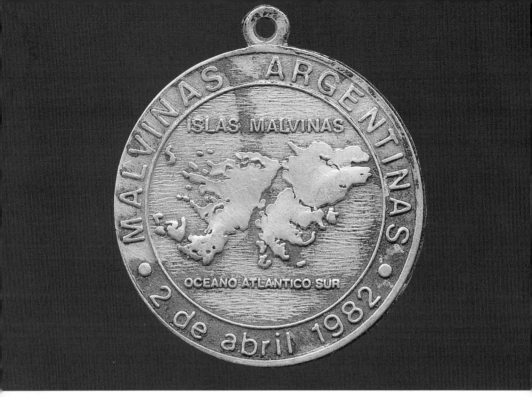

44. A commemoritive medallion minted in 1982 to mark the Argentine invasion.

45. A town once unspoiled by war. In this view from the harbour, Stanley shows itself as a pretty, neat little town.

The news-cum-propaganda would be slipped into a TV diet of elderly films, episodes of Fawlty Towers looted from Governor Hunt's private video collection and an apparently endless supply of Tom and Jerry cartoons.

Sitting side by side, Patrick Watts and Norman Powell would alternate reading to camera in Spanish and English. The scripts, archived at FIBS, suggest frequent struggles between the two to re-write the news. Apparently typed by Norman Powell, they would sometimes be heavily marked with Patrick Watts' scrawl, correcting the Argentines' poor syntax and sometimes changing slightly the balance of the news.

The bulletin broadcast at 8.00 pm on 14 April was fairly typical. It led with the news that Treasury officials from Buenos Aires had arrived to discuss the integration of the islands' economy with that of the mainland. The leader of the party was quoted as saying that the Government was minded to give the Malvinas duty free status. Plans were in hand to establish a branch of the national bank of Argentina in 'Puerto Argentino'. Finally, viewers were assured that food supplies in the stores were at an adequate level.

Two days later the TV station carried brazen propaganda: the captain of HMS *Invincible* had asked the Brazilians for permission to break the journey south with a visit to Rio de Janeiro. Morale was low among the soldiers and sailors aboard the carrier because, claimed the report, "many realised that any future action would have political character in defence of Mrs Thatcher's government". The report was, of course, rubbish.

Radio announcements obviously penned by Bloomer Reeve, or at least translated by him for Menendez, had an uncharacteristic chill about them. It is likely that, while he was prepared to quietly do as much as possible to help the locals, the image he presented to other Argentines had to be tougher. Certainly, when writing for the radio, he sounded like a fully qualified representative of a dictatorship. When a local man ripped the wiring from his Land Rover in front of soldiers who intended to commandeer it, Bloomer Reeve got the young man off with a furious warning, but the following announcement was broadcast.

A serious incident occurred recently during which a vehicle requi-sitioned by Argentine Forces was damaged by a civilian.

The civilian population of Puerto Argentino, ex-Stanley, are reminded that the Military Government will protect and respect them in every possible way as established by the Geneva Convention. However, the Military Government also wants to

113

make it perfectly clear that any transgressions to the issued edicts or any act of disturbance will cause the application of severe measures accordingly and also contemplated by the Military Law.

Another radio announcement reminded Islanders that they were expected to show due respect for uniformed Argentines:

Two young men, Robert Finlayson and Glen Ross, yesterday committed an offence against members of the Argentine Forces. On this occasion the punishment has been light, taking into account that they are young and that it was the first time that an offence of this nature had occurred.

This announcement is being broadcast with the purpose of making it perfectly clear that any kind of friction between the local people and the Armed Forces has to be avoided.

The offence had been a petulant and fleeting encounter between two lads, both apprentices at the power station, and an Argentine General. Speeding past the general and his bodyguards in a Land Rover, one local had, so the general insisted, spat at him.

A further draconian announcement made it clear that motorcycles, symbols of defiance for young men who sped around Stanley buzzing soldiers, were banned.

But some locals had a way of popping such pompous bubbles. A cheery notice from Bill Etheridge, the Postmaster, followed on immediately from the grim communiqué, and restored smiles to faces:

Word has been received that airmail posted here is reaching the UK regularly. The latest despatch was on 22 April and has arrived. Keep in touch with your friends through the Post Office.

With his responsibilities for health, Barry Hussey had been dealing with the King Edward Memorial Hospital (KEMH). Senior Medical Officer Dr Daniel Haines was in nominal control and he now had on his staff several Argentine civilian doctors. Senior among them was English-speaking Mario Lazar who was familiar with the staff from a brief period as a locum at the hospital a few years before.

The KEMH had had its baptism of fire on invasion day when the doctors performed emergency surgery on three Argentine soldiers who had been shot at Government House. Two of the men died in the hospital and one was still in a critical condition when his comrades took him away. In addition the doctors treated about a dozen other Argentine soldiers for less serious gunshot and shrapnel injuries.

The Argentines had established a field hospital in a large building near Government House and had also taken over half of the KEMH. The civilians had succeeded, however, in keeping control of the best wards, the operating theatre and kitchens.

Throughout April the staff prepared for the worst. To do this it was important to work with the Argentines, but Daniel Haines seemed unable to establish a working relationship. Instead he was argumentative and openly hostile. They were clearly reluctant to entrust their people to his care and some wondered whether he was planning some form of active resistance.

Dr Alison Bleaney had taken a few years off from her job at the hospital to raise her two infant children, but she had helped treat the Argentine wounded on 2 April and since then had popped in and out of the KEMH to help when necessary. She became increasingly alarmed by Daniel Haines' bizarre behaviour. He insisted, for example, that London was sending coded messages in records played on *Calling the Falklands*. The Paul McCartney song Ebony and Ivory was popular at the time and he was convinced that a particularly important message was hidden in the words of this song. If there was a message, no one ever decoded it.

It was clear that, one way or another, Daniel Haines would not be left in control of the hospital for much longer.

Bloomer Reeve needed a barometer of the Islanders' mood. As he explained, he found this in some of his old friends from happier days.

> Some of the people were very kind to keep the friendship going. The others were afraid to come near us because of what the rest of the Falklanders would say.
>
> We had a great help from Monsignor Spraggon. I think he was the second person to come and see me.
>
> I asked Phil Summers [previously Dick Baker's assistant and head of the Defence Force] to stay [in his civilian job]. I said, 'These are your interests, I need you here.'
>
> He thought a while but eventually said, 'OK, I'll stay.'

An attempt was made to create a semi-formal forum for the discussion of the community's fears, needs and complaints. Sticking to his principle that it was the locally born people, the 'Kelpers,' second-class citizens under British rule, whose views mattered, he invited a few of the locals to meet General Menendez. They were unelected, but a reasonable cross-section of the Stanley community. Nap Bound was one and he later wrote:

With the departure of our Chief Secretary we have been trailing round rather like a ship without a rudder. However, I was asked by Bloomer a few days ago if I would like to join a small group of Islanders he was inviting to meet him and the General.

I readily agreed to air our views about the situation we now find ourselves in and suggest remedies which might lighten the burden of the people, many of whom are suffering from uncertainty and fear. There are so many things happening which frighten and worry many people which, with a little thought, could be alleviated or even removed.

The meeting lasted all morning, and we spoke about the possibility of evacuating civilians from Stanley when things get too hot; the improvement of camp communications and camp medical requirements, which at the moment are practically non-existent; the immediate education problems; the management of the broadcasting station; compensation for damage to property, and many other things.

Of course many of the questions and suggestions were too complex to get an immediate response, but they were all considered important. I came away with a feeling that our efforts had not been entirely wasted.

The group consisted of a cross-section of the community, excluding expatriates. They were Ning King, Olga Coutts, Harry Bonner, Neville Bennett, Billy Morrison and myself. I have no doubt that some people will point a finger of suspicion at us, but my only concern at this moment is to help our people through an extremely difficult situation.

The meeting may have been held with the best of intentions, but few tangible results came from it.

There had already been a number of incidents that proved how vulnerable Islanders were. A machine-gunner with a twitchy trigger finger had riddled Monsignor Spraggon's home, blowing the toilet away from beneath the elderly cleric and leaving him in a stunned but uninjured heap on the floor. The soldier went on to plough a path of destruction through Spraggon's library. For years afterward the priest would amuse guests by holding up a particularly dense theological volume, in which a bullet still rested. "See this!" he would say. "That bloody Argentine got further through it than I ever did."

Similarly, a machine-gunner defending troops in what had once been the Stanley senior school fell asleep over his gun and ventilated a nearby cottage in which two single women lived. Remarkably, neither was injured.

If this kind of damage could be caused before the British even arrived, something needed to be done urgently about civil defence. A few people took the initiative. One was the truculent Government mechanic Ron Buckett. Terry Spruce, Assistant General Manager of the Falkland Islands Company (FIC), was another, and he was supported by one of his line managers, Mike Bleaney, the husband of Dr Alison Bleaney.

They requested a meeting with Bloomer Reeve to discuss the problem. The Argentines doubted that the British would risk attacking Stanley and causing casualties among civilians, but the locals had a more realistic idea of British military strategy. Bloomer Reeve recalled the conversation.

The three laughed, and one said, 'Look Carlos, it's the English you are talking about. They'll come to finish you off even if we are in the middle.'

So we decided to find strong houses that could serve as refuges. We found only 17, and they started working on the plan to distribute the civilians among these houses. They did a very good job.

We kept one building in reserve, the Colony Club. The problem with the Colony Club was that it was stocked with too much alcohol, so I said, 'This is the last resort. If the hospital at any time exceeds its capacity, we'll take the Colony Club. But for the time being we'll keep it empty.'

The designated shelters were marked with a large red 'X' within a circle, and the letters 'DAP,' standing for *defensa aerea pasiva* (passive air defence). The meaning of these symbols was to be communicated to the British and to Argentine soldiers. In the event, the British did not learn about the scheme and many Argentines thought 'DAP' was some mysterious anti-Argentine graffiti daubed on buildings by a local resistance.

However, the stone cottages and other buildings, including the *Upland Goose Hotel*, were built like fortresses. With window recesses filled with bags of sand or flour, they would be able to withstand all but direct hits from bombs or artillery.

Organisation of the community began to flow from this core of self-motivated citizens. At an early meeting, responsibilities for the care of some older and more vulnerable members of the community were distributed among about a dozen other citizens.

Terry Spruce offered the company's large concrete block-built supermarket, the West Store, as a reserve shelter and he worked with

117

the hospital to assemble emergency-survival packs for each DAP house. Terry carried a particularly useful pass issued by the Argentine Navy, enabling him to enter the FIC's waterfront compound in search of supplies. Apart from basic medicines and bandages, the emergency packs contained torches, batteries, candles, matches, paraffin lamps and water containers. Spruce, Bleaney and Buckett distributed the packs, and made sure that every safe house had at least one short wave radio capable of receiving the BBC World Service.

Others in the civil defence group listed the citizens who remained in the town and their chosen shelters.

Some of those involved in the informal civil defence organisation amused themselves in quieter periods by designing and photocopying flyers that ridiculed the Argentines. When official posters appeared around town urging troops to keep the town clean by using waste bins marked 'MALIMA' – (*Mantenga Limpia Malvinas* – keep the Malvinas clean), Ron Buckett came up with his own variation. His cartoon depicted a diminutive local in woolly hat and wellington boots, with the stump of a fag hanging out of his mouth, kicking an Argentine soldier towards a British Marine, who in turn cartwheeled the man into a MALIMA bin. Photocopied under the nose of Colonel Dorrego in the Public Works Department, the flyers were pinned to walls and lamp posts around the town. As quickly as they were removed, more would appear. Another common poster depicted the Peanuts character Snoopy dancing ecstatically, above the words, 'Happiness is being British'.

Ron Buckett's wife Nidge emerged as a dynamo, doing far more than her fair share to care for the more vulnerable people of Stanley. Patricio Dowling was the cause of her first mission, just a day after the invasion. He was still searching for the Marines who slipped through the Argentine net on 2 April and had visited an elderly couple on the outskirts of town, apparently in the belief that they might know something about the Marines' whereabouts. They called Nidge, she convinced Dowling that the couple knew nothing that could help him, and he left. "This made me realise that some people were going to need help," she recalled.

Nidge took over a Government-owned Mini van, painted a red cross on it (probably a liberal interpretation of the appropriate use of the symbol) and, often aided by her friend Susie Packer, began visiting the pensioners. She would organise their safe accommodation, take them food and medicines from the hospital (demand for Valium skyrocketed) and generally reassure them. When necessary, she banged on the doors of Bloomer Reeve and Barry Hussey's offices, demanding help or recompense for someone whose rights had been abused. Both men usually did what they could to help.

She was not shy of confrontation. On one occasion Nidge was among several locals arrested and marched into the police station. There was a sharp exchange of views, and Nidge poked a soldier in the chest. As the situation threatened to escalate, Captain Romano, the soldier who had been commanding the police since the ignominious departure of Dowling, stepped into the office and stopped it. Aware that she was sometimes too pugnacious for her own good, Nidge was grateful. "Leave Mrs Buckett alone," said Romano, smiling. "We know exactly what she thinks of us."

Romano became an ally, and later, when a curfew was introduced, he issued both Nidge and Susie Packer with a pass so they could venture out during the hours of darkness. They checked in with him every morning, and would call Romano if they needed his help. Sometimes the officer would call them to help him liaise with locals. More often than not he would collect the women in his Mercedes Benz jeep. It seemed to Nidge that, free from Dowling, Romano had the welfare of the people of Stanley at heart. But occasionally his confidence would take them into situations that were more dangerous than she liked. During one nocturnal expedition to check on a home at one end of the town, the police vehicle slipped off the road and became bogged down. Romano insisted that they walk back through Stanley, notwithstanding the presence in the shadows of hundreds of nervous Argentine soldiers. "It's the middle of the night," protested Nidge. "We could be shot." Romano seemed to think otherwise: "No, no, not shot. Not with me."

The next morning when the two women checked in at the police station, Romano was, as always, there to greet them. Susie gave the officer a big fake grin, and said: "Morning, pillock." Romano smiled back happily.

Nidge is convinced that in the final days of the occupation, after her family was forced to move from their house because of its vulnerability to shellfire, Captain Romano kept an eye on it. In any case, it was not disturbed by Argentine troops, and when the Bucketts returned to it, they found somebody had left what seemed to be a gift. It was a silver 'bombilla', the traditional silver straw through which Argentines drink their typical mate infusion.

Bloomer Reeve and Hussey, supported by a few others like Romano, were as loyal as any Argentine, but they interpreted their duty as looking after the physical needs and safety of the people their country had subjugated. Even 19 years on, Terry Spruce became emotional when he recalled the help received from Bloomer Reeve and his right-hand man.

119

If there were any problems, or we felt that the Argentines were doing something undesirable towards the population, we would go to Bloomer Reeve and, where he had control, most things seemed to stop.

We were not friends then. We knew each other and that was it. But after the conflict, if I had seen him and Hussey walking down the road, I'd have gone straight up to them and shook their hands. Because they were tremendous in listening and controlling the Argentine military forces where they could.

Towards the end I saw Bloomer Reeve in tears. He was having problems controlling the forces and he wasn't sure how much longer they were going to allow him to stay here. It would then become a full military operation – and we would be the ones to suffer.

Shared dangers and self-help brought the community together. People who had bickered for years became firm friends, often sharing their food and other comforts.

Compassion didn't always stop at the political barrier. Common decency made it impossible to ignore the plight of the conscripts. Nap Bound observed in one of his letters:

> Most of them are out in the mountains and around the beaches where they have just dug themselves into the wet peat to get whatever shelter they can from the wind and cold. I really wonder what would happen if we suddenly had a typical cold wet April night followed by a day or two of wet north-easters. They are not kitted out for sub-Antarctic conditions and already morale is low.

Jill Harris, a motherly housewife, was regularly approached by hungry young men in shabby uniforms. She recalled the begging approach of one pathetic soldier:

> He knocked on the door and rubbed his tummy and said 'I'm so hungry!' He was a very tall, thin lad, so I gave him a cheese sandwich to get rid of him. He was so grateful.
>
> They were not allowed to beg and there were military police on the streets, so he hid in the bushes until they had gone. Then he sat behind a tin fence and ate the sandwich. He wasn't going to let his friends know he had it. He never ever came back.

Such encounters were common. Yet after the war Islanders were shocked to find huge stocks of tinned and dried food that the army seemed unable or unwilling to distribute to its men.

A few Islanders reported seeing bodies grouped by the side of the dirt road just outside Stanley, presumably those of soldiers who had died of exposure. Carlos Bloomer Reeve confirmed that, during the early days, some soldiers did die through lack of shelter and warmth, although he claimed that conditions improved later.

In occupied Stanley, April was a traumatic month for Islanders, but in terms of international diplomacy little of substance was happening, despite the efforts of some of the most powerful players on the world stage. It was a time of phoney war.

Remarkably, the first British naval units had departed Britain or been diverted southwards from other global duties within just a few days of the invasion. The P&O cruise liner *Canberra* had been requisitioned, packed with Royal Marines and was following in the wake of the first warships by 9 April. But with other key units still to be mobilised, and 8,000 miles of ocean to cover, Britain could do little more than assume a highly righteous diplomatic stance.

The UK's delegation to the United Nations argued successfully for international support, while hammering home the message that there *would* be a counter-invasion if Argentina did not withdraw to the mainland. London continued to insist that the task force was being mounted to secure Islanders' liberation, although, considering the ambivalence that London had shown towards Islanders in the past, it was at least arguable that damaged national pride was really driving the ships south. Importantly, though, in the eyes of the British public the issue was one of justice and freedom for fellow Britons – even though few had even heard of the Falklands until 2 April.

In Washington, Ronald Reagan and his Secretary of State Alexander Haig had apparently shrugged off Galtieri's disdainful refusal to listen to reason when Reagan had phoned him on the eve of the invasion. To the frustration of many in Britain, the US did not immediately come down on the side of the British. But it was a difficult situation. The only foreign policy issue that really mattered to the US was the ideological battle between communism and capitalism. Argentina had been useful in battling left-wing extremism (the brutal methods of the military government did not appear to concern Washington), and of course Britain was a major Cold War player. But there were some potential benefits in this. The Americans knew that they alone stood any chance of gaining the attention of both parties and they might be able to make them see sense. Reagan tasked Haig to negotiate some kind of compromise which would avoid what must have seemed to be a ridiculous neo-colonial sideshow.

The Secretary of State dutifully embarked on an exhausting schedule of visits to London and Buenos Aires. But neither Thatcher nor Galtieri would offer any significant compromise.

In the past Islanders had had a part to play in diplomatic procedures regarding their own islands. But now the importance of their homeland had transcended their parochial interests and wishes. The future of the Falklands was now a matter of national honour for two major countries, and involved the most powerful country in the world. Polite consultations with Islanders did not enter into anyone's plans.

By the middle of April, most elements of the task force, from nuclear-powered hunter-killer submarines to tiny trawlers adapted for mine sweeping, were at sea. First – largely as a show of strength that might yet make the Argentines pull back from all-out war – South Georgia was to be recovered. Then the Falklands.

On 17 April the commander of operations, Admiral Sir John Fieldhouse, flew to Ascension Island where he chaired a planning conference with the task force commander, Rear Admiral John 'Sandy' Woodward, and commanders of the Commando Brigade who would fight a campaign on land.

At about the same time in Buenos Aires, the military junta was considering a complex peace plan cobbled together after much long haul shuttling by Alexander Haig. The plan proposed the withdrawal of both Argentine and British forces, followed by a period of joint administration with three flags, those of Britain, Argentina and the United States. There would eventually be consultations with the Islanders and a return to negotiations over sovereignty. But there was no promise that Buenos Aires would ever see its flag fly legitimately over Stanley.

The Argentines procrastinated, secretly convinced that they were capable of beating a British force operating so far from home. When, on 19 April, a much-diluted proposal was sent to Britain for comment it was dismissed outright. Frustrated and tired, Haig still continued to negotiate, but he did so with little conviction. Ultimately diplomacy led to naught. The course was set inexorably for conflict.

A kind of awkward tolerance had been maintained between occupied and occupiers. Bloomer Reeve seemed able to sell his benign interpretation of military rule to hawkish colleagues as long as the British did not attack. But on 26 April they did. South Georgia was forcibly recovered and the Argentines seemed to accept that fighting for the Falklands was inevitable.

Now the hard-liners, still apparently opposed by Bloomer Reeve and Hussey but with decreasing effect, had a perfectly reasonable logic: Argentina was at war and the locals were loyal to the enemy. Indeed, they *were* the enemy.

That morning a particularly aggressive and professional squad of special forces, which had recently arrived by air from Argentina, mobilised through Stanley, setting up road blocks and arresting a large number of men and boys who happened to be on the streets. Up to twenty at a time were lined up in the Police Station garden, guns trained on them.

The Canadian, Bill Curtis, was among those arrested and he was convinced that at least some of these troops were mercenaries. They spoke Spanish, he said, but with American and German accents. "I can tell a gum-chewing Yank," he insisted.

This was a curious allegation. In the aftermath of the war there were persistent rumours of mercenaries captured or shot on the mountain-tops. But the Argentines always denied they had foreign fighters. They pointed out that Argentina is a society of immigrants, many of whom retain their mother tongues.

In any case, Bill Curtis remembers that the men – he estimated sixty of them – meant business.

> One feller pulled out his gun and stuck it to my head. He said, 'Turn around,' and marched me across the street to the police station. The police chief looked at me and said, 'What problems have you got into now?'

Bill's wife Barbara was at her desk in the Public Works Department when she received a call from a shopkeeper who told her that she had seen Bill being marched away. Barry Hussey had previously helped her and Bill, and she hoped he could do the same again. Hussey hurried to the police station and demanded to see the Canadian. Bill Curtis remembered that he received some heartening advice: "Go straight home. Get in the house and you stay there. I'll take care of these guys. Everything will be OK."

The influence of the doves may have been waning, but a naval captain's insignia still counted for something. Within minutes the hard men had also released the rest of the locals.

That day's drama was not yet over. At about 4.00 pm a handful of Islanders were disturbed at home or at work and told they had half an hour to pack their bags and prepare for a journey.

The group had little in common, although it was possible to see why paranoid Argentines might see them as a threat. Brian Summers, Gerald Cheek and Owen Summers were all active members of the

123

Defence Force and were known for their marksmanship. Velma Malcolm was a pub landlady getting on in years, who was a leader of the Falkland Islands Association, an anti-Argentine pressure group with many influential supporters in Britain. Stuart Wallace had been a popular elected councillor, but was not known as a firebrand. Perhaps the least surprising prisoners were the Senior Medical Officer Daniel Haines and his family.

In Argentina in those days unexplained arrest was one of the government's terror techniques. It was often a precursor to something infinitely worse. Certainly the locals arrested that day had good reason to be afraid. Velma Malcolm later wrote:

> A big, burly, bumptious bugger said, 'You're going to camp; you and your husband.'
> I asked why and was told, 'The authorities will tell you. Hurry up, there is not much time.'
> I then went upstairs to get a case and pack some clothes, when I discovered he had drawn his pistol and was standing over me. I said to him, 'You don't need that gun, I'm not likely to do anything silly.'
> Whereupon he said, 'Are you afraid?'
> Drawing myself up as tall as possible I said, 'No,' and hoped he did not hear my knees knocking.
> Then he went on to say, 'We know all about you. We know you don't like Argentines.'

Cable and Wireless employees Stuart Wallace and Brian Summers were called into the office of their new Argentine boss, an Air Force intelligence officer, Comodoro Mendiberri, and told that they were being detained because there were men in Stanley "who wished to kill them". This seems odd, but considering the much tougher attitude that now prevailed among the Argentines, it was possible that a hard-line faction was intending to neutralise some locals, while a more moderate faction was acting to protect them.

Some detainees were told they could take their families with them if they wished. Not knowing what lay ahead, this was a gamble. As Gerald Cheek remembered, the manner of his arrest gave no re-assurance.

> Three or four policemen jumped out of their vehicle and ran up to the house with pistols drawn and one was shouting, 'Come on you've got to go!'
> I thought I'd ring my parents to tell them, but as I went to get

hold of the phone he screamed he would shoot me. 'You drop that telephone!' He was very upset.

Gerald believed that he was bound for Argentina and an unknown fate. He opted not to take his wife and two daughters.

I grabbed a suitcase and put a few things in while they were screaming and shouting.

I'll always remember that I was going down the path with these guys, their pistols drawn, and I saw Peter Biggs in his garden. I said, 'Peter, we've got to get that Union Jack up again as quick as we can. Look at this lot!'

At the airport they took us straight to a Puma helicopter. We knew then that either we were going to be thrown out over the sea or we were being taken somewhere not too far away.

Velma Malcolm, who spoke some Spanish, overheard one soldier tell those who were guarding her that he favoured a more permanent solution:

'I'd like to shoot them all, the fat ones, the ugly ones, the thin ones – all of them.'

The Puma headed west across East Falkland, and after about 40 minutes descended over the twin settlements of Fox Bay. The detainees were incarcerated at Fox Bay East under the control of an army engineer battalion.

Concern in Stanley about the forced deportations was profound. No one knew where the detainees had gone and there were rumours that many more arrests were on the cards. Some even said the entire population of Stanley was to be moved.

This was a rumour that had some basis. Bloomer Reeve said later that the high command had seriously considered moving the 500 or so civilians out of Stanley into an internment centre somewhere else in the Islands. This would have neutralised the threat from illicit radios, resistance and infiltrators. However, the idea was dropped when it was appreciated that there was nowhere to incarcerate so many people, and the army did not have the materials or time to build a camp.

Bloomer Reeve moved to calm nerves with this broadcast communiqué, but he offered no rationale for the arrests.

The population is informed that today the military government of the Malvinas, South Georgia and South Sandwich Islands has decided to transfer momentarily some inhabitants of Puerto Argentino to a rural zone. This measure was taken due to the military operations that the British government has imposed and for strict security reasons.

Patrick Watts had managed to put a few questions to Bloomer Reeve and added to the official announcement that there were no plans to deport the rest of the population.

Nevertheless, the grim notice that followed a few minutes later was worrying:

The situation has now reached a stage where the Argentine government and the Armed Forces must fully enforce the law of the country. Anyone who assists in any way the enemies of Argentina will be subject to the code of military justice and their actions judged by the competent authorities. Therefore it is in the interest of the population to remain calm and not to create situations which will be seen as a breach of the peace.

The announcement went on to say that new regulations had been introduced "with the objective of protecting the civilian population and to prevent them from interfering in military operations". A curfew would apply with immediate effect. All civilians had to be in their homes or agreed DAP shelters, with windows blacked out, by 6.00. They would not be allowed to emerge before 6.30 the next morning.

A rubicon had been crossed and the unspoken message to Islanders was now clear: Argentina is at war; you are the potential enemy. Cooperate or else.

That day Nap Bound wrote:

I do not pretend that I have not been worried and perhaps a little frightened occasionally during the past weeks, but for some unaccountable reason last night I experienced a true sense of fear and impending disaster. It can only now be a matter of hours before the wrath of the Royal Navy is launched on the occupying army, and there just has to be bloodshed.

Chapter Seven

Radio Resistance

Radio communications were a vital adjunct to life. In 1982 the manually operated telephone system radiated only a short distance from Stanley, and hundreds of Islanders on West Falkland and the tiny island farms relied on the government-administered radio-telephone system, the RT.

The system was far from ideal: there was no privacy, and conversations, no matter how personal, were monitored by almost everyone within a 100-mile radius. Children were educated over the air and doctors would advise their patients within earshot of 2,000 other people. No one using either the government-managed short wave radio telephone network or the far less formal citizens' band 2-metre band network could afford to be coy.

But it was not only about medical advice and education. Radios gave a sense of security and belonging, and most of the time the RT, the 2-metre network and the more complex long-distance 'ham' short wave sets were used simply to chat. The buzzing sets soothed the feeling of isolation, bringing scattered communities closer together.

The Argentines were well aware of the value of radio communications to the Islanders but their claimed intention to maintain the framework of normal Islands' life could not extend to radio communications. They harboured an almost pathological fear that Islanders were spying on them and would use their sets to communicate with the British. They became more obsessive about this risk as the occupation went on – not without reason.

In the wake of the invasion, they moved quickly to take the official RT network off the air and issued instructions that ham and 2-metre radio operators in Stanley and in the isolated settlements should dismantle their sets and aerials.

The edict was moderated for those living in more remote corners of the Islands when medical staff pointed out that people could die if the regular morning radio surgery was not maintained. So the short morning session alone continued, always under the watchful eye of the Argentines.

The Stanley hub of the RT system was a run-down shack next to the Fire Station on St Mary's Walk. In peacetime, the station was staffed from early morning to early evening and a listening watch was kept overnight in case of emergencies. Principal operator Eileen Vidal would sit over the microphone jotting down telegrams, noting shopping lists to be passed on to the Co-Op or the West Store, and patching callers into Stanley's telephone system. In between, she would dispense her amiable mix of friendly chat and world-weariness.

Highlight of the listening day was between 9.00 and 10.00 am when Eileen would surrender her seat to one of the three doctors from the King Edward Memorial Hospital a few hundred yards down the road. Each farm had a well-stocked medicine chest and the doctors would prescribe drugs from it. If necessary, they would arrange for the patient to be brought into Stanley on one of the light planes of the Government Air Service.

There was an unspoken protocol about the doctor's hour. Complaints from piles to panic attacks were rarely the stuff of gossip. After all, the purveyor of one person's embarrassing news might easily be the next person to reveal his or her health secrets.

On the very morning of the invasion, middle-aged and motherly Eileen Vidal carried out the first act of Islanders' defiance, establishing a trend of subversive radio transmissions that would be a continuous thorn in their side.

John Fowler, Director of Education, had gained permission from the Argentines for farm children attending the school in Stanley to contact their parents by radio and let them know they were safe. An Argentine patrol arrived at Eileen's home to take her to the radio shack.

After an hour or so of sometimes almost hysterical conversations the parents were reassured. Argentine guards were eager to get the children back to the hostels and John Fowler wanted to organise their evacuation from Stanley.

Suddenly Eileen found herself alone. The armed Argentines had barely slammed the door when a perfectly timed signal came through. "Stanley, this is HMS *Endurance*. Do you read? Over."

Some 800 miles away to the south-east, Captain Nick Barker in command of the lightly-armed ice patrol ship HMS *Endurance* was involved in a game of cat and mouse with the Argentine Navy. His Royal Marines were on South Georgia preparing to defend the island (they would later shoot down a helicopter and damage a corvette before surrendering) and he desperately wanted to know about the situation in Stanley. The question that must have been uppermost in his mind was had the Argentines invaded? If not, he might return to the Falklands and help defend them.

The message that Eileen Vidal shouted into the ether was stark: "For God's sake, stay the hell out of it! There are enough ships out there to blow you out of the water!"

Endurance's skipper ruled out a heroic but futile attempt to return to Stanley, but he could act as a relay station, passing on any useful military intelligence to London. Eileen found herself fielding complex questions and relying on what she and her family had been able to see from their vantage point at the top of town:

> I told them as much as I could about the Argentine ships and the number of troops in Stanley, and about the aircraft and helicopters. I knew it was a bit risky, but I did the best I could.
>
> They just said they'd pass it all on to London and thanked me. I signed off quickly because I thought that at any minute somebody would come charging in. I was lucky that morning.

She did not know it, but her message to *Endurance* may have been the first information to come from the Falklands after the invasion. The powerful short wave transmitters operated by Cable and Wireless had failed the night before and the British Government had no firm information.

Endurance resumed radio silence and vanished again among the fjords of South Georgia, waiting her chance to strike back.

The official radio telephone station would not be used again for covert work, but a few daring local ham radio operators were ready and willing to take over.

On Saunders Islands, off the north of West Falkland, farm manager Tony Pole-Evans was remote from the action, but he had listened to accounts of the developing situation on the Falkland Islands Broadcasting Station and on the BBC World Service. He heard the edict ordering all owners of radio equipment to cease transmissions and dismantle their transceivers and antennas. But believing that he was in a relatively safe area, he decided to ignore it. Far from curtailing his ham transmissions, he stepped them up.

Tony removed his most obvious aerial, a 45-foot high mast used for the 2-metre citizen band system, and replaced it with an antenna within his house. The new arrangements cut down the range radically, but still enabled him to talk to farm settlements around the West and as far away as Lafonia on the East. He left a relatively small aerial in place for his short wave ham radio work. This meant that he could continue to talk with many locals who had kept their 2-metre sets operational, and use the ham rig to maintain transmissions to his friend Les Hamilton, some 8,000 miles away in Scotland.

The calculated risk was well judged. No Argentines landed on Saunders, although Pucara ground attack aeroplanes and helicopters regularly flew over the settlement, and they lingered long enough to indicate they were taking an interest in anything going on below.

Les Hamilton in Scotland was a former British Army signaller, and when he heard Tony's voice come through his headphones on schedule the day after the invasion, he knew that he might be able to gain some useful information and pass it on to the Ministry of Defence in London.

He and Tony agreed to avoid the use of call signs or any other clues that might help the Argentines identify the source of the transmissions, and they shifted their operating frequency just outside the normal ham frequency band. This reduced the likelihood of any equally loyal amateur in Argentina monitoring their messages and reporting them to their authorities.

Islanders in the Lafonia area of East Falkland told Tony over the 2-metre network when the Argentines moved into Goose Green, and in approximately what strength. He passed this on to Les Hamilton, who in turn fed it into the Ministry of Defence in London.

Similar high-value information came from refugees from the Fox Bay area of West Falkland, who made their way to Saunders when the Argentines took over their settlements. They gave Tony the actual number of men that had landed and described their equipment, which included helicopters. The information was passed on.

Tony's daughter was living on nearby Pebble Island, where the Argentines quickly set up an important base for light transport and ground attack aircraft. The 2-metre network came into its own again, as he recalled:

> She talked to me for a day or so after they arrived on the island, and gave me numbers and types of aircraft. The numbers of planes actually on the island varied, but she could tell me what types they were: Pucaras, Mentors, Pumas and Skyvans. Then they confiscated all the radios on the island, and I didn't hear any more from her.

Pebble Island subsequently became the target of a classic SAS raid, and most of the aircraft were destroyed on the ground.

There was also a fairly large garrison at Port Howard on West Falkland, and although it had been difficult to glean much information about the enemy presence there, Tony was able to transmit a broad-brush picture to Les Hamilton.

Just once did this cool radio operator's pulse quicken with a hint of fear. He was working the 2-metre frequencies one evening, when he looked out a window and saw a torch moving towards the house. Convinced the long-anticipated Argentine patrol had arrived, he threw the radio sets in a cupboard and the 2-metre antenna out the window. But the men who knocked on the door were friends: three men of the Special Boat Service, accompanied by Tony's son David. The special forces soldiers had been watching the north of West Falkland from high ground on Saunders, but had now decided to request accommodation in farm buildings. The Pole-Evans family were delighted to help, and the SBS remained on the island until they were picked up by a trawler following the Argentine surrender a week or so later.

Apart from the move away from normal ham frequencies and the careful avoidance of names and other verbal clues that could direct attention to Saunders, Tony and Les took remarkably few precautions. They transmitted at the same time most days – 4.20 pm – and on the same frequency. "I wasn't really that concerned," said Tony, years later. "But afterwards I realised I'd taken a bit of a risk."

He certainly had taken risks, but possibly not as serious as those faced by a fellow ham operator who was working from Stanley – the very centre of the Argentines' main garrison.

Sixty-five-year-old Bob North, a ham operator by night and a debt controller by day, in North Yorkshire, reacted with great excitement when he heard the voice of Stanley lighthouse keeper Reg Silvey crackling faintly through his headphones. He recalled the moment:

It was about 20.00 hours GMT, two days after the invasion. I had been calling on the 15-metre band and was coming to the end of a conversation with an American when I heard another station trying to contact me with a VP8 call sign. I suddenly realised that this was a South Atlantic station and it could be in the Falkland Islands. I signed off rather abruptly with the American station, I'm afraid, and told the VP8 to repeat his call, which he did, telling me that his call sign was VP8QE, his name was Reg, and that he was in Port Stanley. Could I get some urgent messages through to his relations?

The content of the broadcast was mundane enough, and Bob North was pleased to pass the messages on by phone. But the moment was significant, because Reg, redundant since the invading forces extinguished his paraffin light on Cape Pembroke, was taking the first step of a defiant campaign that would increasingly frustrate the Argentine Forces.

Thrilled with the contact, Bob North rattled off his own questions. Was Reg free to transmit? Would he be arrested by the invaders?

Reg told his new friend that he was fine, but that the Argentines had banned the use of amateur radio kit. Believing he had already pushed his luck, he said that he would be back on the air at around the same time the next evening, but that North should use no call signs or names. In future the transmissions would be entirely anonymous.

Reg suspected that there would be a team of radio specialists in Stanley monitoring the airwaves and they would probably be tasked to detect illicit operators. He had already seen two military vans sprouting strange aerials and he thought they could be used to pinpoint transmissions.

He was correct. Later the vans would be used intensively to search for him and the other illicit radio operators. He gambled, however, that the accuracy of the direction-finding equipment would be compromised by the topography of Stanley. To get an accurate fix on a transmitter, the direction finding equipment would need to operate across a reasonably flat surface, and Stanley, built on the side of a steep ridge, was anything but that. It was, he figured, a risk worth taking.

Reg Silvey had lived in the Falklands since 1969. He came to the Islands from his home in the east of England to work for the British Antarctic Survey, maintaining a radio link with the scientific bases on the Antarctic Peninsula. He was a somewhat introverted man, a bachelor who was neither popular nor unpopular. But the Islands were the ideal place for him. They were peaceful and unspoilt. Over 14 years he grew to love them.

Technology in the form of teleprinters operated by communications specialists Cable and Wireless eventually made him redundant from the British Antarctic Survey, but he found a new and satisfying niche as a watch-keeper at Cape Pembroke Lighthouse, some six miles from Stanley. At the lighthouse he polished the brass and pumped the kerosene for the ancient light and found time to operate his ham set.

When he was off duty he lodged with fellow radio ham Charlie McKenzie and his wife Maude in town, sometimes enjoying a few more drinks than might have been wise at one of Stanley's more notorious drinking clubs, the *Gluepot*. But then the Argentines arrived. He said later:

I was furious because they had ruined my whole life, all in one day. They had destroyed not just my way of life, but everyone's. It was all gone. I don't know, but perhaps I went a bit crackers.

When it was announced over 'Radio Islas Malvinas' that all radio operators must surrender their kit, Reg resolved to stay on the air behind a facade of compliance. The Argentines knew the identities of all hams as licences were recorded in the Post Office. If he and his friend and landlord Charlie McKenzie did not hand in their rigs then Argentine soldiers would soon be knocking on the door.

It took more than an invasion to keep *Gluepot* members from their bar and it was here that Reg met another friend, George Betts. George was captain of the small coastal supply ship *Monsunen* and the vessel had just berthed in Stanley after a journey back from the western islands. George kept a small Atlas battery-operated transceiver on the ship. He treasured the set and, with no plan in mind other than to save the equipment, he hid it in the Falkland Islands Company's warehouse. He resolved that, if asked, he would tell the Argentines that he had left it on *Monsunen*'s bridge from where one of the Argentines now crewing the ship had stolen it.

Reg was delighted at the opportunity this offered. But most locals were now banned from the dock area, which was swarming with soldiers. George, however, had an official pass and said he could recover the radio. The skipper winked and said, "I'll let you know."

The next day the *Gluepot* regulars were discussing the rapidly developing situation in the bar (which they now called the war room), when George Betts approached Reg. "I should go and look in the shed around the back if I was you," he said. Reg did so and found there, hidden beneath kindling and peat in a pot-bellied stove, the Atlas transceiver. He placed it in a plastic carrier bag, covered it with a few innocent items of shopping and took it back to Charlie and Maude McKenzies' cottage. He told Charlie that he had the radio, but kept the secret from Maude.

It was time for some pantomime antics. Charlie and Reg gathered the rest of their kit together and lugged it to the Town Hall, where a uniformed officer dutifully ticked it off against the records and issued receipts. It would be returned when the crisis was over, the two men were told.

"Charlie and I created a fuss handing the kit over," recalled Reg. "I wanted them to remember that I had handed my kit in. I said I was extremely upset and I didn't see why I should do it."

The amateur dramatics continued at home. The McKenzies' garden was dominated by a huge antenna which had to come down. "We wanted them to remember this too," said Reg. "They had a helicopter which was patrolling low over the town. They circled Charlie's house while we were dismantling the aerial and we were waving at them. They definitely saw us."

Two small but serious challenges remained: now that the big aerial had been so obviously dismantled, how could Reg transmit? And he did not have a 12 volt battery to power it. Help with the power source came again from the *Gluepot*. During a session in the war room, he quietly mentioned his problem to two friends, Christopher McCallum and Les Biggs. The two worked at the hospital as drivers, and the Argentines usually allowed their marked Land Rover into any part of town. That evening the hospital Land Rover pulled up outside the McKenzies', and Reg took delivery of a new, fully charged battery. It powered his set for the remainder of the war.

The answer to the aerial problem was, said Reg, brilliantly simple:

> I realised that I could make the washing line into an aerial. It had a steel core, stretched across the garden, and I simply connected up to the set when I wanted to transmit. The matching to the transmitter was terrible, but that didn't matter.

Reg was generally on his own in the McKenzies' house. Maude was an auxiliary nurse, and both she and Charlie were spending much of the time at the hospital because shift work meant working odd hours, and the presence of so many troops made commuting difficult. He was reasonably sure that he would not be disturbed, but took another risky measure to give him a little more security. He managed to get hold of a notice, signed by General Menendez, indicating that the house had been cleared by the military police and should not be entered by Argentine forces. The notices had been produced on Stanley's ancient printing press for official use, but, thanks to a casual run-on by the local printer, extra copies were circulating.

Following his initial contact, Bob North listened out dutifully on the 19-metre band and was delighted when the faint signal from the Falklands crackled into his headphones. This time the transmission was brief, anonymous and serious. Bob was to inform the Ministry of Defence that Stanley Airport (clearly visible a few miles away from Reg's upstairs window) was occupied by Argentine troops and it was being used to receive supplies and ammunition. There were no Islanders in the area and it could be safely attacked.

Bob contacted the Bridlington police station and they sent around a motorcyclist to collect the information and take it to London.

Reg Silvey had crossed into serious spying. The information he was sending to Britain was of real value and the Argentines were aware that someone was transmitting. The direction finding vans were trying to get a fix on him.

The next night the voice from the Falklands began listing numbers and abbreviations that Bob North did not understand. Reg curtly told him to note them anyway and pass the information on to the Ministry, where they would be understood.

The letters were obvious abbreviations for weaponry ('AA' signified anti-aircraft emplacements), and numbers were map co-ordinates taken from a large-scale map of Stanley that the authorities, gathering all the available information about Stanley, would certainly have. He recalled the transmissions with satisfaction:

> I told them that the Argentines had an anti-aircraft missile launcher by the gate leading west from Stanley out towards the Stone Corral. Harriers attacked that, and I would like to think that was because I gave them the coordinates.

The Argentines raided houses on a daily basis. Usually they were restrained and sometimes even courteous, but they meant business and houses would usually be ringed with armed men.

Carlos Bloomer Reeve said later that the communications experts were convinced that transmissions were emanating from the area of the West Store, the supermarket where, in the final stages of the war, dozens of Islanders sheltered. This was a considerable distance from Reg Silvey's home, so either the direction-finding equipment was every bit as inaccurate as Reg had hoped or there was another transmitter, perhaps, Reg speculated being operated by special forces who may have infiltrated the town.

There were, however, occasional indications that the detectors were getting close. Reg was amused that another *Gluepot* drinking friend and near neighbour, Bob Peart, seemed to be getting more than his fair share of the searches. Bob would turn up in the war room for a drink before curfew, furious that soldiers had held him at gunpoint while they searched his house 'yet again'. He never knew that the likely source of his problems was leaning on the bar a few feet away.

The risk could be managed. The notice signed by Governor Menendez discouraged searches, but Reg's safety was ultimately down to caution. Transmissions – by voice if atmospheric conditions were good and by morse if they were bad – would usually last for no longer than 15 seconds. The calls were frequently 'blind' (transmitted without the time-consuming protocol of establishing formal contact with another operator) and would often be scheduled for the early evening when the Argentine radio experts were busy trying to jam the BBC World Service's *Calling the Falklands*.

Transmitting was always a perilous procedure, as Reg explained:

The trick was to transmit while watching out the window for the military police. From the back window I could see right down James Street. They searched house by house and I always knew roughly where they would be. As soon as I saw them, I was out of the house and away. By the time they got to my house, I was probably in the *Gluepot*.

After a few weeks Reg doubted that Bob North was receiving and relaying all of his messages, but he believed that at least one other operator in Canada was listening and passing on the intelligence. MOD was aware of the transmissions around the 19-metre band and may have tasked the GCHQ intelligence-gathering station in Cheltenham to tune in.

Reg Silvey was never arrested. He was not even subject to the arbitrary arrests and house searches that plagued so many citizens of Stanley. He continued to be a headache for the Argentines, fuelling their obsession with transmitters and tying up their valuable assets until the very end of the war.

Reg and Tony Pole-Evans on Saunders Island were the only Islanders who operated a clandestine radio link with the outside world throughout the war. But others were active briefly until just after the invasion.

Bob McLeod, living at Goose Green, was one, but he was put off the air when the enemy soldiers began their notorious occupation of that settlement. Bob had, however, been very popular with amateurs seeking a VP8 contact and Reg Silvey admitted that he slipped Bob's name into some of his broadcasts in an effort to confuse listeners. Among the ham community this may have led to the radio hams' legend of 'Radio Bob': for years the two clandestine broadcasters of the Falklands were referred to as such.

It is hard to say what would have happened if the Argentines had caught the men red-handed and arrested them. General Mario Menendez said later that they would have been 'considered spies', and ominously suggested that the traditional treatment of spies would have applied. Indeed locals were warned that anyone found collaborating with the British would be subject to 'the code of military law'.

Carlos Bloomer Reeve fought the cases of locals who had been arrested for minor acts of disrespect. But he admitted after the war that anyone committing a truly serious misdemeanour, like spying, would have been beyond his reach.

An indication of the gravity with which radio misbehaviour was viewed was revealed on 1 May when the vanguard of the British Task Force attacked Stanley Airport and Goose Green. After weeks of phoney war, it was hoped that a lethal display of bombing and shelling would convince the Argentines to step back from the brink.

Making radio contact with the occupiers was an important part of this strategy and, quite by chance, it involved Robin Pitaluga, the owner of Salvador, a sheep farm on the north of East Falkland. He was listening on 4.5 megahertz, the normal frequency for inter-island RT conversations, when the task force flagship came on the air. Robin takes up the story:

> Suddenly we heard HMS *Hermes* trying to get in touch with the Argentine garrison in Stanley to tell them they hadn't a chance and they should surrender before there was any more bloodshed. They would, they said, send a helicopter to Stanley to pick up the Governor and commanders in chief of the various services.
>
> The Argentines weren't answering, and in our ignorance we assumed it was purely a communications problem, and tried to help out. We called *Hermes* and said that we would try to through to the Argentines. However, we couldn't get through to Stanley either. But all that chat on 4.5 megs *was* picked up by the Argentines in Stanley, who were hearing everything but just not bothering to answer.
>
> Shortly afterwards two very heavily armed helicopters landed on the farm. They did a very thorough check of all the buildings, looking for the British soldiers they were convinced were hiding there. And then they arrived at our house and made us tell them everything that had been going on. They insisted that I should go to Stanley. They were so cross that we had used the radio and spoken to the British ships. That really sickened them.

The soldiers loaded Robin and all the farm radios they could find into a Puma helicopter that was already overloaded with men. The aircraft took off for Stanley, hugging the sides of ridges and valleys to avoid the Harriers that were active for the first time over the Falklands.

The helicopter touched down at the old Royal Marines base at Moody Brook during a bombardment, and both Argentines and Islander sheltered there for an hour before heading down town in a jeep. Twice they had to abandon their vehicle and dive to the ground in a hail of indiscriminate Argentine firing.

Eventually two officers were found at the military police station; a bombastic and aggressive officer resembling Cervantes' anti-hero Sancho Panza and a far more helpful and friendly officer, Captain Romano (see chapter 6), who a little later would help to defuse the situation.

The Argentines were bruised, angry and more distrustful than ever of the locals. Things were getting ugly. Robin recalled what happened next:

> I wrote out a statement but they didn't believe a word of it. Shortly afterwards I saw the more senior one of the two tear it up and throw it away. Another very nasty-looking character had come in and he drew an ugly-looking knife out of his belt and pointed to me. He drew it across his throat before putting it in his belt and disappearing.
>
> Then there was a lot of shouting and noise in the front garden of the police station and I could see they had half a dozen local chaps down on their knees in the wet grass. I recognised several of them. The Argentines gave them a thorough bawling out. I believe they'd been in a pub.
>
> The major told them what he thought of them, and threw his helmet onto the concrete path in fury.

Robin Pitaluga was ordered to a trench a few hundred yards away on Victory Green. There another captain took over and took his pistol from its holster. Robin was convinced his time had come and he would die on this pretty green just a few hundred yards from the *Upland Goose Hotel*, which was owned by his sister and her family. His memories never faded:

> He put his pistol against the back of my neck and then I heard the clicking of the mechanism as he pulled the trigger. I thought sooner or later it must go off but it didn't. I thought, 'Well, if this is the way I've got to go, I've got to go.' He did that about five or six times. It was just more of their terror stuff.

The officer's sadistic humour satisfied, Robin was then thrown into a dugout shelter occupied by two young conscripts. They were told to tie him up and, if he moved an inch, to shoot him. The Islander and the Argentines remained packed into their tiny dugout all night. Eventually the rifle barrel that had been shoved in his face was removed and once the younger of the two men even untied his hands.

After a cold night, interrupted by troops shooting at shadows and a bombardment of the airport, the soldiers brewed some coffee and shared it with their captive. Things looked a little better, but then he was returned to the military police station, where the more aggressive police officer renewed his bawling.

The Argentines were still smarting from the attack and they were dangerous. When Bloomer Reeve belatedly heard of the farmer's arrest he sent the Air Force intelligence chief and head of communications, Vice Comodoro Mendiberri, to the police station. Mendiberri was told to order the civilian's release and get him to the *Upland Goose Hotel*, out of harm's way.

After a fraught discussion, the decent Captain Romano came to release the prisoner and walk him to the *Upland Goose*. He said, with some understatement, "The authorities were not happy with your behaviour yesterday, and if there are any further problems, the consequences will be very grave. You are to remain here until the end of hostilities. Don't move anywhere without our permission."

Romano appeared almost as relieved as Robin that the situation had been defused. And, for his part, Robin was prepared to accept the terms of his house arrest. Spending the rest of the war under house arrest in the *Upland Goose* was rather better than a chilly trench. Or a cold grave.

The 2-metre network, the Falklands' citizen band radio, was ubiquitous. Every homestead had two or three: one for the house, another in the Land Rover and a hand-held one to be kept in the pocket.

Argentine radio equipment was far less efficient (as, indeed, was British kit), and while it made sense for the new military government to confiscate the sets for security reasons, it was also clear that they wanted to use them.

The Argentines stationed volunteer civilian observers from the mainland in key locations around the islands to spot enemy air or sea activity and report it to Stanley. Radar coverage was surprisingly good, but there were plenty of blind spots and strategically placed civilians could be very useful. The confiscated equipment was quickly redistributed to the observers.

But the little 2-metre sets were so common that the Argentines were never able to confiscate them all, and, as already described, people on more distant farms and islands continued talking to each other from time to time, sometimes turning the power down to avoid detection.

However, at Port Louis, just 30 miles to the north of Stanley as the crow flies, a handful of radio enthusiasts used their 2-metre sets in a manner which can only be described as aggressive.

The brains behind the plan was Mario Zuvic, a Chilean of Yugoslav origin who had emigrated to the Falklands a few years before. Like many Chileans, he hated Argentina even more passionately than the Islanders and, as a refugee from Stanley staying with his friends Andres and Celia Short, he plotted what could be done to disrupt the enemy.

An electronics wizard who could not keep his hands off a radio, it was not long before he and equally enthusiastic Andres had erected a crude, concealed 2-metre aerial in the branches of a tree.

As the occupation wore on and no one, British or Argentine, seemed to take any interest in Port Louis, Mario, Andres and Andres' father, Peter Short, took more and more interest in the conversations they could hear on their set. Every night they would listen to the Argentine observers on the hilltops. One group, just a few miles away, always came through clearly.

Often at night the Argentine signallers in Stanley would patch the observers into their long-range radios and the Argentine phone system. The lonely men would chat, sometimes emotionally, to their families on the mainland.

The Chilean and the Islanders decided they could take advantage of the network to confuse the enemy. Mario Zuvic recalled how they did this:

> We made the Argentine controller of the 2-metre network in Stanley think that we were one of their missing lookouts – after the landings it had gone quiet, probably because they were captured by the British. We were sending morse signals and even convinced the Argentine controller to send a recovery team to collect the observers who were supposedly stranded in the hills. I am convinced we misled them for two or three days.

That was a pleasing waste of the Argentines' time. Jamming the Argentine transmissions, the civilians reasoned, would be even more damaging. They knew that to avoid detection this had to be done in an arbitrary and unpredictable way. Otherwise, any direction-finding equipment the Argentines had would get a fix on them. This did not seem to be working against Reg Silvey in Stanley, but projected over flatter terrain, the beams might quickly get an accurate fix on Port Louis.

It was easy. They simply scanned the band until a conversation was detected, then pressed the switch transmitting an obliterating tone at maximum power. It was obvious from monitored conversations that the jamming was infuriating the Argentines.

Their work reached a climax on 8 June immediately following the disastrous Argentine attack on the Royal Fleet Auxiliary ships *Sir Tristram* and *Sir Galahad* at Fitzroy, some 35 miles to the south-west. Observers using 2-metre equipment had spotted the landing ships and brought in Skyhawk bombers that pounded the ships. Fifty-one men died and many more were seriously injured. It was the single most serious blow that the British Army suffered and it slowed the advance on Stanley. Mario Zuvic described the impact on the Port Louis radio operators:

> We didn't know exactly what was going on because they were using a code. But there was a lot of commotion on the day of the raid, and we found out what had happened that afternoon from the BBC. We realised that we could have jammed them and stopped the signal about the landing ships getting through.
>
> So the next day we could hear them getting ready for something similar. I said 'Now we can actually do something,' and we started jamming them badly. The whole day they were unable to pass information to and from Stanley. Messages which should have taken seconds to get through were taking them hours, because we were at it continuously.
>
> Every time a guy spoke, we put the button down and we'd leave it there for half a minute. Then he would try again and we would jam him once more.
>
> We were sad that we hadn't done it so well the day before, but we just didn't know what was going on. There were a lot of code words being used, and we didn't know if they were talking about Stanley or Goose Green or whatever.

At the time there was speculation about why the Argentines did not press home their attacks on the Fitzroy beachhead. The landing site was in a state of chaos and long-range artillery or further air attacks from the mainland would have seriously compounded this. Perhaps no such action was taken because the observers in the mountains to the north of Fitzroy were shouting ineffectively into jammed radios, unable to pass on their information to Stanley.

Delighted and afraid in roughly equal measures, the three men listened to the Argentines speculating about the source of the rogue signals. With his fluent Spanish, Mario translated for Andres and Peter.

The next day, as British Forces regrouped and prepared to resume their advance, the men at Port Louis had their breakfast and told their wives some story about going out to do chores around the farm. They headed straight for their concealed radio and aerial, again determined to throw a spanner in the Argentine works. But during the night the Argentines in Stanley had prepared their direction-finding equipment and after just half an hour of transmitting the obliterating tone, Port Louis had been pinpointed as the source of the signals.

"*Ya los tenemos,*" came the shouted Argentine voice. "We've got them!"

141

And the civilians knew they did, because the voice shouted out the coordinates which matched the settlement of Port Louis perfectly. It was a terrifying moment and the men had no choice but to switch off their transmitter immediately. They could do no more to frustrate the Argentines and perhaps they had already gone too far. They knew that the enemy was not likely to come overland to Port Louis because since the main British landing at San Carlos on 21 May and their advance across East Falkland, the route to the settlement around Berkley Sound was virtually under the control of British paratroops. A visit by a helicopter also seemed unlikely as the Argentines were on the back foot, and most of their helicopters had been destroyed.

But a visit from the deadly little Pucara ground-attack aircraft did not seem out of the question and they might just be in range of the Argentines' 155mm howitzers. As Mario Zuvic explained, "They could have just turned a gun to that bearing and blasted the whole place to bits."

But probably the Argentines knew that the rogue transmitter was effectively neutralised and any punishment attack would be a wasteful diversion from the main effort against the British, who were now approaching in a north-south pincer movement from the Fitzroy and Estancia areas.

The locals had the last laugh when the observers on the hilltop just a few miles from Port Louis came under heavy British naval barrage. Not even stopping long enough to put on their boots, the two men ran from their position, stumbling into Port Louis a few hours later, asking for shelter and communications with the garrison in Stanley. With convincing innocence, the locals lied that they had no radio with which to summon help, and anyway the Argentines were now cut off from the Stanley garrison.

They let them sleep in a shed for a few hours, and sent a brief call to Brookfield Farm, a short cross-country drive to the west. An SAS patrol was there, and they told the civilians to bring the Argentines in.

The visitors appeared to be unarmed, but they might have had a concealed pistol or grenade. Keeping a shotgun and rifle within reach, Andres and Mario banged on the door of the shed and woke the men. "You are behind British lines," they said, "and we have been instructed to take you to the British soldiers nearby. From there you will be taken to a prison ship."

The younger and more junior man was ecstatic. He smiled from ear to ear. His colleague, a regular NCO, was less happy, but resigned to the situation. "If it has to be, it has to be," he said. "Let's go." If they had a weapon it remained out of sight.

They clambered into a Land Rover, and an hour or so later the party drove into Brookfield Farm. There appeared to be no one around, but as Mario and Andres approached the farmhouse a 'copse of low shrubs' stood up and revealed itself to be the special forces.

The Argentines were searched, given some clothes and marched off to captivity. As he walked away, the junior soldier was still smiling. As, indeed, were the men of Port Louis.

Chapter Eight

Goose Green

Even compared to Stanley, the village of Goose Green was tiny. The population swelled a little during the summer shearing season and dropped during the winter, but it was normally a self-reliant and fairly happy community of about ninety people.

Goose Green was the flagship farm of the powerful Falkland Islands Company – the FIC. Brook Hardcastle, the company's camp manager, with responsibility for farming activities across East Falkland, lived in the much smaller neighbouring settlement of Darwin. His deputy, Eric Goss, looked after the day-to-day management of Goose Green's several dozen workers and hundreds of thousands of Corriedale sheep.

Although the settlement was small, the farm was huge. Goose Green's sheep wandered across hundreds of thousands of acres of gently undulating grassland. It was bordered by three other, rather smaller, FIC ranches, Fitzroy, Walker Creek and North Arm.

Goose Green's ugly shearing shed was, and is, an industrial installation, a factory where animals come in at one end and wool comes out the other. But the bright red and green corrugated iron roofs and white walls of the houses are an attractive splash of colour on the drab landscape of 'white' grass and diddle dee shrubland.

There was a company-owned store, which operated mainly 'on tick', debts being deducted from pay packets at the end of each month, and there was a spartan community hall with a bar, where dances or darts matches were held in the winter. On the roof of the hall was a tiny steeple revealing its occasional role as a church. Services were held once or twice a year at best; whenever ministers bothered to visit from Stanley.

Life at Goose Green was generally pleasant enough. The company-owned houses were well-maintained and each had a vegetable garden. There was horse riding, fishing in the rivers and creeks, and hunting upland geese and ducks. Archery had become a craze, and there were even occasional riotous attempts at polo.

144

Pay was poor, but that didn't matter much. The farm dairy provided cheap milk, and mutton was virtually free. The large school had been built by the FIC during the early 1950s when the company was rich from the sale of wool to armies fighting in Korea. It had been a boarding establishment, giving a very basic education to children from farms across the Islands, although by 1982 camp children were being encouraged to study in Stanley and the red timber building was inhabited by just one teacher and a handful of local youngsters.

The lives of single men were darker and more troubled. Their bunkhouse and their welfare were shamefully neglected. With little to do at weekends, most of the young shepherds and labourers would sign for their supply of liquor from the store and settle down for long drinking sessions. It was a wild life for them. Once a young Islander was fatally stabbed in the bunkhouse.

To the Argentines, Goose Green *per se* could not have seemed like much of a prize. If they held Stanley, they held the seat of government and a colourful town steeped in history. If they held Goose Green . . . well, they held a few locals and a lot of sheep. But the settlement had one real benefit. The flat land around it boasted good grass runways and it was situated near the centre of the Islands. A base there could command a wide expanse of land and sea.

Brook Hardcastle had been visiting Ronnie Binnie, his manager at Fitzroy, on 2 April. When he heard that the Argentines had landed he reasoned that they could be moving on to the Islands' second largest settlement soon. It took him six hours of hard driving to push through the muddy ruts back to Darwin; time to reflect on his several decades in the Islands.

The peace of the place was something he valued deeply. He never thought he would see men fighting each other here. Now, though, he was searching the skies, worried that some maverick Argentine pilot might attack a Land Rover alone in the expanse of the camp.

It was a depressing ride home, and when he got there he found the eighty-eight residents in a sombre mood. They had listened to the remarkable radio coverage of the fall of Stanley and the authoritarian edicts in Spanish and English that followed. The only good news was that camp children who had been going to school in Stanley were being sent home: they would be on their way out of Stanley soon.

Brook and Eric Goss discussed what they should do. It was clear that the Argentines planned to be in the Islands for good and no one should think about getting in their way.

They did not, however, call a meeting of the residents of Goose Green and Darwin. Instead, small groups of Goose Green people got together to discuss the crisis. David Gray, whose job it was to maintain the settlement's power supply, recalled that there was no serious talk of resistance.

> I think we were of one mind about not opposing them. We knew what they were capable of and, as Stanley had surrendered, and Rex Hunt was being shipped out, the battle was, lost. At least for the time being.
>
> We collected all the farm weapons together, locked them up in the shearing shed and just sat and waited for them to come.

Eric Goss had decided that Goose Green probably had two more days of freedom. It would take the Argentines a day or so to consolidate themselves in Stanley, and their next priority would probably be to establish a presence on West Falkland, or 'Gran Malvina,' as they called it. They would not be steaming up Choiseul Sound towards Darwin Harbour before Sunday the 4th. His estimate was spot on.

Not for the first time the Islanders' network of short-range 2-metre radios came into its own. Early on Sunday Yona Davis on Lively Island, at the entrance to Choiseul Sound, broadcast a warning. Calling whoever might be listening, she reported that a black cargo ship had just passed the island heading west. It was flying the Argentine flag. Goose Green could expect visitors in a few hours.

The ship was the *Isla de los Estados*, a vessel of some 1,000 tons which was no stranger to Falklands waters. Over the last few years she had made occasional bona fide commercial visits, and on one occasion had visited Goose Green to load surplus sheep for sale in Argentina. (This was one of her last journeys: a few weeks later the ship was shelled by a British frigate and sunk with all hands as she attempted to run the Royal Navy blockade.)

A few miles from Goose Green the *Isla de los Estados* stopped. Then from the east came the throbbing beat of helicopters. Large troop-carrying Pumas swooped in, flying low and tactically. They landed on the grass airfield and rapidly disgorged heavily armed troops.

Peeping cautiously from houses, the locals saw the men dodge from one timber and tin building to another, weapons raised, obviously securing it for the safe arrival of the seaborne force. A section of Royal Marines was still on the run and the Argentines feared that they may have been holed up at Goose Green.

Argentine propaganda insisted that they had come as friends and liberators. If they believed this, the troops must have been disappointed. They saw no sign of life. Certainly there was no jubilant crowd of serfs ready to turn on their British bosses. Even when the *Isla de los Estados* was given the signal to berth at the jetty, the settlement resembled a ghost town.

Around 90 troops, thought to be professional Marines rather than raw conscripts, came ashore with their equipment and supplies. The first few ashore consulted a map and made their way to what they believed was the manager's house. Clearly their intelligence was out of date. It had indeed been the manager's home once, but not for the last decade.

An Argentine officer, a young Lieutenant, Juan Gomez Centurion, summoned his reserves of gravitas and prepared to make a rehearsed speech not to Eric Goss or Brook Hardcastle, but to the storekeeper, Keith Bailey, who now lived in the old manager's house. Keith interrupted the soldier and told him that he could oblige with a can of baked beans or even some shotgun cartridges, but he wasn't authorised to hand over the settlement.

He agreed to take the officer to Brook Hardcastle's home in Darwin on his motorbike. The Argentine clung desperately to his helmet, his dignity and to Keith himself as the small motorbike jolted along the most rutted and muddy route possible.

At Darwin Brook Hardcastle emerged casually from his big house. His attitude seemed to suggest that an outbreak of tick among the flock would be more troublesome than this. Gomez Centurion was, Brook recalled, formal and pompous, aware of his role in history.

> He had a prepared statement, and spoke English very well. 'We are your friends,' he said. 'We are here to free you from colonialism. You will carry on your life as usual and we shall build a big base here at Goose Green and we shall protect you.'

Brook Hardcastle was known for his frank and argumentative nature. There was no better excuse for a quarrel than this. He told Centurion that it was a funny way for 'friends' to arrive and, far from him and his men giving Islanders protection, he expected Britain to do that.

The men exchanged a few more truculent words before the Argentine was bounced back to Goose Green on Keith Bailey's motorbike.

Once there, Gomez Centurion ordered the residents to line up by the jetty head, where they were counted. He introduced himself to Eric Goss, who quickly took a strong dislike to the man:

> He bragged about being involved in the dirty war in Argentina. He said, 'I can pick out a guilty face in a crowd of five thousand and shoot him.'

Because he lived about a mile from the main concentration of military and civilians, Brook Hardcastle did not become the main point of contact for the Argentines. Instead, Eric Goss took the brunt of the occupiers' increasing demands. Within a few days their numbers were swelling and he was under pressure to provide accommodation. In the hope that they would stay out of the settlement, Eric asked Andy Clarke to vacate the big Darwin School. The teacher moved his few pupils into the community centre and the Argentines entered the school. They crammed hundreds into a space designed for no more than fifty.

Brook and Eric agreed that farm life should continue as normally as possible. Sitting at home worrying about the future would do no one any good. The busy summer was over, but under the guise of routine farm chores, they were able to frustrate the Argentines a little and prepare for worse times ahead. Eric Goss:

> We had 27 drums of petrol on the farm at that time, and we hid them. We put some in the wood shed, covered over with fencing batons. And hid others by the killing house. In the end there was just one drum left in the petrol shed.
>
> We disabled our best tractors, particularly the one with the McConnell arm [mechanical digger] on it.
>
> Once they came to my door and I was told, 'I want two tractors with trailers delivered to the school at ten o'clock'.
>
> Denzil Clausen and I drove two crappy tractors up there and Gomez got very angry. 'You take this rubbish back and bring me your best tractors. I want better tractors than this or I will shoot you,' he said.
>
> He was definitely mean enough for that. We'd immobilised the best tractors, but we drove the next best ones up there. When we got out of them, we had to walk away and I could feel the skin on my back crawling.

The Argentines were irritated by a pedantic determination to record all the farm supplies commandeered by the Argentines. This, reasoned Eric, underlined that the locals were cooperating under duress. After the war this was interpreted by some journalists as profiteering, but even though everything taken from farm stocks was recorded and signed for in duplicate, the Argentines never paid their bills.

On 14 April, ten days after Goose Green's take over, the Argentine Air force flew in their first Pucara attack aircraft. The planes were twin turboprop ground attack machines, designed and built in Argentina.

Armed with machine guns, rocket pods and even napalm, the Pucaras were potent, especially against helicopters.

Day by day more troops and equipment arrived. The relatively small initial garrison was multiplied almost tenfold by men of the 12th and 25th Infantry Regiments, a battery of anti-aircraft artillery, engineers and helicopter crews. Air Force personnel took the Argentine presence to around 1,500 men.

The hugely augmented garrison came under the dual control of Lieutenant Colonel Piaggi for the Army and Wing Commander Wilson Pedrozo for the Air Force. The two were markedly different characters. Piaggi, of Italian descent, was big, completely bald and walked with a swagger. He liked to be called Kojak.

He needed, however, more than a macho stance. As the pressure on Goose Green was ratcheted up by the British, he found it difficult to cope and, according to Carlos Bloomer Reeve, he became unbalanced and suffered some kind of breakdown. The imprisonment of the civilians was his initiative.

Wilson Pedrozo, who was descended from English settlers in Argentina, was, on the other hand, controlled and urbane. He always wore leather gloves and a smart uniform, and he struck Brook Hardcastle as a 'stuck-up snob'. But he spoke English well and seemed more favourable to the local people than Piaggi. However, commanding the smaller Air Force detachment, he had less authority than his Army counterpart.

Civilians were in the way. They were ordered to black out their windows and troops visited all houses to confiscate the ubiquitous 2-metre radio transceivers. The blackouts became an obsession. Eric would often be disturbed by a knock on the door and told to accompany a squad of nervous soldiers as they visited a house from which a chink of light was showing.

They remained oddly reliant on and even respectful of the farm manager, which gave him scope for mischief. Often an English-speaking officer would ask him what the BBC World Service was reporting. When the Argentines surrendered on South Georgia, Eric gleefully informed the soldier of this:

I said, 'The Union Jack flies over South Georgia.'
'How did that happen?' he asked.
I said, 'Like this,' and I put my arms above my head. 'Surrender!'
He got in his Rover and was away. About an hour later a patrol of thirty or so came along and proceeded to confiscate every radio receiver, because the World Service news was demoralising their troops.

149

Both men, Piaggi and Wilson Pedrozo, had their work cut out. Piaggi, the army's man, planned and supervised the digging of trenches and bunkers and the laying of minefields, commandeering whatever civilian materials he needed. Wilson Pedrozo presided over the gradual build-up of fourteen Pucaras and their fuel and ammunition dumps.

For two weeks there was a generally peaceful, if tense, co-existence. Then on 1 May everything changed. Early that morning Stanley Airport was bombed by a lone Vulcan bomber. A few hours later Harriers from HMS *Hermes* and *Invincible* swept low over the runway dropping the much feared anti-personnel cluster bombs that the Argentines called *belugas* and insisted contravened the Geneva Convention.

Another group of three Harriers attacked Goose Green almost simultaneously. Seventeen-year-old Kevin Browning was visiting friends and was looking out their kitchen window towards the entrance to the harbour as the raid commenced. He could hardly believe what he saw.

> There were two black dots travelling very quickly and so low that they had to lift up to go over Darwin Boarding School. Then there was an almighty wallop as they hit the runways.

The Argentines had anticipated an attack and had moved helicopters onto the greens within the settlement. 20mm anti-aircraft guns were also on the highest state of alert and the 14 aircraft were dispersed around the grass runway, but it was not enough. The British planes laid waste to at least four Pucaras and killed seven air and ground crew. One pilot was taxiing for take-off when the Harriers unleashed their storm of fire. Pilot and aircraft were destroyed.

Housewife and mother Eileen Jaffray was terrified, as she made clear in a letter written to her mother.

> Our house was hit in the first attack, but luckily it was the conservatory and smashed most of the glass. I'd just got the boys downstairs as the Argies landed their helicopters right around the houses, so we thought something must be on. Gran and Ingrid were downstairs and still in bed. Next thing there was a God-almighty bang, the house felt like it was coming on top of us and you could hear glass breaking and stuff fell off the wall. It's something no one will ever forget.

The Argentines were furious. Later they would take some revenge on the Harriers, shooting one down over Goose Green and killing the pilot, Lieutenant Nick Taylor. Meanwhile, though, they lashed out at the local people who had goaded them with their sullen lack of co-operation. For some, the attack was proof that the locals had been passing vital intelligence to the British, probably using a hidden radio. It seemed too much of a coincidence that the new airbase should be bombed just a few days after the last aircraft flew in.

It was far more likely that the intelligence had been gathered by the SAS or the Royal Marines' Special Boat Service. There had been enough suspicious movements and odd lights in the Sound to indicate that they were around. Eric Goss had been called out one night to explain the lights. Although he suspected the truth, Eric managed to convince the Argentines that the flashes were a curious local phenomenon (that he invented on the spot): moonlight reflecting off seaweed-covered rocks at low tide.

Piaggi later claimed that the move he now took was to protect Islanders from the rage of air force men, who had lost so many colleagues. But few believed that. In any case their action was swift. Squads of Argentine soldiers surrounded every house in the settlement. Any semblance of courtesy had gone, replaced by barked orders: *"Out! out! out!"*

Entire families stood outside their homes, afraid to move, as the houses were searched for the non-existent radio. David Gray was among them:

We weren't sure what was going to happen. My little girl, Joanne, said to me, 'Daddy, are we going to be shot?'

I tried to reassure her, but when you're surrounded by men with guns pointing at you, you don't know. They were very nervous.

The little groups were moved at gunpoint to the hall in the centre of the settlement. They were joined from Darwin by Brook Hardcastle, his wife Eileen and Hooky and Iris Finlayson, who ran the house and gardens.

They were told they would be visited by Piaggi. They waited. And waited. There were 115 individuals; 72 adults and 43 children, including twenty-six refugees who had gone from the frying pan of Stanley into the fire of Goose Green.

When, after a few hours, no one, least of all Piaggi, had arrived to advise when they would be allowed home, somebody tentatively tried the door. It opened, but an armed sentry brandished his weapon and slammed the door shut again. Then they really began to worry. Brook Hardcastle:

How could 115 exist in the hall? There was nothing to eat. There was a little bar there, so we weren't short of beer or whisky, but there were 32 children under the age of 15, there were two people who were over 80. And there was a young child there, Matthew McMullen, who was 3 months old. There were all sorts of problems appearing out of nowhere. There were no clean nappies for the baby. We had water, but nothing to eat. And there were no beds.

As far as Piaggi was concerned, they were out of sight and out of mind. His promise to meet them had been hollow. It was three days before any Argentine with authority visited them. During this time conditions were barely tolerable.

That first night people lay down to sleep on the floor as best they could. Some had managed to grab heavy coats as they were ordered out of their houses and they covered themselves with these. But apart from a few cushions that were given to the smallest children and to 'Nannies' McCallum and Ferguson and 'Bikey' Anderson, there was nothing to relieve the discomfort. One consolation was that the small oil stove functioned and there was an electric kettle. There was water and the two toilets were working. But for how long could these minimal facilities be maintained?

Initially the children saw their imprisonment as something of an adventure, but by the next morning even they were uncomfortable, hungry and upset. There was a small stock of sweets and chocolates in the bar and, as the second day passed, these were passed around.

Late in the day, with still no sign that anyone was concerned about them, some of the men peered from the windows of the hall and succeeded in attracting the attention of a few air force officers.

Willy Bowles, a refugee from Stanley, spoke some Spanish and, with Chilean-born shepherd Oscar Velasquez, he explained to the men that they had been locked up for some 24 hours with no food. The officers indicated they would help. They returned after dark, saying that permission had been obtained for just one person to leave to collect food. Brook Hardcastle had driven his Land Rover to the hall from Darwin, so he used it to collect the supplies. He drove the 50 yards to the store, where the air force officers indicated that he should hurry. He stumbled through the unlit building, grabbing whatever came to hand. Brook's shopping trolley dash netted little more than crackers, Spam and beans, and this was to be the only food the internees had for several days.

Brook convinced the Argentines that he should also collect as much bedding as possible. Some houses had not yet been taken over by the troops, and he entered these, grabbing as many blankets and pillows as possible. The final stop was the shearing shed, where fleecy sheep hides were pegged out to dry. They were smelly and greasy, but anything was better than another night on the floorboards. He stuffed them in the Land Rover too.

A few days later Keith Bailey was also able to make the dash to the store and eventually such visits became routine. The 'shopping' trips were always at night and in darkness. As a result Keith often came back to the hall with more of the hated beans and Spam. Fresh food was out of the question.

In spite of the discomfort and the diet, Willy Bowles remembered a positive spirit, and even a feeling of defiance.

There were some lads in the hall who would get worked up. But eventually even they calmed down, and in the end everyone agreed, 'We're all in this together, so let's face it together, and we'll get ourselves organised.'

The junior officers, who occasionally looked in, repeated the mantra that the locals had been locked up 'for their own protection'. The truth was, of course, that the Argentines were terrified of spies and fifth columnists. In any case, with the civilians out of the way, there were more houses for Argentines and there would be no more ridiculous duplicate invoice books waved every time they helped themselves to farm property.

Although there was no suggestion that the civilians were hostages to be used as bargaining chips or a shield, they were quite definitely imprisoned illegally. The Geneva Convention required the Argentines to send a list of the internees to a neutral authority, such as the International Committee of the Red Cross, but they made no such effort. They also ignored (or were ignorant of) the convention's requirements that occupiers interning civilians provide bedding, shelter, food, hygiene facilities, and separate quarters for men and women. Most worryingly, they had imprisoned the civilians in a building which was extremely vulnerable to attack, and this was clearly banned. Piaggi, Pedrozo and their men were ignoring the international rules of occupation and war in some style.

Falklands farming communities could never be described as egalitarian. Feudal was the word more often used to describe a system which was headed by the all powerful managers. Kevin Browning – a very junior member of the community – said the system that had existed outside was largely maintained in the hall. Brook Hardcastle and Eric Goss maintained their leadership roles without opposition. Kevin recalled:

The old pecking order prevailed, and in the camp in those days you did what you were told. There were some very intelligent people in that hall and they were not used because they didn't have the status. I cherished the moment when I realised the bosses had to be there with us. It was like Liverpool supporters finding themselves in the Manchester United end of the stadium.

As the days passed the prisoners took on responsibilities according to their skills and knowledge. Teacher Andy Clarke did his best to maintain some rudimentary classes. Spanish speakers Willy Bowles, Oscar Velasquez and Brook Hardcastle's daughter Janet established a working relationship with the guards.

Mechanic Mike Robson had been used to getting his hands dirty, which was fortunate, because he volunteered to keep the two horribly over-stressed toilets working. They backed-up frequently and Mike was considered a minor hero. Soldiers delivered drums of sea water for flushing toilets.

Kevin Browning did his bit to entertain. He blew the dust off a 16mm film projector and screened the only two films in the hall – again and again. One was the drama *Soldier Blue* and the other was a British-made black and white film from the 1950s. He quickly forgot its name, but the movie had a strongly patriotic soundtrack, and when the cast burst into Rule Britannia, he turned the volume right up.

After ten days of the Islanders demanding to see either Pedrozo or Piaggi, a young Air Force officer, who spoke a little English, entered the hall and told Willy Bowles that he was "responsible for their morale and welfare".

This was Captain Sanchez, and Willy Bowles, gregarious as ever, struck up a useful relationship with the officer:

> I said, 'You're a bit late, old chap, but better late than never.' Sanchez was a gentleman. He was very worried about us. He obviously had children of his own and he said to me, 'We've got to get this thing sorted out.'
>
> I explained to him that we needed more food, and other supplies from the store. From then on it began to get easier. He used to call in every day and ask for me, so my rusty Spanish gradually got better.

Sanchez arranged for a few men to be let out occasionally to slaughter sheep and gather vegetables. Several women at a time would also be allowed to prepare food in the 'galley', the large kitchen where meals were normally prepared for the bunkhouse men.

Both women and men were strictly controlled. Nevertheless, spirits were lifted. The cooked fresh meat and vegetables made a huge difference.

Thanks to Sanchez, an Argentine doctor began making occasional visits. He seemed genuinely concerned about the health of the children and the three men and women in their eighties, who, like everyone else, were losing weight.

Eventually the two commanders of Goose Green visited. They lamely repeated that the Islanders were locked up for their own good. Piaggi, Willy Bowles recalled, seemed ambivalent, but Wilson Pedrozo was worried. They gave no indication that the internees would be released.

Everyone in the hall feared that water, power or fuel supplies might be cut off. Then the outlook would be grim indeed. Dave Gray requested and was given permission to refuel and maintain the generator each day, always under armed guard.

Designated the 'water man', Eric had the perfect pretext to leave the hall regularly. He would keep the supply of fresh water flowing to the hall, and, in return for this freedom, he agreed to help the Argentines maintain their own fresh water.

Actually, he did as much as he could to *damage* their supply. His favourite trick was to wait until his guard was enjoying a cigarette and a chat with another Argentine, then turn off the water supply to a house. It would be some time before the boilers in the peat stoves ran dry and were damaged beyond repair. House after house lost its hot water and heating.

The officers did not hesitate to take what they wanted from the store. They were especially fond of the stock of Mateus Rosé Portuguese wine. But when ordinary soldiers broke in they were outraged. Eric complained bitterly about one such theft, but soon wished he had ignored it. The alleged looters were arrested and the prisoners were ordered to the windows of the hall to witness summary justice. They were horrified as two scruffy and skinny soldiers, clearly malnourished, were dragged on to the green, badly beaten and forced to crawl past a line of tormentors who jabbed them with bayonets.

The BBC offered merciful, if brief, escape. Ray Robson and Bob McLeod, both keen amateur radio operators, cobbled together two broken radios to make one that worked. In the early evening the only batteries in the hall would be reverentially removed from Dolly Jaffray's torch and the young men would retreat to a quiet corner to tune into the BBC World Service. While they listened, a crowd of prisoners would talk loudly near the main entrance to conceal the crackle of the radio from the guards. Later Ray and Bob would pass on the latest news and any personal messages for the internees that had been broadcast on *Calling the Falklands*.

A welcome ritual was the nightly 'tot'. The rum, whisky and vodka in the tiny bar was rationed to one drink per adult a day. After that Brook would address the other prisoners in a school assembly-like meeting, telling them what Eric and the interpreters had been able to achieve that day and what information had been gathered. Finally he would lead them in a prayer.

Poor sanitation and diet were taking their toll, recalled Kevin Browning:

> Everyone smelled, and we were suffering from diarrhoea. You would turn up at the door of the toilet and there'd be a queue of seven just like you. Then the little kids would come though and they just had to go, and you let them. The toilet was often blocked and there was no toilet paper. The obsession with the toilet filled your life. And malnutrition was kicking in.

Regardless of the discomfort and suffering there were few arguments. The prisoners pulled together and generally got on well. Kevin Browning could not remember a single quarrel, although there were some people who hadn't talked to each other before the invasion, and they did not break their silence in the hall. Kevin attributed the general harmony to the women; one in particular:

> Eileen Jaffray always had a smile, and nothing was too much trouble for her. All the women were much stronger than the men. They held it together. They would be the ones who would calm any difficult situation, reminding us that nobody was bigger than anyone else in there. We were all hurting and there was enough trouble outside.

Throughout the occupation, Goose Green suffered attacks from air and sea. Naval bombardments took place at night, while Harriers could attack at almost any time during the day. The Argentines could do nothing about the warships but had some effective anti-aircraft artillery.

It was assumed that the British would not deliberately target the red-roofed civilian buildings, but a mobile radar had been located between two houses and that was a plum target. Even if the British missed the houses and the hall, panicking Argentines might spray bullets indiscriminately. It was obvious that a better shelter was needed and the Argentines were not going to provide it.

The prisoners lifted floorboards in the hall and excavated into the building's foundations. The 'bunkers' were effective, but dank and uncomfortable, so much so that some preferred to take their chances above ground. Nevertheless, when the Harriers zoomed in or the Royal Navy began their nocturnal shelling, the majority would rush for these holes.

The Argentines had noticed that Harrier attacks usually occurred when the runways were busy and were usually preceded by mysterious radio transmissions. Although the transmissions were almost certainly emanating from special forces in the area, the Argentines were convinced the locals were still spying and, somehow, transmitting.

Armed soldiers would burst into the hall at any time, conducting searches and head-counts. No one escaped the searches, including four-month-old Matthew McMullen. They would look in his nappy while the watching adults hoped Matthew had a special surprise for them.

The head counts could slip into dangerous farce. Brook Hardcastle remembered one such inept visit:

> People were told to step out of the hall one at a time, and as they did so, an officer was counting, '*Uno, dos, tres, quatro . . .*'.
>
> Then a couple of people went back in the hall before they had finished. June McMullen said *she* wasn't going outside with Matthew because it was too damn cold, and the whole thing became a shambles. The Argentines got extremely excited.
>
> Keith Bailey was giving one officer a bit of lip – we were getting a bit more brave by this time – and so the officer just cocked his rifle, and pointed it at him and said, 'Who do you think you are?'
>
> There were times when anybody could've got shot, because they didn't care two hoots for the value of life.

As a known amateur radio operator Bob McLeod was a prime suspect. The Argentines had found photos of Bob in Falkland Islands Defence Force uniform and this seemed to prove that he was spying. One night a squad of belligerent Argentines arrived looking for him.

They liaised, as usual, with Willy Bowles, whom they seemed to trust. "We've got a man in the hall who's a spy," said the senior officer. It took Willy almost an hour to convince them that Bob had been in the hall with everyone else for weeks and, anyway, they had confiscated his transmitter soon after they arrived. The soldiers were eventually convinced, but they left warning that "war is war" and "spies are shot".

Local legend has it that every civilian at Goose Green was imprisoned for the entire month of May. In fact a few were released two weeks before the settlement was liberated.

Brook Hardcastle deliberately played on the Argentine officers' sense of snobbery, pointing out that it was not right for he and his wife to be confined to the same squalid living space as the staff. Eventually the Argentines accepted this and the Hardcastles and Gosses were back in their houses by 15 May. A few days later Brooke negotiated the release of his domestic staff, Hooky and Iris Finlayson.

Arguably, Brook did indeed think that he should not be living in such squalor. But his release served a useful purpose. Immediately after leaving the hall, he drove the five miles or so to Burntside shepherd's house where Kay and Gerald Morrison had remained undisturbed. Brook found that the telephone line between Burntside and Fitzroy was still working and he immediately called Ronnie Binnie to tell him what had been going on. He appealed for help and Ronnie said he would get word to Stanley.

Ronnie discussed the matter with Diane and Kevin Kilmartin at nearby Bluff Cove farm, and Diane penned a note to Terry Spruce at the Falkland Islands Company offices in Stanley. A few bold locals had Argentine passes allowing them to make occasional journeys between the town and Bluff Cove. The next time a driver came through Diane passed him the letter. It said:

At present we are safe and have no resident troops.

Ron spoke to Brook Hardcastle on the phone this morning, and he gave Ron the following information: since 1 May 115 people were confined in the hall at Goose Green. Brook was released yesterday, but the others are still confined. Everyone confined has kept well, but all have weight loss. Houses have been looted and foodstuffs stolen. Brook asks for a shipment of general stores as soon as possible please! All telephone lines have been cut.

Farm is a complete shambles, dead carcasses everywhere. Cows have been blown up by mines. All fences in a bad state.

Hundreds of Argentine soldiers are dug in on the Bluff. Rockets are mounted on tractors, and there are very good anti-aircraft guns.

Terry Spruce felt this was a case for Monsignor Daniel Spraggon, who had the ear of the high command. Together they went to see Carlos Bloomer Reeve and told him that something had to be done. The

Argentine agreed and said he would send an envoy to Goose Green to liaise with the locals and their captors. He seemed to hope that fellow air force officer Wilson Pedrozo, at least, could be persuaded to release the internees.

The chain of events becomes foggy, but it seems he or General Menendez instructed that two officers should make the dangerous journey to Goose Green and urge the commanders to moderate their regime. Around 18 May a Colonel Shermino made the helicopter journey from Stanley and a Captain Rello flew in from Port Howard on West Falkland, where there had been much less friction between locals and Argentines.

Under pressure, Piaggi and Wilson Pedrozo agreed to start a dialogue with the internees. Willy Bowles and Eric Goss were approached and asked to meet the Argentines at the galley.

Eric Goss told them exactly what could be done to relieve the situation:

> I said, 'If you want to build a better relationship, get your troops out of our houses and let our people move out of the hall.'
>
> 'Oh no,' I was told. 'You are in the hall for safety.'
>
> I said, 'We are not! I have seen five aircraft shot down around here. If one of them happened to hit the hall, we are all blooming fried. Let us disperse around the settlement. It doesn't matter what happens then. Some of us will survive.'

The pressure seemed to be having some effect. The locals were told that six houses could be released, but when Eric and Willy visited the homes they found that just three were even remotely habitable; those belonging to Eric himself, the Anderson and the Gray families. The Argentines had wrecked the other homes. Plumbing systems had broken down (perhaps, in some cases, due to Eric's sabotage) and men had looted and rampaged through them.

In addition, the place had simply become unsafe. There were defensive trenches throughout the settlement, artillery pieces between houses and unexploded bombs, including the supremely lethal British cluster bombs, scattered in the grass. It was tempting to agree with the Argentines that it might, after all, be safer in the hall.

Nevertheless, on 18 May Willy and Eric took their families and one old lady, 'Nanny' McCallum, back to the Goss's house. They believed that, outside the hall, they could do more for those who were still imprisoned.

The Andersons cautiously moved back into their home with elderly 'Bikey' and the Lyse family from Stanley. The Grays gambled that they would be safer in the hall, but a single man, Denzil Clausen, said that he would move into their house.

For the vast majority of the prisoners, however, there was no choice. They remained under lock and key.

Both those within the hall and outside it worked on their defences. The floorboards were lifted in the Goss house and a shelter was created in the concrete and stone foundations. Emergency exits were excavated, but later, during the battle, these had to be barricaded to stop panicking Argentines from getting in. Nanny McCallum declined the invitation to try the bunker, preferring her own well-padded shelter between two large deep freezers.

There was time for a little negative propaganda. The Argentines had heard that the Gurkhas were heading for the war zone and they were curious about the little Nepalese warriors. Eric told them that the Gurkhas were indeed fearsome men. Willy remembered that they were susceptible to the old joke about the Gurkhas:

> Eric would say, 'When you wake up in the morning, just shake your head. If it falls off, the Gurkhas have been around.'

During that final ten days the intensity of air raids and bombardments increased. Despite the attacks, a few aircraft remained operational throughout and huge stocks of napalm were built up near the runway. Later it was revealed that General Menendez had banned the use of this horror weapon by Pucaras based in Stanley, but the renegade command at Goose Green had no such scruples and used napalm on the attacking Parachute Regiment, although it had little effect.

Surprisingly, the emissaries, Colonel Shermino and Captain Rello, remained, apparently still hoping to arrange the locals' release. It seems likely that tension was growing between them and their hosts, who were far more concerned about surviving British attacks than being nice to civilians. Certainly, Eric Goss could see that the two were highly nervous.

On 21 May the mediators attempted to organise a meeting with the internees. As Eric Goss accompanied them to the hall, the settlement outskirts came under heavy attack from ships in Falkland Sound. A series of shells landed nearby and the Argentines dived into a bunker, while Eric ran on towards the hall. Eventually they joined him there, but, amid the ongoing shelling, the two men were too nervous to address the Islanders. The last effort to resolve the situation achieved nothing.

On 28 May the 2nd Battalion of the Parachute Regiment began their attack on Darwin and Goose Green.

As they stormed through Darwin Brook Hardcastle looked through his kitchen window long enough to see a soldier lob a grenade into his unoccupied garden shed before pressing on through his garden in the direction of Goose Green.

In the centre of the main target the locals knew the climactic moment had arrived. Raymond Robson and Bob McLeod had, as usual, patched together their old transistor and heard the BBC World Service rashly report that the Paras were south of the mountains and heading in their direction.

The battle has been chronicled many times and there is no need to repeat the story here, except to say that the single battalion was severely outnumbered and outgunned. Seventeen Paras died in the attack, including their commanding officer, Lieutenant Colonel 'H' Jones, who was awarded the Victoria Cross for a suicidal but gloriously brave attack on a machine-gun post. The Argentines, outnumbering the Paras by about three to one, lost around fifty men.

It was a close-run thing and if the Argentines had shown more resolve they might have driven the British back. As it was, their surviving Pucara aircraft rained down machine-gun fire and even napalm. Anti-aircraft guns were lowered to their minimum elevation and raked cannon fire across the advancing British troops.

That much is well known. Not so well known is the role played by civilians in negotiating the Argentine surrender. The civilians in their bunkers had become exhausted by almost nineteen hours of combat raging around them. Eric Goss described the stress and the view as he briefly looked out of the house:

> The sheer noise just exhausted you. We had three howitzers firing by the wool shed, not fifty yards from our house and a 500-pound bomb exploded seventy-five yards away, shattering most of the windows. Star shells lit the place like daylight. The troops would see where they wanted to head for, then scurry through the darkness. When they were all in position again there would be another burst of star shells; it was amazing to watch.

Eventually, the deafening noise of heavy weapons being fired from Goose Green and mortars and small arms coming in had subsided somewhat. It seemed that the last line of Argentine defences were still holding and the British were pausing to regroup.

An Argentine officer dashed across the dangerous open ground to call Eric Goss to a meeting. The Argentines needed his help to establish a dialogue with their attackers and discuss a ceasefire. He was taken to the main HQ, where he found the senior Argentines. Eric:

They were all there. Even the representative of the Navy. There were 14 officers in that room and they wanted to make contact with the British forces.

'How close are they?' I asked. The answer was that they were between the school and us.

I said, 'Give me back my 2-metre radio.' So I was escorted upstairs, where they had this set. I tuned it to the local calling channel, switched it on and called out, 'Is anybody receiving this? It's Eric Goss in Goose Green wanting to make contact with anyone out there.'

Allan Miller [the farm manager] at Port San Carlos came right up, and he got a British officer.

When a British officer took the microphone from Allan Miller Eric told him that the Argentines would be waiting on the airstrip for a British delegation at 7.00 am the next day, the 29th. The message was acknowledged curtly and the officer said it would be relayed to the Paras.

The night passed in a truce that was broken only occasionally. Eric was escorted back to his family, but every hour the nervous Argentines summoned him back to the HQ where he would again call Allan Miller at Port San Carlos to check that the British had not imposed any changes to the plans. Invariably the British officer would use the contact to underline the need for surrender: "Call it quits, or we'll get really tough," was one message that Eric Goss had to pass on.

Denzil Clausen, who had moved into the Gray's house, came to wish that he had stayed with his friends. He had found a radio receiver and tried to tune in to the BBC World Service. As he spun the tuning dial, he picked up an amateur radio conversation. This was overheard by some Argentines who, convinced he was directing British fire, smashed their way into the house. They beat Denzil up, bound him and dragged him to a garage near the jetty, where he thought he was going to die.

They said the same thing again and again: 'You have a transmitter. You are transmitting to the task force.'

I said, 'No. It's not me.' But they wouldn't believe me. I was held there while the fighting was on. There were bullets coming through just above where I was lying.

There was one Argentinian fellow there to guard me, and he put a rifle to my head and I heard him cock it. I thought, 'Well, this is the end.' I knew he meant business, but, thank God, for some reason he didn't pull the trigger.

Eventually he was thrown back into the hall with the other internees.

Fearing that the airstrip meeting might only establish a truce for the collection of dead and wounded from the battlefield, Eric Goss decided he would write a formal note to Wilson Pedrozo appealing for a surrender that would save both Argentine and local lives. He handed it to the officer before the delegation left for the airstrip. He was unimpressed. Wilson Pedrozo had almost certainly decided to surrender anyway, but why give Eric Goss the pleasure of thinking he had given in to an Islander? Eric recalled the conversation that followed:

'It's none of your business, Goss, and anyway you are to come no further.'

I stood by the gate which led off the green. There had been an Argentine in a foxhole at the end of the gorse hedge. His helmet was out to one side and his entrails were hanging out. I thought he's not guarding anything now, that chap.

I watched these chaps walking up towards the flagpole. From the direction of the British lines there were two Argentine prisoners and a British Officer coming along with a white flag.

The surrender was negotiated by the flagpole on the airstrip and within a few hours approximately 1,400 Argentine men had thrown down their weapons and lined up to sing their national anthem in a final, pointless act of patriotism.

Eric Goss watched from a distance as the surrender was formalised and then he returned to the hall, where 100 people awaited freedom.

There was an outpouring of elation, gratitude and relief. But such was the mess of weaponry, unexploded ammunition and even dead bodies outside that few dared to leave the hall. Most of the small stock of spirits had been drunk in the nightly 'tot' ritual, but a few bottles had been saved to celebrate the liberation. Now, as the Paras arrived, civilians and soldiers swigged the liquor, laughed, shook hands and embraced.

It was not all over. When they returned to their homes they found that anything of value had been stolen; items with no value had been smashed and human excrement was smeared on walls and floors. More seriously, there were booby traps. Kevin Browning was about to remove urine-drenched blankets from his bed, when a soldier told him to stop and move away. There were two primed grenades in the bed. In another house a tempting can of Coca Cola was left on a table, its bottom removed and a grenade placed within, its pin removed. Even children's bikes were wired to grenades.

A few locals witnessed one of the final tragedies of Goose Green.

The day after the surrender some of the Argentine prisoners were put to work clearing an ammunition depot. The depot exploded killing one man outright and leaving another burning to death. The flames kept rescuers away and, in an act of mercy, a Para shot the soldier dead.

Kevin and a friend went to work clearing the corpses from the settlement and the paddocks. They tucked 9mm pistols into their belts and, helped by Argentine prisoners, loaded 39 bodies into their tractor and trailer, and took them to a shallow mass grave. Twenty-four years on, his feelings have mellowed, but then the job gave him some satisfaction:

> I was delighted to bury the fuckers at the time. I had developed this hatred over the weeks. The grave wasn't that deep and it was so full of water that the bodies floated.

There is a curious postscript. One of the envoys sent to sort out the friction between Islanders and occupiers was found dead at Goose Green. Electrician Dave Gray, who saw the body, recognised it as one of the two-man team, but could not say whether it was Colonel Shermino or Captain Rello. He had been shot in the back. Did one of the men who tried to help the locals so upset his compatriots that they killed him?

That is one question that the locals could have put to Piaggi or Wilson Pedrozo, had the Argentines not been evacuated immediately to a prison camp at San Carlos. They might also have asked them, "Was it all worth it?" But there could have been no adequate answers. In the end, the two months of occupation at Goose Green had been for nought.

The Argentines had simply shown themselves as stereotypical South American machos – men who were strong with the weak but weak with the strong.

Chapter Nine

Local Hero

Constable Anton Livermore was the sole surviving member of the Falkland Islands Police Force. He walked the streets of the town in his dark blue uniform and checkerboard-rimmed cap, a - reassuringly British icon among a sea of camouflage and olive-drab.

Apart from a small squad of Special Constables who had been recruited hastily on the eve of the invasion and turned out less frequently as they seized opportunities to leave Stanley, the 19-year-old was alone with the enemy.

Helping the odd drunk home after pub closing time and breaking up brawls at the Town Hall hops had been the standard fare pre-invasion. Now he now faced a far more demanding challenge, treading a narrow line between helping Islanders to cope with the stress of occupation, and liaising with the Argentine military police.

It was a dangerously ambiguous role. If he stepped too far in one direction he would be justly accused of collaboration. Defend his compatriots too openly and the Argentines would remove what little authority and influence he had.

The Police Chief, Ronnie Lamb, had been deported soon after the invasion and the only other full-time police officer, a young and inexperienced woman constable, had left voluntarily. Chief Secretary Dick Baker, whom the Argentines had allowed to remain in Stanley for ten days after the invasion, asked Anton to stay in uniform to defuse potentially serious clashes between locals and Argentines. And he had symbolic value: for many Islanders a uniformed British bobby would be a comforting reminder of old times.

Carlos Bloomer Reeve agreed and said the young man should not be expected to compromise his loyalties.

And so when the Argentine military police moved into the tiny station they found one bobby still there. A cautious relationship was established and as the weeks went by Anton came to appreciate that the Argentine military police were not all bad. One young MP in particular, the friendly and smiling Captain Romano, made life tolerable. Romano, clearly a disciple of Carlos Bloomer Reeve, was genuinely concerned about protecting Islanders from undisciplined soldiers.

The young captain would often check that civilians and their property were safe. Sometimes Anton would be called on to help with such work, and it seemed to him that this was justified: he was helping some Argentines but he was helping his own people too.

But Major Patricio Dowling was something else. As described in chapter five, Dowling was in charge of both the police and the intelligence cell for the first weeks of the occupation, but he concerned himself far more with intelligence than day-to-day police work. That was left to Romano and other junior officers. Dowling succeeded in scaring every Islander with whom he came into contact – including Anton Livermore.

He recalled being summoned to the secret policeman's office to discuss his new role:

Dowling said, 'You will collaborate with us!'

I said I'd help them, provided it helped us, and that was it. But there was no way that I was going to turn in my own kin. No way!

He told me my life story: who my family were, where I'd gone to school, the works. I had been pretending not to speak Spanish but he knew that I had spent two years at school in Argentina. He knew a lot about a lot of people.

Dowling hoped that once Livermore had been forced to compromise his principles, he would collaborate. With this in mind, Anton and one of the few remaining special constables were ordered to accompany a squad of troops on a mission to arrest Peter and Emily Short, both ham radio operators who Dowling wanted to interrogate. Riding roughshod over the agreement by which Anton worked at the station, Dowling told him that he *must not* come back without the Islanders.

Anton had heard that the couple were preparing to flee for the camp and he hoped desperately that they had done so. If they had left Stanley he could not be blamed for coming back to the station empty-handed. He recalled a tense few minutes at the Shorts' home:

I knocked on the door. No answer. Then I overheard the intelligence officer say to one of the conscripts, 'If they try anything funny, shoot them.'

166

We searched the house, knowing it was pointless, and headed back out. The guns were raised, pointing at us. I said, 'Look, they're not home. We'll look in the garage. If his Land Rover is not there, they've gone.' We persuaded them to look inside the garage and they saw the vehicle had gone. Sighs of relief! We all returned to the station. I had similar arguments with them many times.

The pressure was becoming intolerable, so, three weeks after the invasion, Anton Livermore approached Terry Peck and asked for help to end his relationship with the military police. Terry been elected to the Legislative Council the previous October and had once been Chief of Police. He had returned to the force as a special on the night of the invasion and had since been involved in his own intelligence work. Anton had also passed him snippets of information gleaned from overheard conversations and papers left on desks.

Terry discussed the issue with Monsignor Spraggon, who agreed that Livermore needed to be extricated. He, in turn, discussed it with Carlos Bloomer Reeve, and, as he did so often, the senior Argentine helped. The police and the intelligence cell were formally told that PC Livermore had been released from his duties.

As luck would have it, Livermore found a way of repaying Terry Peck's favour. Just before leaving the Police Station for the final time he overheard Dowling discussing Terry. The Argentines had dug a defensive trench in the Police Station's front garden and picked the same soft area of earth in which the police had buried their more sensitive files. Dowling had uncovered many documents signed by Terry Peck when he was Police Chief.

One of the Chief's secret duties (which Terry Peck found distasteful) was to observe and report on local political agitators, including councillors and the few Argentines who lived and worked in Stanley. The information was collated at Government House and may have been passed back to London. Seeing the personal dossiers, Dowling probably reasoned that if Peck was capable of spying on Argentines then he could do the same now.

As he cleared his desk Anton Livermore heard the Argentine discussing plans to find and arrest Terry Peck the following morning. Anton made his way as quickly as possible to Terry's home and said simply, "They're after you. Get lost!"

Terry Peck had been planning his departure from Stanley for some time. In his early 40s, he was a short, tough and gutsy maverick, with a reputation for acting first and asking questions afterwards. He'd been held hostage on the hijacked Argentine DC4 aircraft back in 1966 (see chapter one) and didn't relish the thought of being captured by them again. After the invasion, he reasoned, it was better to find out what he could about the Argentine forces and then throw in his lot with the British Army. He decided to bring his escape plan forward and would do so with the help of Pat Whitney, a government driver who had obtained permission from Bloomer Reeve to carry mail and supplies across the boggy terrain to the hamlets of the North Camp. Throughout the generally peaceful month of April Pat had shuttled to and fro. His service was appreciated greatly by the isolated farmers.

After telling Monsignor Spraggon that he was "thinning out for the hills", the ex-chief of police borrowed a semi-automatic pistol and a few hundred rounds of ammunition from his brother and hid them between the inner tube and tyre of a spare Land Rover wheel. Trumping up some reason why the wheel was needed, Pat was asked to carry it to Rincon Grande on his next North Camp run. Terry asked if he could ride along behind the Land Rover on a motorbike. Pat realised Terry was on the run and was pleased to help.

It was virtually the last chance for such an escape. As the Task Force approached, the Argentines were becoming stricter. Pat had already been told that he was to report to the Argentines and he believed that his pass was about to be withdrawn. He was taking no chances and after this trip he would remain in the camp.

There were two routes out of Stanley, the easier one north of the Two Sisters mountains and the other one south via Ponies Pass and across Mount Challenger. Pat knew that the Argentines maintained a checkpoint on one route or the other, but rarely on both. A short run to a vantage point south of town confirmed that there was no check-point at Ponies Pass.

Meanwhile, at the west end of Stanley, Terry Peck was 'liberating' a Suzuki motorbike from the garage of an expatriate who had fled the Islands. As he emerged from the garage he noticed a small convoy of Mercedes Benz jeeps passing west along the road. In the lead vehicle was Dowling. "He's going west," thought Terry, "so there's no way *I'm* going that way."

Then Pat Whitney arrived at the house in his Land Rover fitted with oversize tractor-grip wheels. "We can't go the Two Sisters way," he said.

"No," replied Terry. "I've already changed my mind about that."

Early on 21 April, the Queen's Birthday, Pat led the way out of town, his Land Rover loaded with food, mail and an extra wheel. Terry stopped briefly at the radio station where he slipped a note through the door. He had already told his grown-up children who lived in Stanley that he was going to be lying low for a while, but he had had no contact with one daughter, Christine, who lived on West Falkland. In his note he requested that Patrick Watts or one of the other local broadcasters play John Lennon's song *Imagine* for Christine.

He was quickly back astride the whining motorbike and racing to catch up with Pat. There was no checkpoint, but there were natural obstacles. The late autumn weather was saturating the camp. One stream was so swollen that the men had to carry the Suzuki across the torrent in the Land Rover.

There was no way of knowing whether the Argentines were aware that Terry had fled, or whether they were so determined to arrest him that they were on his trail. But he feared they might be. There were a worrying few minutes as the men crossed Mount Challenger when helicopters several miles to the south unleashed a hail of fire on an unseen target. Up there on the mountain the Land Rover and bike were painfully exposed. It seemed, however, that the gunships were enjoying some target practice and they soon flew on.

In the mountains the two men split up, Pat agreeing to drop off the spare wheel at Rincon Grande a few days later. He continued on his mail and food run, and Terry headed for Long Island Farm, the home of Neil and Glenda Watson.

North of Mount Kent there was a closer encounter with another Argentine helicopter. He forced himself to continue driving normally across the open countryside as the aircraft circled him until, eventually, it too flew off.

The Queen's Birthday is a public holiday in the Falklands and is usually marked with parades and parties. Anticipating that the locals might be provoked to protest against Argentine rule if the Queen was slighted, General Menendez cannily announced that respect would be paid to the monarch. There would be no parades, but it would be an optional holiday.

At Long Island farmhouse they needed no permission to celebrate. More than twenty North Camp farmers and refugees from Stanley were knocking back whisky and rum, toasting the Queen, when Terry Peck strode in. He gratefully accepted a whisky.

The partying Falklanders did not hear the first faint throb of a Puma helicopter. By the time the machine was swooping in and flaring for a landing it was too late even to think about making an escape. Within seconds the house was surrounded by troops. No one was sure whether Dowling was among them. Certainly the Watsons would have recognised him from his earlier visit to arrest the fugitive Marines. But perhaps he was taking a back seat this time.

Terry assumed that they were looking for him. Unable to come up with a better hiding place, he simply dodged into the bathroom, locked the door and sat on the toilet with his trousers undone. It seemed hopeless, but if they entered no one could look more innocent.

The Argentines searched houses often but badly. Now they idly looked into most of the ground floor rooms and checked the names of those in the Watsons' lounge, but did not even try the door of the toilet.

They left as quickly as they had come and within minutes the Islanders were behaving as if they had never been interrupted.

As Terry left the farm he enjoyed a fleeting vision of innocence that bolstered his determination to fight.

We had the second dram, and after that I left and headed for Green Patch. It was strange that day. There was absolutely beautiful bright sunshine and I remember some of the children were out on the sand beach, running through the breakers.

At Green Patch that evening he found that the locals and the dozen or so guests from Stanley were expecting him:

People had guessed I was on the run. Reputation travels ahead of you, and they put two and two together.

Some Royal Navy men from *Endurance* had been stationed there doing survey work before the invasion, and I was able to commandeer some of the warm gear they'd left behind, including a good pair of boots and two sleeping bags. Then I went out to the peat banks with Pete Gilding and Terry Betts and recovered some of the rations that they'd buried there.

I got my head down that night in the cookhouse where Pete and Jackie Gilding and their two girls, Sarah and Debbie, were living. I got up before daylight and got my Bergen packed intending to head on.

He remembered, though, that Lottie Williams, his elderly ex-mother-in-law, was on the farm, and leaving his kit at the bunkhouse he strode off to pay her a brief visit. This was a mistake:

I hadn't been there any more than five minutes when in flew this bloody Argie helicopter again. The same people got out of it and surrounded the place. All 25 or 30 of us were herded into Jock and June McPhee's house.

I was concerned because they started questioning people about where they'd come from, what they were doing on the farm and so on. Then they called me over.

First thing this Argie Officer said was, 'Have you got any weapons?'

I said, 'No, of course not.'

He asked me what I was doing there, and I said, 'I'm a travelling plumber and live in Stanley normally but I go out to the farms to help people with their plumbing and heating.' He was writing all this down.

Then there was great excitement. Some of his men started shouting and I thought 'What the hell's going on now?' So we looked out the back window and there was this little Argentine sergeant coming along carrying my bloody camouflage smock!

We learned later that Debbie or Sarah Gilding had seen my Bergen in the bunkhouse and pulled some of the contents out, including my smock. Jackie finally convinced them that all this stuff had been left behind by the sailors from *Endurance*. I breathed a sigh of relief when they didn't point the finger. I was very grateful to Jackie for covering for me.

After quite casually holding the people of Green Patch at gunpoint for an hour, the soldiers boarded the Puma again and it took off. It was still not clear whether they had been searching for anyone in particular. However, according to *La Gazeta Argentina*, the mimeographed Spanish news sheet produced for the troops in Stanley at about that time, the high command were convinced that British special forces had landed in advance of the main force. It is probable that they were searching for men who did not appear to be locals.

At the time Terry had a strange feeling that they knew who he was. He wondered if they were giving him enough rope to hang himself. If he did anything rash Dowling would have the excuse he needed to get rough.

As Terry Peck left for Rincon Grande, some 15 miles away, a dense fog descended on the North Camp. The fog hugged the moors and mountains on and off for several days. For a man on the run it was a blessing.

He arrived at Rincon Grande at dusk and left the motorbike about three miles away from the settlement before walking cautiously in. Pat had left the spare wheel and the weapon at the agreed location and, now armed, Terry sneaked into the single men's bunkhouse where a lone shepherd was sleeping soundly. An empty bottle was by his side. Judging by his experience over the last two days, associating too openly with people seemed to attract attention, so, after a few hours in a bunkhouse bed, he slipped away again before dawn. None of the residents knew he had been there.

Later that morning, from a promontory some three miles away, Terry watched as the Puma helicopter flew in to Rincon Grande for another search by Dowling's men.

He made for Geordie's Valley some three miles from the settlement, where, before the war, he had spent many days fishing. There were no buildings in the valley and no reason for the Argentines to check it out, but there was natural shelter from rocks and peat banks, fresh water and geese on a nearby pond that he might kill for food. He concealed his motorbike beneath the diddle-dee bushes and laid low.

The fugitive had achieved his initial aim. He was safely out of town, was armed, had transport and food. Thanks to the Navy, he even had some good weatherproof military clothing.

It had already been a dramatic adventure, but had Terry Peck read one Alistair McLean novel too many? Were the Argentines *really* after him? And would he have been in danger had he been arrested?

Carlos Bloomer Reeve said nineteen years later that he had not sanctioned Terry Peck's arrest and was not aware that anyone was searching for him. But he admitted he did not have total control over the intelligence officers and others who saw Islanders simply as the enemy.

Anton Livermore had definitely heard Dowling discussing plans to arrest Terry and, during his hunt for Bill Luxton, Dowling had already shown that he could chase his quarry across the Islands.

Terry Peck's worst fear was that he would be arrested by the hard-liners and "taken on a one-way helicopter trip over Berkeley Sound". Had he been captured, it would probably not have been that bad. Monsignor Spraggon or others would have appealed to Bloomer Reeve for help and the latter would probably have saved him from such summary punishment.

At the very least, however, Terry would have joined the seven other 'troublemakers', all prominent anti-Argentine activists, potential community leaders or key Defence Force members, who were imprisoned on West Falkland (see chapter 11).

But at that time no one could be sure of anything. By 25 April, four days after the Queen's Birthday, South Georgia had been attacked and retaken by British troops, and the mood among Argentine soldiers was becoming very dangerous.

Terry had visited three settlements in three days and on each occasion Argentine troops had swooped in close behind him. Now he decided to spend the coming days in the open, observing and waiting for news of the British.

Geordie's Valley was to be his home for ten tedious days. It was damp and chilly, but, thanks to the two Navy sleeping bags, it was tolerable. Just. His ration packs did not contain the usual solid fuel spirit cooker and lighting a smoky diddle-dee fire was dangerous. The cold rations became boring and barely generated enough energy to keep the cold at bay. Terry's spirits were being sapped away and eventually he decided to throw caution to the wind and light a morale-boosting fire.

> I'd just got this meal all cooked up when I turned and knocked the bloody lot over. I saved my mug of cocoa but the stew went all over the place.
>
> The old spirits had hit rock bottom. I had always hoped that I'd meet up with some special forces, but it hadn't happened.

Demoralised, Terry packed his meagre camp, abandoned the bike and began walking towards Brookfield Farm, the cluster of two houses and a shearing shed that was the home of Trudy McPhee. He desperately needed some sustenance and some warmth.

When he got near the homestead he realised that Brookfield's population had been swelled dramatically by families that had left Stanley for the presumed safety of the camp. An extra 16 people were living in the two houses and a small crowd of children were playing noisily on the green. He was unshaven, caked in dirt, wearing an odd assortment of military clothes and carrying a weapon. If the children saw him they would be terrified. And this time, if the Argentines were around, they would certainly not believe that he was a travelling plumber.

Trudy was preparing a meal in her kitchen with refugee Connie May, when she caught a glimpse of a bearded and filthy figure scuttling past the window. She recognised him:

> I said, 'That was Terry Peck! He just went past the window!' Sure enough he came in, looking a bit silly.
>
> He asked if we would mind giving him food each day, dropping it at different places. I said 'Sure, no problem,' but I didn't want the children to know because I felt it would be putting pressure on them.

Terry tucked back as much food as he could. When the children headed for the house, the women pushed him into the bathroom, and

173

he slipped through the window a few minutes later, still clutching bread and cheese.

Brookfield, Trudy and the refugees from Stanley were a godsend. He spent the next few weeks lying low during the day in the outlying fields, waiting for news of the British landings and planning mischief. One foggy day he walked to Green Patch and realigned the markers on the settlement's grass airstrip, hoping that any aircraft using it would crash.

At night he would sleep outside in the shelter of a sheep pen, in the sheds or, when the cold became too much, in the warm generator house, next to the engine. Sometimes, in the evenings, he would come into Trudy's house.

The Argentine helicopter tours of the North Camp were now infrequent and it seemed safer. Knowing that they had a fugitive in the area added some welcome spice to the lives of those at the farm. At times it was almost fun. The women insisted that their guest had a bath and a hair cut. He was soaped up and enjoying the luxury when the door opened and Trudy threw something across the room at him. It landed in the bath with a splash. "You forgot your rubber duck," she laughed. The rubber duck became a running joke and it was soon adopted as his code name.

The scrubbed and sweetly-smelling man must have been much more pleasant company, but there was an unpleasant pay-off. Back at his camp site, Terry prepared for the night:

> I pulled open my sleeping bags and thought, 'What the hell's this stink in here?' I shook them thinking some bloody animal had died in there, and then it dawned on me: these were my body smells lingering in the sleeping bags.

Gail Steen had left Stanley with her children and her husband Vernon (who would later play a remarkable part in the assault on Mount Longdon) and was now sheltering in the North Camp. Ingeniously, she forged a new identity for Terry. He had an Argentine 'white card' with him. Buenos Aires had issued the document in the 1970s when it was agreed that all travelling Islanders should carry them, in accordance with the despised Communications Agreement. Gail recalled how she doctored the card to change Terry Peck into 'Jerry Packer': "I altered Terry's white card using an old typewriter. His photo was taken and I remember making use of the pattern on his jumper to merge the rubber stamp on the corner." A liberal application of grease and a severe crumpling made the forgery look like a well-worn document. It might not have passed muster at an immigration desk, but an Argentine soldier could be fooled.

During the short days Terry would range as far as Green Patch settlement. Watching from the hill above one day, he saw Peter and Jackie Gilding and their two daughters leave their house. He could not resist the temptation of sneaking into their kitchen to brew a cup of tea. He should have known better: something always seemed to happen when he visited a North Camp hamlet. As he soaked up the warmth from the peat stove he heard the unmistakable sound of an approaching boat, its outboard engine screaming.

He looked out cautiously and recognised Neil Watson from Long Island Farm and one of his Stanley guests, Mike Luxton. They were friends of the Gildings and had motored up the coast to exchange gossip and information. Terry guessed that they would walk into the Gildings and make themselves at home. He hid and waited until they were sitting comfortably, before emerging with the panache of a pantomime villain. The effect was pleasing.

When peace was restored, the three men swapped information. Mike and Neil were fascinated by Terry's adventure and Terry was particularly interested in the Argentines, who he knew had a company or more of soldiers dug in on the hillside above Long Island Beach, an obviously good site for a British amphibious landing.

There is a local legend that treasure was buried on the beach in the 18th century, but now Terry wondered if there might be other valuables in the area. He was thinking of the Royal Marines who had surrendered there two days after the invasion:

> I said to Neil, 'Do you think the Marines would've hidden their weapons when they surrendered?'
> He said, 'I know exactly where they are.'
> So I said, 'Fine, can we get them sometime?'
> I made arrangements to join them at the farm the next day.

The weapons were buried in dunes at the southern end of the beach. The Long Island men routinely drove down there to collect water from a stream and, with Terry Peck wedged in the front seat of the Land Rover, they did so again. As the containers were filled, Neil indicated where he had helped the Marines to bury rifles, grenades and 66mm rocket launchers.

There was no sign of life in an Argentine observation post just 500 yards away, but what was the soldiers' routine? Did they man the OP at night? Terry volunteered to watch it that night and later, under cover of another water-collecting mission, he was dropped off in the dunes. With his mind more on the threat from the observation post, he slipped into a freezing stream. Soaked to the chest, he spent a miserable four hours establishing that the Argentines had abandoned the OP.

When Neil, Mike and Neil's 13-year-old son Paul returned to the beach, they found Terry cold and wet but confident that they would not be seen. Nevertheless, Argentine troops were certainly no more than a mile away and the job had to be done silently.

They were soon scraping away sand from the bundles of weaponry. Terry recalled that the stealth did not last:

> We were getting over this big dune when two of us fell arse over head with all the kit, which made a hell of a noise. But the Argentines didn't seem to hear us.
>
> We covered up our footsteps as much as we possibly could and got back to the farm.

Back at the house Neil pulled the wood panelling away from his kitchen chimney and the precious weapons were concealed there for the night. The next morning the cache was cleaned and checked over. Despite a month in the sand, it was in good condition.

Neil was gung-ho and wanted to put the kit to use that night. He'd been a sergeant in the Defence Force and knew one end of a self-loading rifle from the other. The tank-busting rockets were new to him, but they were throwaway weapons with printed instructions.

Terry was much more cautious. He knew that such an attack might be satisfying, but there was bound to be retaliation and there were two wives, four children and a grandmother at Long Island to consider. Instead Terry thought the kit should be kept for later, when, all going well, the men would be able to help regular troops with their advance on Stanley.

Soon afterwards, on 21 May, Isobel Short at Port San Carlos was heard on the 2-metre radio network making a guarded but highly significant comment. "We've just received a lot of friends," she said. Later the BBC confirmed that a major landing was under way at San Carlos Bay. Terry, now Rubber Duck to his friends, thanked the people of Long Island, left some of the ex-Marine weapons, borrowed Mike Luxton's motorbike and set off. He was now very well armed with grenades, 7.62 rifle, a pistol and ammunition.

On the way west he dropped by Brookfield and told Trudy and the others that he was on his way to meet the British. He was given a hand-held 2-metre radio transceiver and told to call when he met the British. He promised he would.

Terry Peck had the strength, determination and sheer guts to carry his mission through. Few others in the North Camp were able to commit themselves to such an extent, but they did what they could and Terry Peck never forgot them.

Apart from those who hosted him on the farms, there were people like Keith Whitney at Rincon Grande, who ferried Terry and the bike across Salvador Waters in his inflatable boat, ignoring the risk of being spotted by a patrolling Pucara aircraft. A boat would have been fair game for the Argentines.

Then there was 14-year-old Saul Pitaluga at Salvador.

Saul rode his own motorbike ahead of Terry, guiding him along the unfamiliar track to San Carlos. Eventually the youngster's clutch cable broke. He said a cheery goodbye to Terry and disappeared in the darkness, loudly crunching the bike's gears.

Abandoned and isolated Lorenzo House offered tempting but dangerous shelter. There was, however, no sign of Argentines, so Terry entered and lit the peat fire. As his clothes steamed and sleep threatened to overtake him, something strange happened. The telephone rang.

The few lines radiating across East Falkland from Stanley were shared and farmers on the same line were able to speak to each other without going through the Stanley exchange. Terry lifted the receiver and listened. Tony Heathman at the Estancia was talking to Adrian Newman at Douglas Station, not far from Lorenzo. They were talking in thinly veiled terms about Terry. Tony was trying to establish if 'Rubber Duck' was at Douglas.

They must have been amazed when the man himself came on the line. Adrian was able to say that a squad of Argentines had just rampaged through his settlement. They were retreating from San Carlos after shooting down two British helicopters and had locked up the locals for 24 hours before leaving in a stolen Land Rover, taking two local lads with them.

The next morning he motored the short distance to Elephant Beach House, another empty shepherd's house, and boldly cranked the handle of the telephone. In Port San Carlos Jimmy Ford picked up the phone. Terry asked him to tell the most senior British soldier he could find that he was coming in that morning. He was armed and looked about as dodgy as it was possible to be, but they were not to shoot him.

The Argentines could have been listening, but it hardly mattered now. He pressed on.

Coming over the ridge above Port San Carlos he saw what he had dreamed about for weeks. Long lines of British soldiers were marching inland from the beachhead. When he got a little closer he could see they were wearing the red and green berets of the Parachute Regiment and the Royal Marines. It was a moment of personal triumph:

I was riding through them! I was frantically waving to everybody and they were waving at me, because they'd had the message passed on to them, that this guy is friendly; no shooting him!

The next three days were a blur of debriefings. The intelligence officers of 3 Para were the first to grill Terry. They were heading where he had come from and every little bit of information was snapped up. He drew them maps of Argentine positions around Stanley and Long Island and described their weapons and equipment.

Every time he thought there might be a chance of a long, sound sleep he was taken to another Army unit to face more interviews. Again and again he recited his facts and figures. During one meeting he noticed prints of photographs he had secretly snapped soon after the invasion and sent back to Britain with a departing government contract officer. They had obviously found their way to the right people.

He was drawing a sketch map of Stanley on his second day at Port San Carlos when he was approached by the second in command of 3 Para. He recalled the conversation clearly:

In walked Major Roger Patton. He said, 'Terry, would you be willing to come and join us in the front line and act as a guide?'

I said, 'Nothing would please me more. The sooner I get to Stanley and the kids the better.'

So come daylight he and I flew in a Scout helicopter to Teal Inlet and then, after about an hour there, I was on the march with the battalion itself.

The goal was Estancia Farm. It was a long hike to the east and lay just a few miles from Stanley. The route would almost take Terry home, but before he would see his children again some obstacles had to be overcome; specifically several thousand enemy soldiers – and a rocky ridge called Mount Longdon.

Chapter Ten

The Fighting Farmers

Terry Peck's knowledge of the Argentine dispositions around the north camp, the routes to Stanley and the local people who could be called upon to help was indispensable. It was decided that he could be of most use attached to 3 Para's D Patrol Company, the 60-strong unit whose responsibility it was to move ahead, establishing the whereabouts of enemy forces and their defences.

The company had recently had an axe hanging over it. Many strategists, particularly those with one eye on savings, assumed that, in the days of aerial and satellite intelligence gathering, there was no need for dangerous foot patrols in enemy territory. The OC of the Patrol Company, Major Pat Butler, thought otherwise and he was determined that his 'old-fashioned' team would prove their value.

Pat Butler met Terry Peck at Teal Inlet and they immediately began planning Patrol Company's move forward to Estancia. This farm had already been identified as a staging point for 5 Infantry Brigade's attack on Stanley.

Patrol Company were to travel well ahead of the main force. Seeking as much speed as possible, they planned to follow the deeply indented and rocky beaches of Salvador Waters rather than cross the swampy moorland. Once in the target area, they would check out Estancia and the mountain of the same name, which rose to the east. This would need to be held if the farm was to be a safe base. Later, the patrols would reconnoitre the 'gap' between Mount Kent and Estancia Mountain, through which troops and traffic would later be funnelled.

Special Boat Service men moving in fast rigid raider boats would also be under Para control: when they reached Estancia it would be that group's responsibility to cover the northern approaches to the farm.

Patrol Company, with Pat Butler and Terry Peck in the lead, remained with the bulk of 3 Para as they marched out of Teal Inlet along an established track. At the large steel bridge which spanned the Malo River the sixty men of Patrol Company slipped away towards the coast.

It was dangerous work. Just a few days before, a patrol of Royal Marines arctic and mountain warfare troops had encountered a group of Argentine paratroops holed up in the nearby Top Malo House. There had been a ferocious firefight.

Pat Butler recalled that, although the Patrol Company was normally a rather cliquish 'club', Terry Peck mixed in easily. Terry had become something of a legend in a very short time and he inspired the company commander:

> I was pleased because we were aware by reputation what Terry's background was. The bloke had extracted himself out of Stanley, had made his way to Port San Carlos, and done his thing on the way. So there was no doubt that here was a man of some calibre.

Paras were not the only soldiers on the move that night. D Company watched the flying tracer and flares as the small Argentine garrison on Mount Kent, which overlooked Estancia, was driven off by men of G Squadron SAS.

A slight pre-dawn glow just made silhouettes of the horseshoe of mountains west of Stanley as the Patrol Company went to ground about two kilometres from Estancia.

Terry already knew that ten refugees from Stanley had moved into the house and were being cared for by Tony and Ailsa Heathman. But was there anyone there who might be unfriendly? He moved in cautiously with a patrol:

> I went up to the house. It was in pitch darkness and quite eerie. I knocked on a window and Tony Heathman immediately answered: 'Who the fuck's that?'
>
> I said, 'It's the Rubber Duck.' There were a few more choice words then: 'Just wait a minute. The fucking SAS have just finished shooting the place up. Now you bastards arrive.'

The Heathmans had been terrified when the SAS squad, apparently en route to Mount Kent, had pumped fire into the farmhouse 'just in case'. No one had been hurt, but the locals lay nervously waiting for another attack.

The weary Heathmans advised that there had been a fleeting visit by an Argentine Army helicopter only a few days before. And before that occasional bedraggled and lost soldiers turned up at the farm.

Tony usually directed them to their own men looking down from Mount Kent.

Ailsa had suspected that their farm would be taken over by the British, but she hardly anticipated a battalion and their support units – some 600 men. She recalled that they were overwhelmed by a scramble for shelter. Sometimes it bordered on the absurd:

D Company made a dive for the shearing shed. But they were quite promptly kicked out. So we put nine of them, a patrol, in our sitting room.

But later that night there was another knock on the door. There was a group of engineers standing outside. 'Have you got somewhere we can stay? We've got sleeping bags but we're wet.'

So we thought the only thing we could do was let them have the kitchen floor. We went to bed and shut the generator off. But D Company were going out on patrol at some unearthly hour of the morning. They got up and fell over all these engineers sleeping on the floor. There was quite a panic.

The soldiers would not accept assurances that water from springs and streams was safe to drink, even though it was discoloured. Falklanders had been quaffing it for generations without any illeffects. But British 'experts' had insisted that it contained liver fluke, and all water had to be treated. So the burden of transporting water was placed on a supply line that was already stretched to breaking point. The locals were amused to see that the troops associated plumbing with purity: they were happy to drink the water that came from the taps in the house, even though it was exactly the same untreated water that came out of the ground. The Heathmans did not let on.

Priority was for the four rifle companies to deploy onto Estancia Mountain with supplies, ammunition, mortars, anti-tank weaponry and as much other heavy weaponry as could be mustered. There they were to dig-in and maintain defences until the battle for Mount Longdon almost two weeks later.

Whereas the 'yomp' had until then had been across relatively flat, if soft, land, the route into the mountains was far more difficult. Getting the bulk of the battalion into position would be hard enough: keeping almost 400 men supplied with food, water and charged radio batteries, while also ferrying heavy mortar and anti-tank ammunition to forward depots, presented a huge challenge.

Helicopters could not be relied upon. Bravo November, the only Chinook to survive the Exocet attack on the *Atlantic Conveyor*, was dangerously overworked and Army Air Corps Scouts and Gazelles could carry tiny amounts. Larger Sea Kings and Wessex were generally busy at San Carlos.

Landing craft began shuttling supplies in from Teal Inlet, where the Paras' quartermaster was based, and a pair of Royal Marines Swedish-made 'BV' tracked vehicles were a boon. But it was not enough.

Terry Peck had the answer. The friends who had supported him during his weeks of rough living were just an hour or so's drive away. He suggested to Roger Patton that the locals had the tractors, trailers, Land Rovers and, above all, the cross-country driving skills to establish and maintain a supply line. The major grasped the idea enthusiastically and within minutes Terry was calling Trudy McPhee on the civilian 2-metre band.

Trudy receiving a message from Terry that, though short on words, was big on excitement:

> He was cagey. He just said, 'Rubber Duck here. Can you get as many drivers and vehicles together as you can and meet us at the Heathmans' as soon as possible?'

This was the moment the people of the North Camp had been waiting for. They had been powerless while the Argentines issued arbitrary orders and came and went from their farms and homes at will. But now the enemy was on the back foot. There was, at last, something important for them to do.

There were no tractors and trailers at tiny Brookfield, so at 04.00, well before dawn on 31 May, Trudy McPhee left for Green Patch settlement, about an hour's drive away. There she dropped into her parents house and told them that she was going to meet the Paras. Jock and June McPhee were worried, and they told her so. But Trudy had strong views.

> There was no way that I was going to miss this! To me, I was doing my bit for my country. And there was just no way I could sit at home.

Trudy collected all the useful vehicles in the settlement and eager volunteers to drive them. Then she drove on to nearby Port Louis and Johnson Harbour for more. She recalled that the response at Johnson Harbour was typical:

> People were really good about giving their vehicles. [The manager] Osmund Smith just said, 'Take it,' and handed over his

Land Rover. There was no guarantee that they'd get anything back.

In the remarkable wagon train that began to form and head slowly south-west there were drivers and vehicles from every farm in the area. Trudy was the undisputed leader, driving a Land Rover, and her partner, Roddy McKay, drove a powerful but old and incredibly noisy caterpillar tractor.

From Johnson Harbour came Bruce May and Claude Molkenbuhr; from Rincon Grande Keith Whitney; from Port Louis Trevor Browning and Andres Short; and from Green Patch came Raymond Newman, Pat Whitney, Maurice Davis, Terry Betts, Mike Carey and Pete Gilding.

Patrick 'Pappy' Minto and his brother Ally popped up from somewhere, and jumped at the chance to help; as did Jamie Bennison, an expatriate Briton who had been working as an advisor in the Government's Agriculture Department before the invasion.

Terence Phillips had forced him to leave his home at Mount Kent Farm, but now he welcomed the chance to – quite literally – get his own back.

The men at Long Island had also been awaiting such a chance and they were armed with the ex-Royal Marines rifles.

Most of the volunteers were driving some form of vehicle; a few 'rode shotgun,' relieving the drivers and ready to manhandle cargo.

At Green Patch Trudy's parents suffered nagging fears. June felt that the troops were trained for such danger, but the locals had no idea what they were getting into:

> I worried about them being shot. Jock said he could accept it because they went of their own free will. But what he couldn't accept was that Trudy was right out in the front.
>
> At night the firing of guns was something awful. You thought there must be hundreds of people being killed.

Standing on the low ridge behind the settlement, Jock realised that although heavy pockets of fog wreathed the area, there was nothing covert about the convoy heading for Estancia. He could hear the diesel engines and the empty trailers rattling continuously. Argentine Pucara aircraft based at Stanley were designed to attack such targets and, if the wagon train was detected, they probably would.

The motley caravan rolled through the Para defences and into Estancia less than twelve hours after Terry Peck sent out his radio message. They were welcomed enthusiastically and tasked almost immediately.

Over the next two weeks Major Roger Patton was to develop a profound respect for the resourcefulness, determination and downright courage of the Islanders, particularly Trudy. He said later:

I don't know how we would have managed without them.

It was something that we hadn't really thought through – how we were going to move this stuff around.

Trudy was the focal point. It needed someone to get a grip of it and she took it upon herself to do it.

The immediate task was to help move some 300 paratroops and specialist support up into their tactical positions on Estancia Mountain. The tractor teams were quickly loading men, rations, ammunition and water, and moving across the virtually trackless terrain.

The teams adopted a virtually round-the-clock rhythm, shuttling supplies and men the several miles to and from Estancia Mountain and establishing depots of mortar ammunition ready for the advance.

Men in the front line had a constant hunger for radio batteries. In the rush to depart the UK, the Paras had been equipped with Larkspur mobile radios, the batteries of which were designed to be recharged from armoured personnel carriers. But in the Falklands there were no APCs, so the Heathmans' generator was pressed into almost permanent use charging the power packs. Every day the local drivers delivered them to the outposts, bringing dead batteries back for recharging.

There were also journeys to the Paras' main depot at Teal Inlet. Although most supplies and equipment were being ferried up from the main depot by Royal Marines boats or by helicopter, very heavy loads of ammunition and fuel often had to be dragged overland.

From the start there was the possibility of an infantry counter-attack from Stanley and raids by marauding aircraft. Roger Patton had even feared that the Argentines might use gas. A precedent for unconventional warfare had already been set at Goose Green with the use of napalm. Towards the eastern end of the tractor-trailer teams' operating radius they came within range of Argentine artillery. It was rarely well aimed, but 155mm artillery shells would drop worryingly close to the supply line.

No one enjoyed special treatment and no one asked for it. The drivers and their crews slept in their vehicles or on thin mattresses in Army tents. Occasionally there might be a warm corner in the Heathmans' house, but they would compete for it with everyone else.

Roger Patton told them to dig trenches for their own protection and the civilians became accustomed to responding to the three loud whistles that indicated a possible air attack by jumping into their waterlogged holes. Most were false alarms, but a pair of Argentine Canberra bombers dropped bombs less than half a mile from the settlement.

When working on the mountain, the drivers would keep a weather eye on the helicopters. The aircraft would usually receive radio warning of impending air attack, which would send them swooping for the shelter of valleys. The drivers would take their cue, abandoning vehicles and diving into the diddle-dee.

Without the visual indicators, drivers caught out could be in for a worrying time. Roddy McKay's clanking museum piece of a tractor became a target for a Skyhawk. A bomb shook him and the vehicle, but the effect was deadened by the soft peaty earth.

Trevor Browning told of a narrow escape during a night mission to Teal Inlet. He, fellow driver Mike Carey and one soldier had been tasked to collect a load of petrol. Normally the civilians would not be armed, but on this occasion Mike Carey and Trevor Browning were given self-loading rifles. There was concern that some pockets of Argentines might have been overhauled in the advance.

With reasonable loads, the journey to and from Teal Inlet took six or seven hours, but a heavy load of drums and jerry cans on a timber sledge (sledges can be more practical than wheel trailers on soft peat-land) was a slow slog.

Fully loaded and moving cautiously through driving rain without lights, the men decided to take a break at an abandoned shepherd's house next to the Malo Bridge. Stopping was a little risky, showing the light of a field cooker even more so, but the attraction of a hot drink was too great. The men were in the shepherd's stables brewing tea when, as Trevor remembered it, all hell broke loose.

We were sitting there, pissing rain hammering on the shed, talking to one another, when all of a sudden it lit up like daylight!

There was this awful bang. The Argies were supposed to be bombing the Malo Bridge. They were miles off, but much too close to us. This Para said, 'I don't know where it's coming from but I'm getting the fuck out of here!'

As I was legging it for the tractor he was shouting, 'Look mate, you're sitting on a fucking bomb. If anything comes near you get off that thing and run!'

I said, 'You don't have to tell me twice.'

The days were long. Trudy would get her briefing in the morning from Roger Patton. One of Roger's fellow officers recalled that, such was her strength of character, that it was not always clear who was giving orders to whom. She would then distribute the tasks to the drivers and their mates. The trailers would be laden – often overladen – with food, heavy ammunition, water and men who were either heading back after a brief break at the farm or coming down for their spell of comfort.

If the troops asked how the locals managed to cross such hostile country with relative ease, while their own transport was nowhere to be seen, Pappy Minto would give them a quick master-class:

'Just put it in four-wheel drive with the differential lock on and give it welly. That's what they are built for! If you feel like the ground is getting soft, don't stop; just give it *more* welly. If it pulls out the other side, it pulls out. If it don't, get somebody to tow you out.'

But even the locals found the going hard. Pat Whitney was a master of the Falklands camp when in a Land Rover, but was less skilled with a tractor and trailer. He remembered pulling a trailer, packed with several dozen troops, up the side of the mountain. A wheel slipped into a rut, capsizing the trailer and tipping men and supplies into the mud. "Whose fucking side do you think you're on, mate?" snapped one angry soldier.

Sometimes the troops were their own worst enemy. Roger Patton was furious when Paras stripped the wooden sides off a bogged and temporarily abandoned trailer. By the time a rescue team returned the next morning the troops had burned the timber for warmth and the trailer was useless.

During the two weeks around Estancia the drivers kept their eyes open for Argentine kit and food, especially anything fresh that might brighten up the dull, constipation-inducing diet of army 'compo' rations. Abandoned positions offered opportunities for plunder. Neil Watson remembered finding one during a visit to a forward observation post.

We found bags of onions in this Argentine dugout. Real, fresh onions! And there was a motorbike, brand-spanking new. We thought we'll collect these goodies and go back. What we didn't realise was that we'd been seen from Mount Longdon – and it was daylight. Next thing shells started coming in very close.

I just flattened out on the ground. Pete Gilding had a bag of onions and Pat Whitney was trying to get the bike going. Pete stopped and said, 'Alright, you can have your fucking onions back!' Pat got the bike going, jumped on it and next thing he was gone!

It was possible to laugh about this later, but other searches for kit and food had no funny side. Pappy Minto was returning from a supply run with his brother Ally when they came across an Argentine Puma helicopter that had been shot down by a Harrier. They entered the burned-out aircraft.

> We were looking for weapons. But it was full of bodies. At first we didn't realise we were standing among charred bodies. It was only when we took a closer look that we saw what they were. It was a horrible thing, but it was something you accepted.

Those who put their formidable shoulders behind the Paras were resolute and strong. Some, like Pappy Minto, experienced and saw things that gave them nightmares for years afterwards, but none backed off from the danger. Terry Peck, no slouch himself in the courage stakes, did not hide his admiration:

> I'd never seen driving like it. I don't think anybody could ever better it. They were just an amazing bunch of people, they didn't glory in it, but they just couldn't do enough to help, and it was so appreciated by the guys in the regiment that I think the admiration they had will always remain with them.

3 Para originally expected to take little more than a breather at Estancia before moving on to their designated target, Mount Longdon. But it soon became clear that more time was needed. Little was known about the Argentine strength on the feature and casualties from an unprepared attack could have been very high.

Even if the Paras had been able to take the mountain in the first few days of June they would have had to hold it for far too long while other units caught up and secured adjacent features. The decision was made at Brigade level to hold fast at Estancia for the time being.

Pat Butler, OC Patrol company, was delighted. His specialists would be able to conduct deep patrols of the approaches to Mount Longdon and even penetrate the defended crags themselves. It was what the company had been trained to do.

Terry Peck was an obvious asset in this task, but so too was another local who had made his way to Estancia. Vernon Steen was an engineer with the Government Air Service and an NCO in the Defence Force. By FIDF standards he was a well-trained man. The Paras gave Vernon a rifle and a uniform, and he joined Terry in the Patrol Company.

Pat Butler recalled the company's *modus operandi* of his twelve standing patrol groups and the important role played by the two local fighters:

> We secured the sole use of Mount Longdon, which meant special forces and others stayed away, and we planned a very detailed close target recce operation. This means putting troops onto the objective and working out in as much detail as possible where the enemy is, what weapons he has, what protection he has in the form of minefields, wire and so on. It is very painstaking work and very dangerous.
>
> This operation was of such intensity that we had to run a system in which one patrol always had the opportunity to dry out and rest. We would have one patrol acting as an 'anchor' in an OP, reporting by day as well. At night a second patrol of four men would move forward onto Longdon.
>
> By night we would always have our men on the hill – that's where Terry and Vernon did their thing. We kept this going between the 1st and 10th of June.

Trudy McPhee specialised in using her Land Rover to support the patrols. She and other local drivers would form up with a convoy of six Land Rovers at around 4.30 pm, just as darkness was descending. Terry Peck or Vernon Steen and their regular soldier team mates would be loaded for a rough trip to their starting points just forward of the British lines. The driving was carried out in the dark and with no lights. To show a light would have drawn artillery fire and the drivers played safe by removing bulbs.

Roger Patton insisted that Trudy change her bright clothes for camouflaged Army fatigues. Otherwise, he told her, a sniper peering through a light-enhancing night-sight – and the Argentines had far more of these than the British – might see her as someone different and assume she was a commander; a perfect target.

Once at the drop-off point the drivers would wait for hours before the patrols returned. As Trudy recalled, the missions gave little chance to recharge personal batteries for the supply runs that still had to be carried out the following day.

> We always used to make sure we'd park underneath the peat banks, because every night around 11 o'clock the Argies would lob a few mortars in our direction. You would hear them whistling over. From whatever time we got them up there until they got back at about 2.00 am was the only time we really had

to sleep. By the time you got back to the Estancia, it was time to take rations up to the rifle companies.

It took guts to support these missions, but the patrols themselves were remarkably daring. As Pat Butler explained, they had to be:

> The whole purpose was to get a feel for the contact we would encounter. There were patrols actually counting people in their sleeping bags in their trenches. That is what we could achieve by stealth.
>
> At this stage there was a conflict of opinion about what we were facing. The view right the way back to London was that there was only a company on Longdon. We had been counting at least three times this number, so we were always of the opinion that we were going to attack a battalion – at least 700 men.

The demands of real operational work were new to most of the Patrol Company, but they had, at least, trained for the role. Terry Peck and Vernon Steen had no such luxury, and yet Terry Peck guided five patrols jointly with an NCO, and Vernon was at the head of slightly less. One or other of them was on the mountain most nights before the battle itself. Nineteen years on, Terry Peck looked back on his nights on Mt Longdon with a sense of awe:

> It was unreal. We would get as close as we possibly could get without spitting in their eye. We're talking tens of metres. Sometimes I got a bit nervy, particularly on moonlit nights.

In such circumstances mistakes were easy to make and Terry made one potentially serious one. He was patrolling with Corporal Pete Hadden when another group of men emerged from the gloom. A no-go corridor had been agreed to avoid blue-on-blue incidents, but Terry had led Hadden's group across it. Recognising the approaching patrol, Sergeant John Pettinger told his team to hold its fire. But Terry was not so cautious and fired several rifle rounds at the 'enemy'. Pettinger was furious:

> When we got back I had Pete Hadden by the throat, but it turned out it was Terry. He'd thought he'd seen some enemy. Which was fine, but I'm glad he didn't hit anything.

John Pettinger was, perhaps, the most daring patrol leader of all. With Private Dick Absalon, a 19-year-old sniper of uncanny accuracy, he virtually mingled with the enemy. The two would leave a machine-gun and radio team some 600 metres down the feature, ready to pour in fire if the Argentines detected the infiltrators. It was agreed that if the two men had not returned by 4.00 am they should be reported missing. This account from John Pettinger of his first penetration of the Argentine defences:

> We spent five hours up there, sometimes within touching distance of the enemy. Some were chatting away, sitting in holes, others were asleep. Suddenly we realised it was coming up to 4.00. When we realised this, we just put the rifles down by our side and sauntered off northwards. We turned west and when we had cleared the position and got through the minefield we ran like hell. We did that on three different nights.

The Argentines must have assumed that the men walking calmly across their arc of fire were their own. Who else would dare do it? On another night Pettinger and Absalon located a gully that took them straight into the Argentine defences. Unfortunately the enemy also used it. John Pettinger:

> There was human crap everywhere, so we proceeded up the gully very carefully. Then we saw the silhouette of a guy walking down towards us. We had practised what to do in such circumstances: as we couldn't afford to open fire, we would have to stab him in the throat and out through the windpipe. That way he wouldn't scream.
>
> A dig in the ribs was enough to say we need to do something about this, and we put our rifles down. Fortunately for him, he stopped about six feet away from us. He dropped his pants and had a crap right in front of us. It was the luckiest crap that guy ever had.

John Pettinger was awarded the Distinguished Conduct Medal for his daring patrols. Dickie Absalon was killed by a mortar blast the day after Longdon was captured. Pettinger reckoned that during the battle the young sniper killed more Argentines than any other soldier, often picking off men almost a kilometre away.

Mount Longdon was attacked on the night of 12 June. There was no softening-up artillery barrage, which would have warned of an impending attack. Silence was to be the watchword. To make sure no one went astray, Patrol Company NCOs and the two local guides were distributed among the other rifle companies.

For the first time the civilian drivers were to go beyond the Estancia Mountain, cross the Murrell River if possible and drive right up to the start line for the Paras' attack. Their trailers and Land Rovers, plus a few Royal Marines' Swedish-built tracked BVs, would be packed with mortar rounds, a medical unit and general supplies. The whole area was well within reach of Argentine artillery and mortars, and the forward zone would be within sniper range.

Roger Patton briefed Trudy and asked her to lead the caravan, walking ahead of the blacked-out vehicles when necessary. He gave her a pair of white gloves and told her to indicate left and right turnings with her hands. He also gave her a field dressing and a hypodermic loaded with morphine. If she was hit or stood on a mine, one jab from the needle would bring relief.

Despite the stress, the tension and his impatience, Roger recalled a few moments of contemplative chat with Trudy before the convoys moved out.

> I remember saying, 'This is a strange way to spend a Saturday night, isn't it?' The two of us were very much there together, and I think she would have come all the way to Mount Longdon, but I really could not take her all the way. With a degree of angst she obeyed her instructions.
>
> We got to Murrell Bridge and the Argentines were firing star shells. It was absolute chaos!

In spite of Trudy's forward scouting and her white-gloved signals, the going across the swampy ground to the east of Estancia Mountain and before the Murrell Bridge was appalling. Vehicle after vehicle became bogged and was abandoned. Three surviving civilian Land Rovers and the Marines' remarkable BVs were the sole survivors of the wagon train and they did their best to shuttle the cargoes from the stricken vehicles up to the front. But Roger Patton was right; it was chaos.

Eventually there was no movement at all and Trudy recalled that the Major was almost apoplectic.

> Roger came up to me and he got really shirty. 'Come on Trudy! Get this fucking lot moving! What's not out in five minutes can bloody well stay here.'
>
> So that's why so few of us actually got through. Loads of them got left behind.

Argentine artillery had zeroed in on the approach to Murrell Bridge. Trevor Browning recalled that he and the Para assigned to ride shotgun in his Land Rover had sunk their vehicle to its axles in mud and had been working hard to dig it out. It seemed they were about to succeed as the shells came in. Trevor:

> There was an awful thump alongside us. The Para shouted, '*Out! Out! Get down!*'
> The shells landed about 50 feet away and they were definitely aiming for us. There was nothing else around for them to aim at anyway. Eight or ten shells came in and we lay there for what seemed a long time but it was probably only about 15 minutes. I was down this hole that was half full of water, and I didn't even feel it. All I thought about was my family.

Once over the Murrell Bridge Trudy was given the sobering news that the land ahead might be mined or laid with trip wires. On the other hand the rising moon and clear sky meant the drivers of the surviving vehicles could see where they were going and Trudy was able to clamber back behind the wheel and make better time.

Roger Patton insisted that none of the civilians could go onto the slopes of Longdon, which would be swept with fire. He described the panorama as 'bare-arsed'. Trudy led the depleted supply train another kilometre to the north-west of the mountain to a treatment centre set up by the medical team. There the supplies were finally dropped.

The nine locals who made it to the Longdon were Trudy, Roddy McKay, Bruce May, Neil Watson, Claude Molkenbuhr, Pat Whitney, Pappy Minto, Mike Carey, Maurice Davis and Trevor Browning. Later they were asked to help at a helicopter landing pad, from where Scouts and Gazelles evacuated the wounded to Teal Inlet. There they remained for the rest of the night, comforting the badly injured men and helping them into the aircraft.

Trudy recalled that the wounded who arrived in the Marines' BVs were often dreadfully injured:

> The first casualty to arrive had been shot in the stomach and I could smell the burned flesh. He was hanging on to me and trying to say something. But he was too far gone. I was horrified. By the time he got to Teal he was dead.
> The next fellow to arrive had his leg blown off. Getting him out of the back of the BV was terrible. God! The screams!

Neil Watson remembered that during quieter periods the civilians and the troops would huddle low beneath peat banks, brew tea and talk. The pessimists and optimists vied with each other:

One guy was called Scotty Wilson. Scotty was really cheerful. He said, 'In two more days we'll be through to Stanley and on our way home.'

Another guy said, 'Or we'll be dead.'

Scotty got killed by artillery fire the next day on Mount Longdon. The other guy got injured.

I think that was the worst day of the war for me because I felt I was talking to men who were going to die. I knew it. That was a weird feeling.

By about 5.00 am, some seven hours after the fighting began, the flow of wounded to the helicopter landing zone had slowed and Roger Patton returned to advise the locals to move back towards the Estancia. He feared that with daylight Argentine mortars and artillery would become more effective. The team arrived back at the safety of the Estancia at about 7.00 as the first glow of dawn was lighting the horizon.

Trudy found herself unable to sleep. The farm house was almost empty now and she felt a sense of anti-climax. She remembered that it was her mother's birthday and decided to do what a lesser person would have done a long time before. She went home.

As 3 Para prepared for the battle Vernon Steen was assigned to B Company, but he continued to work closely with the patrolling team he had come to know well during the preceding days: Sergeant John Pettigrew, the talented sniper Private Dickie Absolon (who was to die the next day) and another private he later remembered only as 'Zip'. The four-man team used their special knowledge of the mountain to lead B Company to the start line.

Terry Peck and patrol commander Corporal Mark Brown did the same for A Company. Pugnacious as ever, Terry managed to have a 'bloody good slanging match' with his colleague when he insisted on pushing further ahead than Mark Brown thought was necessary. Apparently Terry won the argument because Brown retraced his steps and brought the rest of the Company forward.

As he did so, all hell broke loose. A soldier from B Company stood on a mine, waking the Argentines. It was a bitter blow. In ten days of patrolling along these very routes the patrols had not put a foot wrong. They thought they knew the minefields. Terry Peck had been cool and calculating until this point, but the firing that erupted shook him profoundly:

Our 'silent' attack went into the noisiest thing I've ever heard, and I still had that silly thought; 'This is supposed to be quiet!

193

Why is everybody screaming, shouting and making such a noise?'

The shooting coming from the mountain was bloody ferocious. It was so thick and heavy that if you put a finger up it would be taken off. Guys were falling by this time.

You lay down behind a tiny little bog of grass and you thought it was great cover, but all around was the noise of the grass being hit. The bullets were making funny noises hitting the ground. I was taking shit in the eyes and things like that.

Terry grappled with the same battle of will over instinct that every soldier faces under fire: somehow he had to force himself out from the meagre cover and continue to advance with A Company. He clutched his rifle, got to his feet and began running for the next available cover. By this time it was clear that his specialist skills in silent, subtle guiding had become redundant. As Terry ran, crawled and threw himself up the hill, men were dropping, dead or wounded. His memories were visceral:

There was the noise of men shouting and screaming. When you did go to ground you picked yourself up and thought, 'Come on let's go, get on your bloody feet and let's go!' That was the hard part.

There were guys on heavy machine guns without taking their fingers off the trigger. It just pounded out thousands of rounds, one after the other.

Communications had gone, so it was voices alone which kept these guys going. The Toms knew the voices of their corporals and sergeants but I didn't know them. It was total chaos.

I got so far up the side of the mountain and this guy was shot near me. All I heard was a grunt and he hit the deck. Somebody knelt down beside him and I remember him saying it was Steve Hope. This Aussie, Lieutenant Ian Moore, called for medics and I said, 'I'll give a hand to take him back down.' We knew he had a severe head wound.

We carried him down this slope, but sometimes we had to lie across him because of the fire that was coming in. We were catching it left, right and centre. It was lit up like Blackpool. Really horrendous. We got this guy down into a crater caused by a shell. We had eight wounded in that one hole with two medics, that's how big the hole was.

One of the medics was Chris Lovitt. I lost contact with Chris who went up on the mountain helping others and he was shot and killed that night.

Then I went back up the side of the mountain. A Company by now had been forced to the west because the north feature we were to take originally was too bloody steep and machine-gun fire was coming straight down it. So they detoured around the north-west corner of Longdon and made their way up onto the side.

I was asking where A Company was, and I was mentioning one or two guys by name, Mark Brown being one. Someone said, 'He's wounded.' I thought, 'Oh Jesus!'

B Company, which included Vernon Steen, had made it all the way to the first line of Argentine trenches before their cover was blown. They captured soldiers who were still in their sleeping bags. But from then on, as Major Pat Butler explained it, "they took a real hammering". He had a good overall feel for the battle:

They had more than we did. Basically they stood their ground and fought. You had Argentine artillery falling among the rocks, our own artillery falling a little further away, and lots of tracer flying around. They also had their French 120mm heavy mortars delivering quite a lot of explosives into us from Wireless Ridge and Tumbledown.

Somewhere towards the top of the feature a young sergeant with B Company achieved immortality with an act of almost foolish bravery. Ian McKay led a section of men trying to break out from a position in which they had been pinned down. Ian McKay fell dead into the Argentine machine-gun nest, but not before the tenacious soldiers within had been killed. McKay was awarded a posthumous Victoria Cross.

After leading B Company to the battle, Vernon Steen and his colleagues were retasked by Pat Butler to the company's HQ element, under the command of Roger Patton.

As the watery winter sun came up, the Royal Navy bombardment that had supported the Paras ceased as the ships steamed back out to sea and away from the threat of shore-based artillery and Exocet missiles. But a worryingly accurate Argentine artillery bombardment from huge 155mm guns in the centre of Stanley and 105mm pack howitzers on Stanley racecourse continued.

Roger Patton assigned Vernon to guard prisoners at the west end of the mountain. Later he was tasked to help evacuate wounded POWs by helicopter to Teal Inlet, before returning to the Estancia to await further orders. To his regret, he was not called to the front line again.

Vernon is a modest and quiet man, and he rarely talks about that night on Longdon. But his regular army colleagues were in no doubt about the value of his work and Major Pat Butler spoke of both him and Terry Peck with respect. "They fought," he said simply.

Ten hours after going in with A Company Terry Peck was still on the mountain, stunned, like every other survivor of both sides, at the ferocity and the brutality of the fighting:

> The next morning the smell, the carnage. . . it was unreal. There were bodies everywhere. Then you got the reports coming in about who had been killed.

The Argentines had fought hard and well with the benefit of the natural fortifications of a craggy peak. Arguably, better troops would have held the feature, but 7 Infantry Battalion had no reason to be ashamed of their performance.

It is not clear how many Argentines died on Longdon, but the Paras suffered eighteen dead on the night of the attack and a further five as the Argentines lobbed in artillery shells the next day. Pat Butler recalled a stunned and slightly unreal mood among the men as the sun came up on the 13th. Forgetting the dangers, the men began gathering in a highly untactical fashion in a hollow on the north side of the summit.

> It was very quiet, and you could feel the tension go. It was just like listening to 1,000 birds start chirping. At this stage Two Sisters was being fought over still and Tumbledown was still in enemy hands, and people had forgotten that the Argentines could call fire down or we could be counter-attacked. So there was a change of batteries and they were all switched back on again.

Terry Peck remained on the summit with the rest of battalion for a further 24 hours. The only food left was toffees and whatever could be found in the Argentine trenches. They sheltered from the artillery shells among the rocks of the summit and looked down on the epicentre of this war, tiny Stanley. It looked as benign as *The Archers'* Ambridge, but at that moment it was as strategic as Berlin or Moscow.

A day after the surrender, Vernon Steen cadged a lift into Stanley aboard a helicopter. Landing on the racecourse, he walked into the trashed and stinking little town. Some days later, he made his way to the Government Air Service hangar and he saw what had been done to the little Beaver float planes that he had maintained up until the invasion. They lay in mangled heaps of metal on the hangar slip. The huge task of bringing Stanley back to life was just beginning. A few months later Vernon would receive a medal for his work with the Paras, but the real reward was having the Argentines out.

Terry Peck went home when 3 Para reached Stanley, but he visited his comrades daily in their camp in and around abandoned and shell-damaged houses. Pat Butler recalled that Terry reverted to being a peaceful, law-abiding citizen quickly. He was outraged when he found out that the Paras had broken a window to get into an abandoned house:

> He said, 'It's not on, it's not on!'
> I said, 'Look Terry, the boys have got no kit. We've got to get into the house.' We were not being vandals, we were just surviving. He saw the point.

Terry Peck was given honorary membership of the Parachute Regiment and, wearing a red beret and winged cap badge, he marched with the Battalion to a memorial service at Stanley's cathedral. Then he waved them off from the pier in Stanley as they boarded MV *Norland* for the long journey home.

Like many, perhaps all, veterans, his memories refused to fade.

> I don't suppose there's a single day goes by when I don't think of it for a few seconds or more. From my lounge window I can sit and watch Mount Longdon. Some days in the winter the sun reflects on the steel cross.

No one has ever quantified the value of the local assistance in the North Camp. It did not matter much then to the locals anyway. It was just the right thing to do. But twenty years on both Majors Patton and Butler (a retired full colonel and a still-serving lieutenant colonel respectively) know that they made a difference. Pat Butler:

> Without them the outcome would have been the same, but the time taken to achieve it and the loss of life would, quite possibly, have been much, much higher. I have nothing but the absolute deepest respect for them all.

But perhaps the greatest compliment comes from Roger Patton's simple acceptance of the locals as members of his team, who were simply doing their job:

> You treated them as equals. They were willing volunteers and we willingly accepted their offers of help. We were all in it together. There was nothing special about them; nothing special about us. We had a job to do and I think we did it pretty well.

Chapter Eleven

"In two hours you will be free"

About 500 people, less than half the peacetime population, were trapped in Stanley with the Argentines and they shared many of the same dangers.

The town's baptism of fire came on 1 May with the attack on the airport. It had been obvious that the British would try to stop blockade-running aircraft by destroying one end of the air-bridge. Bombing Argentina itself would have been an unacceptable escalation. Instead, the RAF launched a huge Vulcan bomber, armed with some 10 tonnes of bombs, against Stanley airport.

It was a truly impressive mission by a 1950s aircraft on the cusp of retirement. It involved a grotesquely complex Christmas tree formation of tanker aircraft, refuelling tanker aircraft, refuelling the bomber at the tip of the tree; all flying from Ascension Island. Operation Black Buck, as it was codenamed, remains the longest aerial bombing mission in history, and it undoubtedly delivered a loud message to the Argentines, just as it boosted the morale of the Islanders. But the bombs did not put Stanley airport out of action. Just one bomb landed squarely on the runway, and because it was towards one end of the tarmac strip, the skilled and brave Argentine Hercules transport pilots continued to fly in and out of Stanley.

However, 1 May was a shockingly ferocious first day of action. This, taken from one of Nap Bound's letters, is what it looked and sounded like to a civilian in Stanley:

> Our family had been sleeping on the floor of the *Upland Goose Hotel*. We were asleep at 4.30 am when a stick of 1,000-pound bombs was dropped on Stanley airport.
>
> You cannot imagine the shattering noise and the blast that followed. Still in our underclothes and shivering in the winter chill, we peeped out through the windows, but of course it was

black-dark and all that was visible were tardy flashes from the anti-aircraft defences, ineffectively chasing the bomber as it headed for home.

Four hours later the Harriers arrived and all hell was let loose at the airport again. By this time it was daylight and we were able to observe most of the action. The noise was terrific, as the bombs were followed by anti-aircraft guns firing from almost every battery, including the one about 100 yards from us by the telephone exchange.

I was standing at the front door of the *Goose* when an anti-aircraft missile came tearing down the harbour from the west. It travelled at three or four metres above the water for about a mile and then suddenly shot upwards at about 45 degrees. It was not possible to say whether it hit its target or not.

We could see flames and black smoke leaping skywards from the fuel depot just a few yards away from the airport building. The air over the airport was full of blazing flak. I only saw one Harrier but no doubt there were several others.

Things were quiet until about 3.30 pm when the naval bombardment of the airfield started. We could clearly see the shells bursting in plumes of black smoke all along the runway.

We did not feel in any particular danger as we watched this from the first floor of the *Goose*, until something exploded almost over our heads. As you know, the writer's wife is not altogether built for speed, but in an open contest to get back down to the ground floor she led the field by a comfortable four lengths, with me coming an easy second from several teenagers.

Later we heard exactly what had happened. An Argentine Mirage fighter had passed low over Stanley apparently on its way out to attack the fleet, when it was mistaken for a British Harrier. The battery opened up and scored a direct hit and the plane exploded in mid-air.

As Harriers from *Hermes* and *Invincible* pounded the airport area, others attacked the enemy airbase at Goose Green.

The fact that men were now dying was driven home to Christopher Harris, a young carpenter in the Public Works Department. He and his colleagues had avoided most Argentine work, but after the Stanley raids an Argentine arrived with a request they could not reasonably refuse:

He asked us to make crosses for the graves of their guys. The first one we did was for the Mirage pilot who got shot down over Stanley. We made a cross out of a good piece of three-by-three.

We varnished it and someone made a good job of putting the name on it.

When one of them came in to collect it, he said, 'Now you've got to work out a way to mass produce these, because we're going to need hundreds of them.'

So from then on they were pretty basic.

The community grew closer. They watched out for each other and exchanged scraps of news and rumours if they met during the few hours that shops, Post Office or savings bank opened.

They wrestled with feelings of pity for the young conscripts who often suffered the downright inhumanity of their superiors. Christopher Harris and his fellow carpenters watched, horrified, as a conscript was kicked unconscious for accepting a cigarette from them. The NCO concerned then showed them a phosphorous grenade and told they might learn about its effect on human flesh if they continued to befriend conscripts.

Sympathetic as they were to the plight of the young men, no one could afford to watch conscripts stealing their food. Les Harris, Christopher's electrician father, experienced one theft too many. When his garden and poultry pen were raided, he complained bitterly to an officer. He did not expect such a severe response:

> We went back to the house and, sure enough, these soldiers were still there with bags full of our ducks and vegetables.
>
> They were wet and dirty and tiny. They could have only been about seventeen. They were made to walk down the hill and their knees were giving way on them. They were almost on their knees. If ever I felt sorry for anyone it was those two young lads.
>
> That day I said, 'I won't ever tell on any of these kids again.'
> It was heartbreaking.

Many of the professional soldiers showed clear contempt and hostility for the locals. Some Islanders believed that there were mercenaries among the professionals.

Jill Harris ventured forth daily, shopping for her large family. During one such expedition she ran into these frightening men:

> I was in the Co-Op when special forces came rushing in and put us all against the wall. They were just turning the place over and old Bill Berntsen, who worked there, said, 'You can't come in here! There's a notice on the door saying no persons in uniform allowed in.'

201

One soldier spoke English with a German accent. He just pushed old Bill aside and said, 'You've got someone hiding in here,' and they went through to the storeroom.

There were Irish accents among them as well.

Mike Peake and Bill Roberts [both telephone engineers] were also lined up, and they said to me, 'You've got your kids at home, so we'll keep them occupied while you sneak out the door.'

They just started talking very loudly to the Argentines. Anyway I got out and I tried to walk away slowly to avoid attracting attention. It was the longest walk I have ever made.

I had my box of stores, although to this day I don't know if I paid for them.

The Harris's small stone cottage had been designated a DAP shelter, and every night during the hours of curfew, (originally 6.00 pm to 8.00 am, but soon brought forward to 4.00 pm) it was filled to capacity with eighteen other Stanley folk.

Jill remembered not so much tears and fears as laughter and anger:

We all had to be in the house before four o'clock when the black-outs went up. We would prepare a meal for the evening and that would take about two hours to serve.

The old folk were really good about telling us stories and Iola Burns always brought in a game or something for the children. She taught the little ones to tell the time and to play draughts. You could never beat Iola at draughts!

We got searched a number of times. The Argies would burst in with their alsatian dogs. They surrounded the house and pointed guns at all the windows.

One night they charged through the house stepping over sleeping children. One chap had a rifle slung across his back and got it jammed in a door. He was jerking around and panicking, and I started to laugh.

It was amazing what we found to laugh about.

The men who maintained the electricity and water services were local heroes. Located on the edge of Stanley, both power station and water filtration plant came under shellfire. But the men worked on believing that if they stayed at their posts Stanley's essential infrastructure would survive.

Having such responsibility gave them power. Les Harris, a senior electrician, and his colleague Bob Gilbert began interfering with the Argentines' power supply as much as possible. They replaced standard fuses at the electricity transformers around Stanley with lower tolerance fuses, concentrating particularly on transformers serving the main concentrations of troops, the Government Secretariat, Government House and the Town Hall. Locals were inconvenienced, but the electricians thought that, if they knew why, they would not mind. Les Harris described the scheme:

> Between six and eight every night these fuses went. It was guaranteed because the Argentines did all their cooking at that time and would overload the weakened fuses.
>
> They used to send guards to collect us. We'd go down to the transformer, say, 'Yes it's a fuse,' go up to the Power Station, get an even *lower* tolerance fuse, go back, and fit it. All this took time. This went on for about a week and then Colonel Dorrego called me in and demanded to know what was happening.
>
> I said, 'You're overloading the system. If you don't cut the load down it's going to blow up!'
>
> He believed me. He said, 'I'll give you a captain and you go around all our establishments and cut off anything that you think is using too much electricity. Cut the cables off!'

This was officially sanctioned sabotage! The electricians had *carte blanche* to go around the units, wielding wire cutters and rendering useless any appliances that took their eye. They even had an officer to defend them. Les Harris:

> The first things we went for were the cookers. Then their kettles. Some of the things cut off placed hardly any load on the system. Some soldiers would try to argue but the captain would step in, so *everything* went.

Denis Place, a stocky Yorkshireman who had been whiling away his last years before retirement on contract to the Falklands Government, led a team of plumbers and watch-keepers who kept a basic water supply flowing until the very last hours of the siege.

His assistant, Derek Rozee, explained that demand on the system had suddenly multiplied from 2,000 people to four or five times that number. Rationing was the only answer, and he and Denis made sure that the locals, not the Argentines, controlled this.

> The only places with permanent water were the two hospitals [military and civilian]. I had six valves at my end of Stanley and I'd close them down just before 6.00. Denis would do the same

203

at the west end. The reservoirs then had time to recover overnight.

We did get very, very short, but the general public recycled their water. When they'd had a bath, they would chuck their clothes in to wash them. Then they would use that water to flush the toilets.

When you met people on the street you would sometimes have to stand to windward because they weren't bathing much.

The occupation pulled us together. People would say, 'How are things, Derek? When are we getting cut off again? Time's getting on; almost curfew; better get home and fill the kettles up.'

And there was passive resistance. If we could be awkward, we would be. We didn't rush to help them. We would take our time.

Maintaining the flow of treated water from Moody Brook filtration plant to the reservoirs was dangerous work done by a small corps of local watch-keepers. The old Royal Marine barracks at Moody Brook, adjacent to the filtration plant, was now an Argentine base, and British Navy and Army artillery regularly targeted the complex. The cavernous water plant was hit by shells but continued to function.

There was no doubt that, without electricity and water, the suffering of ordinary Islanders would have been multiplied and such essential services as the hospital and volunteer fire brigade would be unable to function. "Our concern," said watch-keeper Charlie Coutts, "wasn't for the Argentines, it was for our own people."

In a letter posted without much hope that it would reach its destination, Nap Bound revealed a community that was under increasing pressure but holding together well:

The bombing of the Stanley area is now just accepted and nobody seems to worry much any more. The other day I was standing outside our front door when a Harrier unloaded two big ones on the installations they have on the Camber Ridge, opposite the town. I have never seen anything like the explosions. Mud, smoke and orange flames erupted skywards to some 400 feet and the blast shook the foundations of our building.

Shops open for only two hours in the mornings, and so far most of the essentials seem to be holding out. But with the amount of livestock being consumed by the invading troops we are threatened with a cut in the mutton supply.

We have been heartened by the news of the Pebble Island raid where our forces destroyed the air base they had constructed for their horrid little Pucaras. They are also based at Stanley airport, and almost daily we see them flying up the harbour at no more than 100 feet, often to the cheers of watching Argentine troops.

Our only reliable information comes from the BBC, although of course we also hear from A sources of the 'wonderful successes' achieved by their troops. There is a standard joke in Stanley: every time a single British Harrier passes over, someone remarks that 'they shot them both down!'

The Stanley garrison has been getting increasingly jumpy and it is not unusual to hear that a burst of machine-gun fire has riddled someone's house during the night. Every day new defences appear round Stanley.

The Royal Navy generally heralded its arrival off the coast at around 10.00 pm with a few dull 'thuds' from the 4.5 inch guns. Seconds later the same shells would land with a loud 'crump'. A few more ranging shots and the destroyers and frigates would begin pouring in shells.

As the nights passed, the explosions moved into the outskirts of Stanley and became far louder and more worrying. The Argentines had no defence against the naval guns and as the sun came up the shelling ceased and troops and civilians would emerge bleary-eyed.

A daring helicopter crew used the perceived safety of dawn to launch a missile attack. Their Wessex aircraft popped up from the Camber Ridge opposite Stanley and unleashed two wire-guided missiles at the Town Hall, where, it was believed, the commanders held a daily briefing. Almost every weapon in Stanley opened up as the Wessex crew coolly guided their missiles into the heart of the town.

In the *Upland Goose* the occupants ran to the main entrance. There they saw one missile wildly careering about the sky while the other was apparently heading straight for them. Passers-by had already thrown themselves into a ditch, but those gathered in the door watched transfixed. As the errant missile exploded over the harbour, the other sped on, missing the Town Hall by a few metres and ploughing into the police station, 150 metres from the hotel. A quarter of the front of the building and much of the roof were blown away.

The locals enjoyed seeing the venue of their arbitrary interrogations blown up. One officer was said to be killed. (Fortunately, this was not the friendly and humane policeman Captain Romano, who genuinely did his best to protect local property.)

A small team of Swiss Red Cross officials, who had arrived aboard an Argentine hospital ship, were deeply impressed. When the missile attack was followed almost immediately by a Harrier raid that narrowly missed the hospital ship, the alarmed officials made hasty preparations to leave.

Carlos Bloomer Reeve had time for little more than cursory discussions with the Red Cross team about measures that might be taken to protect civilians. Plans to shelter them in Christ Church Cathedral, the neutrality of which could be recognised by both sides, were not finalised and never put into practice. But the Red Cross later suggested otherwise and this may have led to a dangerous misunderstanding.

Those Islanders facing internal exile at Fox Bay were having no better time. With blockade-busting ships and boats busy at its jetty, the settlement was a prime target. The Argentine commanding officer, an engineer major, tolerated the prisoners, but found them a nuisance. Stuart Wallace recalled his 'welcome' lecture:

> He made it clear that he wasn't that keen on having us. He said he'd been killing communists for ten years and hoped he didn't have to kill us. It was memorable stuff!

The prisoners were housed with Richard and Grizelda Cockwell, who normally managed the farm. Most other Fox Bay folk had abandoned the settlement.

Brian Summers recalled a relatively relaxed regime at first, allowing the prisoners to dig vegetables and kill mutton. But there were limits. If they tried to go any further than the Cockwells' garden gate without permission warning shots might be fired. Brian described how conditions further deteriorated as the attacks began:

> The really sticky time was the day of the attack on Goose Green. We were all taken into the shearing shed, lined up and told not to cross a white line on the floor. I think had we attempted to cross it they probably would have shot us. They were very edgy and might have done something silly.
>
> They suspected that we were passing information and thoroughly searched the house. They found one of those big music centres and got extremely excited over that. Fortunately they didn't find the radios [receivers] we had hidden away.

Like Islanders elsewhere, the prisoners excavated a shelter in the foundations beneath their home, equipping their bunker with mattresses and food. When an attack began, there was a general scurry for the shelter. There the raids could to some extent be relished. Velma Malcolm:

Whilst it was a little alarming to hear the whistle of shots over the house, it was also exhilarating, and we tended to say, 'That's good, give them some more!' For the last 19 days we never undressed, and slept under the house every night.

When a naval shell crashed through the roof of the Cockwells' house, burying itself beneath the kitchen floor, the prisoners feared it was packed with explosives. Brian Summers leaned down into the hole in the floor and lifted the shell case out. There was huge relief: it was a star shell, filled only with a pyrotechnic compound to light up the night sky.

Desperately short of medical staff and equipment though they were, the Argentines would not allow the two civilian doctors among the prisoners to help. When the captives offered to amputate the limb of a soldier who had been severely wounded, they were turned down. However, judging by Brian Summers' description of the makeshift arrangements, the soldier would have been lucky to survive:

We were going to use disposable nappies as bandages, and Start Pilot [an ether-based product for starting reluctant diesel engines] as an anaesthetic. They [the Haines's] were going to use a hacksaw to actually amputate this guy's leg. But the Argentines wouldn't let them touch him. He eventually died.

In a visitors' book belonging to Tim and Sally Blake of Hill Cove is this entry written in a shaky hand: "Hector Hugo Luna, Nueve de Julio 778 31B." Added to this is in another hand is, "Shot down Argie pilot from Teal River East."

Hector Luna's story reveals that Falklanders did occasionally help the enemy, but only for the best humanitarian reasons.

Luna was one of the many Argentine pilots who flew with reckless courage into San Carlos Bay's cauldron of fire in late May. Like so many others, he had dodged between the mountains and plummeted to almost zero feet for a ride of terror across the Sound. Again like so many others, he had been met by a Harrier, which shot him down.

But, unlike most, he managed to eject safely, and, although suffering from a damaged knee, a broken collarbone and exposure, he hobbled the several miles from the wreck of his Skyhawk to the door of a shepherd's house. He was soon being driven to Hill Cove, where Sally Blake used her limited Spanish and the farm medical chest to treat him.

Sally consulted the doctors in Stanley during the morning medical hour. The broadcasts were always monitored by the Argentines, so they learned that Luna was safe.

The relationship warmed as the pilot realised he was being treated decently. But it cooled again the next day when nearby Dunnose Head settlement was bombed, seriously injuring the manager, Tim Miller, and destroying two houses. Later, the RAF explained that *they* had mistakenly bombed the farm, but the Blakes assumed their friends had been attacked by the Argentine Air Force and they were furious. Tim recalled that his wife fiercely scolded the only available Argentine:

Sally went storming into the bedroom where Hector was and said, 'Now look what you've done! There were women and kids in those houses and you bombed them!' She gave him a hard time. Poor old chap!

When the misunderstanding had been sorted out the farmers and their patient-prisoner became friends. 'Old Hector,' as he became known, was a curiosity and other people from Hill Cove came to see what the enemy looked like.

He told the Blakes that he had cheated death by ejecting from an aircraft twice before and had promised his wife that if he survived this mission he would consider it a sign that he was meant to live and give up the other threat to his health, cigarettes. He still had three Jockey Club filter-tips in a crumpled pack when he left Hill Cove aboard the Argentine helicopter that had come to collect him.

As he boarded the aircraft he told the Blakes, "When this is all over you must come and visit my home."

Sally answered, "I don't think we will be visiting for a while." They never found out whether he kept his pledge to stop smoking.

There is anecdotal evidence that Special Air Service or Boat Service soldiers may have infiltrated Stanley and other occupied settlements. Any such claims have to be treated with caution; locals trapped behind Argentine lines would have liked nothing more than to meet an undercover British soldier, and wish fulfilment might have a part to play in some stories. But British special forces are famously secretive, and if such missions did take place, there is no reason to assume that they would have been officially confirmed or denied in the years since.

Eric Goss, locked in the community hall at Goose Green with 115 other civilians, is convinced that the SAS actually entered his prison. "We had a visit by an SAS man," he insisted, continuing:

He came into the hall and walked around with his arms folded. He wasn't even in a combat jacket, and he looked in every room, but never spoke to anyone.

When he left, Les Billet said to me, 'We've had a visitor.'

I said, 'Yes, I've seen him. I'm not blind!'

'He's one of ours though,' said Les.

Les was an old Desert Rat and he'd recognised that this was some intelligence bloke.

We watched from a window as he went down towards the jetty and just melted into the crowd.

In Stanley, radio telephone operator Eileen Vidal, who had plenty of time on her hands since her service had been restricted to one hour of medical calls a day, believed she spotted an odd 'local' whom she was convinced could only be part of a special forces unit.

I was coming out of the Store and this chap was coming up the steps. I thought, 'Who the devil's he? He's a stranger.'

He was dressed in a parka. I stopped in my tracks when I saw him. He just gave me this grin, then he went on and I went on. I'm sure he was an SAS man. Definitely a stranger.

Reg Silvey, the covert radio operator whose story is told in chapter eight, may have encountered the same under-cover soldier. It may have been fanciful, but Reg had recently ceased his transmissions briefly because of a technical problem, and he wondered if the soldier had been tasked to check that he had not been arrested. He recalled:

I met him on Fitzroy Road. He came up to me and asked if there was a shop open where he could buy something. I said, 'There is, but you've only got about 15 minutes before curfew.'

He said, 'Well, I'd better get out of here then.'

He looked like a local, but he was as white as a sheet. He didn't have a wind tan, and he stood out like a sore thumb. I said to him, 'You're obviously not from here. You know you're not safe.' I asked him if he wanted to come back to my place. But he declined that. He claimed he was in a place on Davis Street, and he may have been in one of the abandoned houses.

Anyway, my family got word back that I was OK.

On Saunders and Keppel, both small islands off West Falkland inhabited by one or two families, special forces made themselves known to the locals. On Keppel there was a unique cooperation between them. Sam and Hay Miller had thought they were alone on the island. Unknown to the Millers, a Special Boat Service patrol, the elite of the Royal Marines, had been watching their house for days. Sam recalled what happened:

The kids were in the sitting room playing cards when suddenly the door opened and this blackened face wearing a green beret came round the corner. 'Pssst! Don't worry, we're Royal Marines.'

I thought, 'Well, God almighty!' Within ten minutes all four of them were inside and the rum was flowing.

Over the next few days, Sam's little sloop became, as he put it, "the smallest ship in the task force". With the SBS officer, he sailed it to Golding Island, close to the Argentine air base on Pebble Island. The officer clutched a shoulder-launched missile, which he planned to use against any nosey helicopter. The Hirtle family on Golding Island had been watching Pebble through binoculars and were able to tell the SBS man what they had seen. It was all very useful.

Back in Stanley, the Argentines searched for some means of picking out special forces from Islanders. On 25 May Radio Islas Malvinas told the citizens that all males between the ages of 16 and 65 were to be issued with ID cards. This was the pet project of army intelligence, a unit that Carlos Bloomer Reeve disliked intensely.

He doubted that the cards could be administered efficiently, and as they were to be produced on the Secretariat's simple letterpress equipment, alteration or forgery would be simple. Bloomer Reeve despised the scheme as much as he did the intelligence men who had conceived it. But he let it go ahead:

It was completely stupid, but somebody thought it was a good idea, and we didn't bother about it because it kept them busy. I never understand intelligence people. Not even Menendez understood them.

The cards, each with blank spaces for photograph, age, discerning features, languages spoken and place of birth, were duly printed and a group of earnest intelligence men toured Stanley listing all men and filling in the cards. A photographer was to follow taking the mug shots, but he never did. Without pictures, the cards were of even less use than Bloomer Reeve had anticipated and if British special forces were involved in nefarious work around Stanley, they continued unimpeded.

Amid the increasing disorder, Carlos Bloomer Reeve continued to walk a slippery tightrope, protecting Falklanders as best he could, while remaining a loyal Argentine air force officer.

An example of the potentially dangerous situations that he defused occurred at the FIC West Store. Stoutly built, central and well stocked with food, the supermarket was an attractive shelter and an increasing number of Stanley people began spending nights there.

Unfortunately, however, the Store had not been listed as an official DAP shelter. It was also one of the areas from which covert radio signals seemed to be emanating. When in early June a zealous nocturnal patrol called on the store and found it thronging with civilians they panicked. There could be any number of SAS or SBS among the locals.

The two dozen or so people inside were ordered outside and lined up facing a wall with arms outstretched. Somehow, word of the tense and dangerous situation reached Bloomer Reeve and he immediately made his way to the West Store. There he found a complete breakdown of communications and twitchy soldiers still levelling weapons against the locals. One of the civilians was the FIC's deputy manager, Terry Spruce:

> You were looking at the cracks in the side of the wall, and shivering. Bloomer Reeve asked me a few questions and I really went for him. He should have known I was looking after that area for the civil defence.

Bloomer Reeve told the nervous patrol that he knew the men and women to be bona fide locals. Furthermore, Terry Spruce had his authority to run the store as a shelter. The troops dispersed, and Bloomer Reeve shrugged off Terry Spruce's cross words.

When Dr Daniel Haines was shipped to Fox Bay Bloomer Reeve asked Dr Alison Bleaney to take his place. Alison had been taking a break from medicine to raise two infant children, but had kept in contact with the hospital in case she was needed.

The Bleaneys moved into the hospital, joining about 100 other civilians crammed into the wards and corridors. As well as patients there were the staff and their families and those who had been forced to abandon their homes. Even some cupboards were occupied at night by sleeping children.

Helped by Dr Mary Elphenstone, Alison had three key responsibilities: to handle the routine medical needs of the town, maintain the daily camp radio surgery, and prepare for whatever emergencies might lay ahead.

Barry Hussey became her closest ally. She and Mary met him every morning and if, as often happened, soldiers placed their weapons too close to the building they would summon him to confirm their authority and ensure that the troops backed off.

211

Little, however, could be done about the Argentine special forces who searched the hospital at around 3.00 am most nights. On each tiresome occasion, the civilians were forced to get out of their beds and be counted.

Three children were born in the KEMH during the occupation. When the daughter of Taff and Jackie Davies slipped into the world, nurse Alice Etheridge produced a Union Flag from beneath her overall and, holding it above Jackie, pronounced that, "No one in this hospital is going to be born under the Argentine flag".

Politics was not usually an issue between the local doctors and the Argentines who had been drafted in to work with them: regardless of nationality, they worked together on the wards and in the operating theatre.

The Argentine staff took it in turns to visit the front lines. Alison recalled that this took a heavy toll on them, particularly the likeable senior doctor, Mario Lazar.

> They would come back so upset about what was happening to the men that we had to *make* them eat and drink. Mario used to take food from the hospital to the front line. He would run the curfew and a couple of times he was shot at. He started drinking quite a bit and in the end he left on the Argentine hospital ship, because he could see what was happening and didn't want to be there.

When reports suggested that a child on West Falkland was suffering from appendicitis, Alison requested his evacuation to Stanley. A helicopter flight was approved and Alison volunteered to travel on it. Either Bloomer Reeve or Hussey – she did not recall which – insisted that this was out of the question as the flight would be too dangerous. According to Alison, they were right. The helicopter was hit by British fire and crashed before it reached West Falkland. [Several Islanders have questioned this account. They did not think the ill-fated medical mission had taken place, and suggested it could have been innocently confused with a successful Argentine mission to the North Camp, where young Allan Steen was suffering from appendicitis. That flight was carried out safely, and the boy received surgery in Stanley.]

Alison's infant daughter Emma unwittingly played her own part. When power to the RT station was cut off, making the camp radio clinic impossible, Hussey took the two women (and Emma) to Menendez where they could plead their case for power to be restored.

Mary did most of the arguing, but the general was not sympathetic. He lost his temper with her. Realising that desperate measures were needed, Alison pinched her baby hard. The loud argument was shattered by the infant's piercing yell, whereupon Alison released a breast and began feeding. This was too much for Menendez, who agreed to get the radio clinic back on the air. Anything to get rid of this troublesome trio.

If there was ever a night to soothe the nerves with whisky and Valium and pray for deliverance it was that of 11/12 June.

As civilians hunkered down behind the thickest walls they could find, small arms and artillery rattled and pounded out of the town itself and those peeking from their windows saw the sky illuminated with tracer, shells and flares.

Around midnight, the frigate HMS *Avenger* directed shells from its 4.5 inch gun into a civilian home. It is not clear why. Most probably the computer control systems had a calibration problem which the forward artillery observers in the hills to the north could not know about. But perhaps, as Carlos Bloomer Reeve believed, the ship was attempting to hit adjacent Sulivan House, where he, Hussey and a few other senior Argentines lived.

Whatever the reason, in the space of a few nightmare seconds two women were killed, another fatally injured, a child orphaned and two men widowed.

John and Veronica Fowler had opened their home to others who needed the protection of stout walls and the support of friends. The house was further from the centre of town than seemed desirable. But was there any safe place in Stanley? John had taken the extra precaution of building a shelter within his family's sleeping area and he had filled all the window embrasures with crates of earth.

Apart from the Fowlers and their two children, those in the house were Steve Whitley, the Government vet (whose gelding shears had been so useful for sabotage) and his wife Sue; Public Works surveyor Harry Bonner, his wife Doreen and their mentally handicapped daughter, Cheryl; and Laurie Goodwin and his elderly mother Mary.

On 11 June, in spite of the dreadful noise of fighting to the west, the families lay down to sleep.

John was woken a short time later by Steve, who told him a shell had landed in the front garden. Shrapnel had entered the house, but the bunker had deadened the sound so well that John had not heard it. Strangely (but these were strange times), all of the occupants other than the Fowler children and Cheryl gathered in the kitchen to make coffee. John felt very uneasy about this:

> I suggested that everybody moved further into the heart of the house. While people were doing that, I popped into the shelter to check on the kids.

I can't describe the sound but I can always hear it. You knew it was coming in. Fortunately for some of us, it was a shell which was set to explode above its target. I think if it had been a shell which had come into the house we would all have died. As it was, it was bad enough.

It exploded and Sue and Doreen Bonner were killed instantly. There was sufficient time for Doreen and Veronica to throw themselves on the ground at the end of Mary Goodwin's bed and to be lying there holding each other. To describe it as a noise is understating it. This tremendous compression just shook the whole house.

I threw myself on top of the children, thinking there was going to be another shell any moment and woke Rachel who said, 'Is this a bad day, Daddy?'

I knew Veronica was still alive as I could hear her shouting. And I could hear Steve shouting. At that stage I had no idea what had happened to anybody else.

When it was over, in the poor light and smoke and with the water pouring everywhere, Veronica said to Doreen, 'Come on, let's go.' But Doreen had died. Just like that: taken with a piece of shrapnel through her spine. She died without a sound, without a word. As did Sue.

Steve was badly injured, but survived. Veronica and John received minor shrapnel injuries, and Harry, Laurie and the Fowler children were unhurt. The saddest survivor of all was Cheryl. Doreen had dedicated her life to caring for her disabled daughter and now this good mother was dead. John Fowler checked on Cheryl: "I remember going along to her bedroom and there she was, as ever, just lying there singing or giggling or whatever she did."

Help arrived quickly from the neighbouring houses; Ron and Nidge Buckett (ever thinking of ways they could help others) from one side and Carlos Bloomer Reeve and Barry Hussey from the other. Water was pouring from ruptured pipes and electrical cables fizzed. But the telephone still worked. Someone called the hospital for help and then tried to persuade the stunned survivors that they must leave the house. John Fowler wanted only to crawl back into his cocoon-like shelter with his family.

Ambulance driver Brian Paul and a few nurses braved the curfew. John Fowler remembered that as he was helped down the path to the road Barry Hussey was speaking to him. John did not remember his precise words, but knew that he uttered something like, "First we took your home, now we are killing you."

This was more than an apology. It was also an expression of profound disillusionment with his country's great but foolish and doomed adventure. Later, in hospital, after Mary Goodwin had succumbed to her shrapnel injuries, John again spoke to an emotional and apologetic Barry Hussey.

I remember saying to him then, 'If that's how you feel why don't you go to Menendez and say, look, we are now beginning to cause the people, whom we are supposedly liberating, to die. Let's call it off.'

He said, 'If only it were that simple.'

The fabric of Stanley could not hold together for much longer, despite efforts by the electricians, water engineers and the fire brigade. The Argentines were drawing their artillery pieces closer to the centre of town and the incoming artillery fire was getting closer. Knowing of the tragedy at the Fowler home, few civilians continued to live in the outer areas of the town, and those who were still reluctant to move into the 'safe' DAP buildings were ordered into them. There were no more hits on houses that were occupied, but the fire brigade still braved the hot shrapnel to pour water onto abandoned civilian houses caught in the cross fire.

The part-time firemen, under the command of Neville Bennett, would often enter the houses to remove personal effects and even food – this was becoming a commodity for which it was worth taking risks.

Sometimes the non-combatant Argentines helped the firemen. On at least one occasion Bloomer Reeve himself worked to move a family's personal effects from a house that was threatened by a nearby blaze.

The noise from the shelling sometimes blunted one's judgement and senses. Jill Harris's son Christopher was a fireman and she recalled that during a lull in the artillery duel he and his colleagues made a dash to Wilfred Newman's house on Davis Street, which was ablaze.

While they were there the shells started landing again, and I thought, 'Oh no, Christopher is up there. I'd better go up the hill and tell them to get off the street' – as if they didn't know the shells were landing.

So I went up to Davis Street and the young Argentines living in the little old house at the top of our yard were telling me to get down. I said, 'No they're trying to get *you*, not me.'

I stood on the fence to look along the road to see if I could see

215

the fire engines, but they hadn't been hanging around. I was the only silly person standing up on the street as the shells were landing.

The images from those days are horrible, sad and frightening. One stays constantly with Christopher Harris:

> There was a boot with a foot in it sitting in the middle of the garden. It had obviously been blown off someone on Davis Street. At the time it seemed perfectly acceptable to find a foot in a boot. But looking back on it was a horrendous thing. And some of the other things . . . the bodies I saw lying around.

Mains water pipes had been ruptured in the fighting and the supply was contaminated with sewage. Diarrhoea was common and the hospital staff put word around that all drinking water must be boiled.

At the filtration plant Charlie Coutts remembered the young Argentines shouting for him to dive into their slit trenches when the Navy's 4.5 inch guns opened up. Sometimes there was not enough time to reach the trench. On one such occasion Charlie was close behind the sergeant of the guard unit as he opened the outside door, heading for the trenches. As he did so a shell burst, sending shrapnel into the sergeant.

It was a similar story at the Power Station, where the Superintendent, Ted Carey, led the watch-keepers and engineers. He recalled a hellish night:

> I was stuck there more or less under constant fire. The shrapnel was coming through the wall, one took a piece out of the side of my pants; another went over my head into the switchboard.
>
> Outside by the engine radiators there were six Argentine soldiers getting some warmth. A shell dropped, knocking my high tension cables down and killing them all. Six of them.
>
> I had to go out. There were bodies and blood all over the place.

He was, however, still determined to care for his station. Ted argued with the stressed head of the Public Works Department, Colonel Manuel Dorrego, that the generators should not be put under the direct control of soldiers, as the Argentine now proposed. Ted was convinced they would only destroy what was left of the system. He searched out Carlos Bloomer Reeve and asked him to talk to Dorrego. Bloomer Reeve, weary and anticipating the inevitable, was frank:

216

"Ted, I will have a word about it, but just carry on, because we won't be here that much longer."

On the night of 13 June the battle for Stanley reached a terrifying climax. In the mountains the missiles, aircraft and artillery of long-distance killing had given way to bayonets and bullets.

The shelling, both from the sea and the Royal Artillery, was bad enough, but what locals feared far more was the chaos that would ensue when the Argentine Army was routed and flooded back into Stanley. Would they make a stand and force the British troops to winkle them out house by house? Perhaps, with a collapse of order, the troops could embark on a spree of atrocities.

Before sunrise on 14 June Carlos Bloomer Reeve, dressed in his air force overcoat and blue-grey peaked cap, gathered the colleagues who had been sheltering with him at Sulivan House and told them that they must move to a safer area. The men made their way through the town, which was illuminated only by exploding shells, towards the *Upland Goose Hotel*, where they were to collect junior members of their administration. It was an icy night and the town's sordid and sad appearance was partly concealed by a little snow.

The ground floor lounge of the *Upland Goose* was littered with the restless bodies of local people, among them the author. All were fighting the fear that returned with every explosion. Bloomer Reeve opened the door of the lounge and from the gloom a voice nervously asked who it was. The reply: "Don't worry. It's me, Bloomer Reeve."

He was not particularly tall, but, dimly silhouetted and viewed from the ground, he seemed to fill the doorframe.

For someone who had loved the Islands, respected the people who lived there, and had done his best to protect them, it was a supremely emotional moment. Nevertheless, Bloomer Reeve was surprised when a woman stepped forward to kiss him and wish him luck. There were, said someone who was there, tears on his face.

Another person said, "You have to surrender!"

"That is not my decision, but our troops are retreating," he said. And then an unforgettable phrase: "In two hours you will be free."

The group of men slipped into the night to destroy cipher equipment at their communications centre and collect more officers.

As the sun came up the dejected remains of the Argentine Army was obvious. Those who had been routed from the mountains were moving to the east, through Stanley. Makeshift ambulances drove slowly through the columns lining the road, and some soldiers helped their staggering comrades to keep moving. Among the wounded, a soldier – it was not clear whether he was dead or alive – lay in a wheelbarrow, pushed by a comrade. A stump of leg was covered with a filthy bandage.

British shells dropped into Stanley Harbour and in the large garden of the school hostel in the very centre of the town a huge 155mm artillery piece continued to propel occasional shells at the British.

At the King Edward Memorial Hospital Alison Bleaney sat dejected and worried. There would be no camp medical session on the radio telephone today. There had not been one for several days, not since the troops moved into the RT station and dismantled the equipment once and for all. Now she had tuned her own portable radio receiver to 4.5 megahertz, the usual civilian channel. If anyone was in trouble at camp she would, at least, hear them. What she could do about it? Well, she would think about that if it happened.

The doctor worried that a plan to concentrate all civilians in the Cathedral, proposed a few days earlier during the visit by representatives of the International Committee of the Red Cross, had gone off at half-cock. No final agreement had been reached, but some seemed to think the plan was being put into effect. Alison had heard such suggestions on the BBC and if the British forces had also heard this they would enter Stanley believing they could flatten everything except the Cathedral.

Suddenly there was a voice on her radio. Somebody was calling the Argentine forces, alternating the message in English and Spanish. This, it emerged later, was a Royal Marine intelligence officer Captain Rod Bell, who grew up in South America. He was urging the Argentines to arrange a meeting and surrender. Bell made it clear that this was their last chance.

Alison knew that it was unlikely that any Argentine would have heard this. As well as closing down the RT station, Menendez had forbidden his troops to listen on the local frequency. She put Emma in her papoose pack and left the hospital to find Barry Hussey. Outside she saw the defeated men from the hills pouring back through the town, but fresher troops were still manning positions with machine guns primed and the lids off boxes of belted ammunition.

Hussey might be anywhere, and she searched for him. The desperate Argentines looked at her oddly, but Emma, strapped to her mother, seemed to neutralise any threat they may have posed.

Eventually Alison found Hussey, but he was not inclined to go with her to the RT station. She pleaded.

I said, 'Look, they are calling! We can talk to them! If you do not surrender now, then all the civilians – most of us anyway – are going to die!' If we were going to go, then his guys were going to go as well. What was the advantage of not surrendering?

218

Hussey finally agreed to go to the station, and they made their way there. Alison had a rough idea of how the RT equipment went together and, after a few minutes of fiddling with cables, the dials lit up. Hussey told her to call the British and to keep them talking while he listened.

Rod Bell came back on the air immediately and repeated his message. This was, he emphasised grimly, the final chance to avoid further major loss of life.

Hussey disappeared to consult Bloomer Reeve and then to discuss the ultimatum with Menendez. He returned after about an hour with Bloomer Reeve. Alison recalled that both were ashen-faced and tense, but calm. They had met Menendez and been given permission to discuss a meeting with the British.

As Emma gurgled happily, Alison continued to pass on the messages to Rod Bell. Neither Argentine would speak to him. She did not remember the messages, but they all pointed to one thing, a cease-fire and surrender.

The young mother and doctor played a key part in ending the fighting, but she gave the credit to Bloomer Reeve and Hussey:

I am absolutely convinced that at the end they persuaded Menendez that the only honourable thing was surrender. I don't think we would be here now if it wasn't for them.

Nap Bound had anticipated that there would be wild celebrations among the civilians when it was all over. But neither he nor anyone else could express joy at what they saw. He wrote:

The scene was pathetic beyond words. I experienced a deep sense of depression and numbness.

I stood on the front road watching a trickle of dejected young soldiers making their way eastwards, dragging their rifles through the filth. Slowly the numbers increased to thousands, all presenting the same terrible picture. Some were wounded and helped along by friends. Others had lost much of their clothing, including their boots.

Small arms, ammunition and mess kits littered the streets. Most of those we saw were young conscripts who were only too willing to be rid of the whole ghastly experience. But now and again you would see the highly trained officers walking arrogantly along in their neat uniforms.

The morning was wet and cold, and as the day progressed the streets were covered in a light falling of snow. As they passed the hotel where I stood, a priest stood on the pavement and blessed many of the injured.

At Fox Bay there was an oddly joyless little celebration between locals and their one-time captors. After surrendering to sailors from HMS *Avenger*, the garrison's defeated commanding officer and a colleague visited the Falklanders. Grizelda Cockwell recalled the meeting.

> The major produced a bottle of champagne out of his jacket and said, 'I told you we would drink champagne to the victory – and the victory is yours. Here is the champagne.'
>
> We all had a glass of champagne; us, the Argentines and a Lieutenant Commander off *Avenger*.
>
> The major made a very gracious little speech, admitting that it was our victory and we had done well. Then they left, and it was the last we saw of them.

Back in Stanley news of the general surrender took a while to filter through the town. Radio Islas Malvinas had ceased transmissions and, with so many people confined to shelters, the diddle-dee telegraph was not working either.

John Leonard, the senior member of the small American community, remembered that several days had passed since he last contacted Bloomer Reeve to report on the safety of his compatriots. During what he assumed to be a lull in the fighting he phoned Sulivan House. Remarkably, the telephone system was still working and he got through on the first attempt.

At the other end of Stanley the phone was picked up and a cautious voice said, "Hello?"

John said, "Can I speak to Comodoro Bloomer Reeve?"

There was a brief pause, then: "Sorry, old chap! No one of that name here. This is the British Army."

When all had been quiet for a while and civilians began to emerge from their shelters, radio telephone operator Eileen Vidal decided to walk west along Ross Road with her daughter Leona to meet the British soldiers. What she saw near Government House barely made her break her step:

> There were two dead Argentine soldiers, laying face down. I can still see a little dirty hand stretched out on the pavement. We felt nothing – which is awful really. I never knew how hard war makes you.

We passed them and by the time we came down the road again somebody had covered them over.

The thing that has stuck with me all these years is that little dirty hand.

Such lurid images embedded themselves deeply in the clay of many minds, and while the squalid detritus of occupation and war were swept away in the long period of recovery and change that followed, they remained preserved.

Digging down through the layers of the years they are revealed again, evoking memories of bravery, stoicism, fear, compassion and even a little laughter.

Eventually, though, one reaches a bedrock labelled 2 April 1982. It was the day, as the late Major Phil Summers of the Falkland Islands Defence Force would have put it, that "It started."

Epilogue

"I remember having a very, very vivid dream in which the shelling started again. Except I knew that this time I was in 10 John Street with large picture windows which were not taped, and there was nothing in the window embrasures. I knew this time that I was going to die. I woke up absolutely soaking with sweat."

John Fowler

In early 2007, as the revised edition of this book is being prepared, it is worth considering the Falklands' relationship with Argentina 25 years on. It has changed greatly in the last few years – and not for the better. It is impossible to conclude that the situation in the south-west Atlantic is anything other than a cold war.

Argentina is consistently hostile towards the Islanders, demonising them by describing their obstinacy as the principal obstruction to the achievement of an agreement favourable to Buenos Aires. The dispute is now higher on the political agenda in Buenos Aires than it has been at any stage since 1982. And while pumping up the diplomatic pressure and populist rhetoric, the Argentines have stepped up economic pressure, obstructing the Islanders' every move to diversify and develop their economy.

Fortunately for the islands, the left-leaning President Nestor Kirchner is no fan of the military. He condemns the military regime of the 1970s and early 1980s for the disastrous war, and has repealed legislation that once protected the military officers who trampled on human rights. Kirchner states that the Malvinas goal will be pursued by peaceful means, but that does not appear to rule out almost any kind of hostility short of actual war.

What a contrast Kirchner's policy is to that which was being developed and pursued by his predecessor, fellow Peronist Carlos Menem. Menem's Foreign Minister, the late Guido Di Tella, surprised everyone in Stanley, London and even in Buenos Aires with his eccentric softly-softly approach. He is now almost fondly remembered in the Falklands: one former councillor described him (only slightly tongue-in-cheek) as 'dear old Guido'.

Under Di Tella's guidance, foreign policy priorities were more mature. He tackled the issues of global significance that were expected of a country that wanted to be taken seriously in the world. He did not, however, forget the Falklands. Indeed he almost seemed to be having fun with them. He established friendships with the Islanders he met at the annual United Nations debate on colonialism, and even sent Christmas gifts to hundreds of Islanders. They were not seduced by the charm offensive but this hand of friendship was a refreshing change, and for a short time it sweetened the bitterness.

His policy was not without success. In 1999 he convinced the Islanders to sign an agreement by which Argentines would be allowed to visit the Falklands and the weekly air service from Chile (which flew over Argentine territory) would be guaranteed. The agreement also paved the way for regular Argentine-British discussions over the shared south-west Atlantic fisheries and for consultations over oil exploration. As something of a sop to sensitive Islanders, the Argentines even agreed to reconsider the offensive nomenclature they had adopted during the war – Stanley, for example, was always referred to as 'Puerto Argentino'.

Many in Stanley felt that the agreement, largely negotiated in secret, was a step too far. There were furious arguments and demonstrations but most of the elected councillors felt it was a pragmatic move. Nothing remarkable occurred as a result. But tensions were lowered enabling the Falklands' economy to further develop and diversify, maintaining the Islanders' status as the highest earners per capita in South America.

But then in December 1999, Menem left power. With him went Di Tella and that lightness of touch on the Malvinas tiller disappeared. Guido Di Tella died just two years later, and there were kind words said about him in Stanley.

The new president, Fernando de la Rua, had inherited an economic house of cards from Menem. The peso was still firmly linked to the US dollar, which had brought inflation under control, and life had become much easier for many people, particularly the middle classes. But all the while the government had been building up huge debts. Private money was flowing out of the country, and when de la Rua took over the economy was in recession. Fearful savers began withdrawing their money from banks in dollars, and the government moved to ban withdrawals. There were riots, the link with the dollar was severed, and the peso was devalued. It was an economic meltdown of appalling proportions. The president fled from the Casa Rosada in December 2001 and resigned. He was replaced by a series of five caretaker presidents, some of whom lasted only days.

Then in May 2003, as Argentina began to claw itself back from chaos, Nestor Kirchner, a former Governor from Patagonia was elected. Kirchner took a little time to get around to stamping his new style on the Falklands dispute, but by 2005, it was becoming evident. He was an Argentine leader of the old school; whose drum-beating Malvinas jingoism formed a backing track to a policy of extreme hostility and intransigence.

What little mutual trust and respect had been achieved through the Di Tella years evaporated as Kirchner's Foreign Minister, Jorge Taiana, virtually abandoned the possibility of joint approach to fisheries control, ruled out further development of air communications between the Islands and Chile, and made it clear that everything possible would be done to discourage international companies from participating in a Falklands controlled hydrocarbons industry. Britain was slammed for its dogmatic insistence that Islanders – an 'implanted' people – should have a veto over sovereignty negotiations. The Malvinas returned to the top of the Argentine foreign policy agenda.

The 'sovereignty umbrella', a political device that protected practical issues of cooperation with Islanders and Britain from contamination by the sovereignty dispute, was folded up and put away. Now almost every issue of mutual concern is contaminated by the dispute. The only issue that continues to make any progress at all – and that is at a funereal pace – is the plan to remove the land mines left behind by Argentine forces. Both countries signed the international land mines protocol, and have occasional meetings to discuss the issue. At the time of writing in 2007, however, not one of the estimated 15,000 mines has been raised.

Falklands registered fishing ships have been harassed and detained and Islanders travelling through Argentina on British passports have faced humiliating delays at airports as officials puzzled theatrically with the paradox of Argentine 'citizens' carrying British passports.

In an extravagant propaganda move, it was announced that a DVD explaining Argentina's 'historical rights' to the Malvinas would be presented to every tourist visiting Argentina, and distributed to

224

foreign politicians, ministers and diplomats through embassies and legations.

A 'Malvinas observatory' was created, consisting of academics, politicians, journalists, diplomats, senior military figures; indeed almost any public figure who had been involved in the issue. A notable exception was Andres Cisneros, who was once Guido Di Tella's deputy, and probably one of the few remaining doves. The observatory was tasked to monitor all activity concerning the Islands, promote the claim and lobby parliaments and governments. Its first task was, reportedly, to consider ways of dismantling the Argentine-British agreement on oil exploration in the maritime zone overlapping each country's territorial claims. Never formalised anyway, it is now moribund.

Sensing the ascendant solidarity of Latin American states, led by left-leaning leaders in Venezuela, Brazil, Chile and Argentina itself, Kirchner has attempted to raise the Malvinas as a matter of regional importance. It had been a familiar issue in the United Nations' Decolonisation Committee for many years, but Foreign Minister Taiana raised the stakes at the annual meeting, by meeting Secretary General Kofi Annan and requesting that the UN boss use 'his good offices' to persuade Britain back to the negotiating table. Taiana was reported to have – rather disingenuously – passed the Secretary General reports on discussions about air services, hydrocarbons, fishing and mine removal – all described as 'confidence building measures to help improve relations with the Islands and the British.' Perhaps reluctant to be taken for a ride, Annan listened politely but appeared not to have done anything.

There was an almost rabid response to the Falklands Government's plan (backed by London) to issue 25-year fishing licences. It was bound to be greeted with hostility, but in the light of the Argentines' hawkish attitude, Islanders and London apparently thought they had little to lose. The licences would be much coveted by international fleets, would help assure future prosperity and make administration of fishing easier. But to Buenos Aires it was yet more unilateral behaviour that ignored Argentine rights and interests.

Kirchner's position on the 1982 war is ambiguous. He has said that it was a huge mistake, but he honours the Argentine dead of the war and the veterans in terms that suggest their cause was just. His Defence Minister, Nilda Garre, said that the issue of the Malvinas had been "manipulated [by] a terrible dictatorship, unleashing a war and snatching a national cause." But she continued: "It was also a war with luminous aspects, the heroism of soldiers, officers and the solidarity from all the Argentine people."

It is unlikely, though, that either she or President Kirchner has many supporters among older military officers. There was palpable tension when Kirchner moved to introduce legislation that would bolster the authority of civilian ministers over the military, and he publicly berated a small number of officers who had taken part in an act of commemoration for military personnel and civilians who died at the hands of guerrillas in the 1970s and 1980s.

Kirchner's efforts to ensure that the military act only under the guidance of elected civilians are a good thing. Without strong civilian leadership, there would be fears that maverick military units could take things into their own hands, perhaps mounting intelligence gathering missions, flag-planting missions of the kind that were carried out in the 1960s, or even attacks on British forces. Some believe that at least one covert landing on the Falklands was carried out. On 27 December 2001, when the chaotic game of presidential musical chairs was getting under way in Buenos Aires, a farmer discovered an inflatable boat on a beach on the north of East Falkland. The boat was upside down and covered with enough sand to suggest it might have been there for some time, but inside the boat were found Argentine military rations, other items of kit that could be military, and at least one satellite phone. There were no bodies, and a two-day search confirmed there had been no shipping accidents in the area. The boat was quickly removed by the military authorities, and taken to the Mount Pleasant base, where it is believed the satellite phones and other equipment were studied carefully. There was an information blackout, and although locals were convinced that there had been an Argentine military adventure, the local authorities and the Foreign Office in London cast cold water on the idea. However they offered no other credible theory, and the results of forensic investigations were not made public. In 2006 the Foreign Office was asked to supply information about the incident under the terms of the Freedom of Information Act. The official reply did not allay fears. Just a few innocuous memos and press cuttings were released by the FCO; the petitioner was told that other papers could not be released. "We have established that the passage of time has not diminished the sensitivity of the issue," wrote an official. "Disclosure of classified discussions with [the] Argentine Government may damage current UK/Argentine relations. It could undermine trust between the UK and [the] government of the Falkland Islands and affect our foreign policy of protecting the security and prosperity of the Overseas Territories."

Only one conclusion can be drawn from this: that the inflatable boat incident did indeed have a connection with Argentina, and its discovery was an embarrassment to Buenos Aires. It seems very likely that the occupants were on a military mission of some kind.

It would be odd, however, if Argentine forces were not gathering intelligence about the British military establishment in the Falklands. National forces must always plan for possible eventualities, and British forces in the Falklands are at least a potential adversary.

Military tension is not significantly higher today, but security at the Mount Pleasant airbase has been increased and the commander of British forces is keen to impress on visiting reporters that he and his staff are not at all complacent. Nuclear submarines occasionally visit the Islands, and when they do local reporters are usually advised, so that reports will reach Argentina.

British forces in the Falklands remain a very credible deterrent. In recent years, their numerical strength has been reduced, but newly acquired strategic transport aircraft and ships mean that the Islands can be reinforced very quickly if necessary. Furthermore, a new warship built especially for the Falklands patrol, HMS *Clyde*, has just been launched and will be on station in 2007. A programme of house building at Mount Pleasant demonstrates that British forces expect to be in the Islands for the long haul.

Islanders do not, on the whole, worry about further Argentine aggression, although when asked, almost all say that they would be *very* worried if British forces were pulled out. Neither are they profoundly worried about the political or economic impact of the deteriorating relationship with Argentina. It is undesirable and tedious, of course, but few Islanders have ever known a normal relation ship with the neighbour, and they are used to its ebb and flow. Prominent former Falklands councillor Norma Edwards confirmed that the situation is, "A kind of cold war." She added: "At present we tend to look upon it all as just a pain in the arse, but if they became more aggressive, then we would have to take – or get the Foreign Office to take – a stronger hand."

Hawkish Kirchner is, said Norma Edwards, at least the traditional face of the opposition, and therefore easier to understand. "You know where you stand with the ones with aggressive attitudes."

Councillor Mike Summers supported the controversial 1999 agreement, saying it had been "a risk worth taking." Unlike Norma Edwards, he regrets that Argentina has now thrown it out. "It would," he said, "now be difficult to see further agreements with Argentina that relied on much trust."

But Mike Summers is comfortable under siege too, and he is prepared to speak plainly. "Argentina is a hostile neighbour," he said. But their "antics and activities" have no effect on the core elements of the Falklands economy. "We have grown beyond [their] ability to kill off the economy," he said. "Sanctions against Spanish fishing companies working on both sides would simply have the effect of making companies choose, and there is plenty of scope for others to take up capacity left by anyone going the other way. Sanctions have to date had no discernible effect on hydrocarbons activity, none on agriculture and relatively little on tourism."

Some analysts suggest, reasonably, that Kirchner is exploiting his people's passion for the Malvinas in the lead-up to presidential elections in 2007. If so, it is a well-worn – and somewhat dangerous – path. Over the years the Malvinas issue has often been revived with bombastic rhetoric and aggressive foreign policy to whip up popularity or divert attention from domestic failures. It happened in 1982. If there are links to the election, then the issue may go off the boil again soon. But Kirchner may well win a second term, and if he feels that his Malvinas policy helped him to victory, he may not want to abandon it. Oil exploration off the Falklands and the possibility of a find might even make moderation impossible.

There are signs that even the British Foreign Office is running out of patience and being less delicate in its statements. They have, after all, almost no room to manoeuvre. Because of the British sacrifice in the Falklands in 1982, they cannot take any position other than one of total support for Falkland Islanders. There is no point in allowing the Argentines to believe anything else. Speaking shortly before the end of his term in the Falklands in 2006, Governor Howard Pearce – a senior diplomat – said: "It is understandable that many Falkland Islanders should interpret Argentina actions as a policy of *de facto* economic sanctions, designed to do damage to the Islands' economy. I have this message for the Argentine Government: if that is your aim, it is bound to fail. Pressure will prove counter-productive."

Governor Pearce suggested there is, quite simply, no solution to the dispute. "The beginning of wisdom for the Argentines," he said, "is to recognise that they aren't going to get anywhere on the sovereignty issue."

But of course that will not stop them trying.

Index